Theologians at Work

Theologians at Work

BY

Patrick Granfield

THE MACMILLAN COMPANY, NEW YORK

COLLIER-MACMILLAN LTD., LONDON

Library of Congress Catalog Card Number: 67-27515
First Printing
The Macmillan Company, New York
Collier-Macmillan Canada Ltd., Toronto, Ontario
PRINTED IN THE UNITED STATES OF AMERICA

ACKNOWLEDGMENTS

Acknowledgment is made to the following for permission
to reprint copyrighted material: *The American Ecclesiastical Review* for "An Interview—Karl Rahner: Theologian at Work," CLIII, No. 4 (Oct. 1965); "An Interview
with Jaroslav Pelikan," CLV, No. 5 (Nov. 1966); "An
Interview—Robert McAfee Brown: The Ecumenical Venture," CLIV, No. 1 (Jan. 1966); *Review for Religious* for
"Interview with Abbot Butler," 26, No. 1 (Jan. 1967); *The
Commonweal* for "An Interview with Reinhold Niebuhr,"
XXXXV, No. 11 (Dec. 16, 1966); *The Clergy Review* for
"Diakonia and Salvation History—Piet Fransen Interviewed," LI, No. 5 (May 1966); *America* for "An Interview With Yves Congar" (May 6, 1967).

Contents

Introduction

THEOLOGY, to the delight of some and to the consternation of others, is "in." Liberated from stuffy classrooms and stuffier journals, it speaks no longer to an elite, but to the millions—and millions listen. Theology has become newsworthy. Hans Küng draws a spellbound audience of five thousand in Washington to hear his views on theological freedom; the "death of God" phenomenon becomes a *Time* cover story and a television "special"; articles on theology appear in *Look, Atlantic Monthly,* and *The Saturday Evening Post;* and the newspapers of the world recount for four years the daily events of the Second Vatican Council.

Theology faces an information explosion of its own. A proliferation of books, articles, and reviews leave those interested in theology financially and intellectually hard pressed in their efforts to keep up to date. Paperbacks and Xerox machines—both habit-forming—make theological material more easily available. Books on theology are best sellers. For example, *Honest to God,* by Bishop Robinson, has sold 350,000 copies in English and has been translated into seven foreign languages; *The Secular City,* by Harvey Cox, has sold a quarter of a million copies and is published in six languages; and *The Comfortable Pew,* by Pierre Berton, has broken all existing publishing records in Canada and is nearing the 200,000 mark. Some theologians have become so compulsively productive that one wonders if they are corporate personalities.

Theologians are on the move and have taken their place in the front ranks of the "restless generation." Thanks to jet aircraft, European and American theologians have become veteran travelers. Universities on both sides of the Atlantic frequently exchange professors. A small diocese in the Middle West thinks nothing of inviting a well-known European theologian to teach at its summer school or to deliver a few lectures. The University of Notre Dame had over a dozen foreign theologians at a theological conference last year—the *mise en scène* for some of the interviews in this book. Conventions in Rome, Ceylon, or San Francisco are sure to attract many foreign visitors. But what is this quest for religious truth, this consuming impulse to know and to communicate things divine?

"Theology," Elmer O'Brien has recently noted, "exists, upright or bent, sick or healthy, nowhere except in the minds of theologians." How does one find out what a theologian is thinking? The most obvious way is to read what he has written. This is not as simple as it sounds because theologians, like all men, reveal themselves, even in their writings, only partially and obscurely. This is not done out of coyness or perverseness. It stems from the very nature of theology which deals with a transspatial and transtemporal reality—the mystery of God. Theologians have come a long way from the time of Eunomius, fourth-century bishop of Cyzicus, who boasted: "I know God as well as He knows Himself." We recall the humble words of St. Paul: "We see now through a mirror in an obscure manner, but then face to face. Now I know in part . . ." (*1 Cor.* 13: 12–13). Theology deals with great words (*Urwörte,* Rahner calls them) that defy complete definition and are wrapped in mystery. Basic words like love, fatherhood, sonship, and justice contain inexhaustible wealth. Every theological formulation is partial and imperfect. Mystery is not that residual core that remains after intensive study of the revealed message; mystery necessarily accompanies revelation and every expression of it. Theology is in continual evolution, and theologians present more questions than answers. How many have said with Dante: "O Speech! How feeble and how faint are thou to give conception birth!"? In theology, translucence and opacity go hand in hand.

Theological writing, then, is an imperfect vehicle of expression. The printed page cannot give the subtle qualifications that the theologian himself has difficulty in articulating. The intellectual odyssey of the human mind is often circuitous, inconsistent, and confusing.

Every man's thought is determined by a myriad of influences many of which cannot be analyzed. Family, education, friends, reading, and numerous half-conscious happenings help shape a person's psyche. The demythologizing of Bultmann, for example, was the result of his attempts to make Christianity meaningful to soldiers in combat. Tillich, who was a chaplain to the German forces in the First World War, says that his "war experiences were very important because they caused the collapse of the idealist elements in me. . . . I changed from an idealist to a realist, a tragic realist."

Theologians, because they are human and engaged in a human effort, are inconsistent. Their path to truth is slow and painstaking. Like all of man's endeavors, theology is fallible and subject to change. One thinks of the several volumes of St. Augustine's *Retractations,* of the differences between *"Thomas junior"* and *"Thomas senior,"* and of the evolution from the "early Barth" to the "later Barth." The words of Orestes Brownson are pertinent here:

> They who knew me in childhood are not they who have known me in the prime of manhood or in old age. . . . Would you become acquainted with the man, you must read the history of his soul— make yourself familiar with his spiritual experiences, his inward struggles, defeats, victories, doubts, convictions, ends, and aims. These constitute the real man, and you become acquainted with him only in proportion as you become familiar with them.

In the past, theological writings reflected the personalities of their authors. After reading Ambrose, Origen, St. Thomas, or Calvin you come away with a feeling for them as persons. It is a strange phenomenon that for the last several hundred years this was not true of most Catholic theology. Newman and Scheeben were exceptions. For the greater part there flourished an impersonal, dialectic, somewhat forbidding style of writing. The manualists were faceless men, victims of a highly structured and formalized approach. This is not to impugn their brilliance or their contributions to theology, which was considerable. It is simply to say that their writings did not carry the distinctive mark of their personalities. Protestant theology, however, for a long time has produced a more personal theology. Barth, Brunner, Niebuhr, and Tillich are outstanding examples. It is only within the last few decades that Catholic theologians have adopted, to any noticeable degree, a personal procedure. The work of Häring, Rahner, de Lubac, and Congar is much more personal than that of their predecessors.

The most effective way to know what a theologian is thinking is to talk to him. If "all real life is a meeting," as Buber suggests, then there is no substitute for direct, personal contact to find out *what* a theologian is and *who* he is. How different it is to know someone personally when we had previously known him only through his letters. We can reach someone in the course of an hour's conversation in a way that we could not hope to duplicate by means of the printed word. It is a common experience in reading theology to say to ourselves: "I wonder what the author means by this statement?"; "Is he influenced here by Cyril's Christology?"; "How would he answer Professor X's criticism?"; and "What kind of a man is he?" A dozen thoughts like this come into our minds. We think how profitable it would be to sit down with the author and talk to him about his theology. However, we realize that this is impossible, and so with a shrug of our shoulders, we get down to the practical task of struggling to understand what he has written.

As a professor of theology, I too desired to meet and talk to the distinguished theologians whose works I had read and studied. This desire was intensified after reading the *Paris Review* interviews with writers. I was fascinated by those emerging portraits. I found them provocative and informative. As I read them, I wondered why the same technique could not be used with theologians. A series of personal, frank, and essentially serious interviews with proven theologians would provide equally interesting and valuable insights. Informal conversations with them would reveal facets of their minds not usually evident in their writings. We would have an intimate picture of theologians as scholars and persons. The more I thought about it, the more I was convinced that the idea was a good one. At first the whole plan seemed rather farfetched, since many of the theologians I would have liked to interview lived in Europe and I had no immediate plans to go abroad. However, by a combination of good fortune, generous and co-operative theologians, and persistence, I was able to "reach the sources." *Theologians at Work* is the result of this endeavor.

I

My immediate problem was to select the theologians to be interviewed. I first drew up a list of about thirty, it was finally reduced to sixteen—the limit set by the publishers. The men selected represent various theological approaches. All of them are, or have been, professors of theology who have written considerably. They come from eight countries (counting George Lindbeck who was born in China). Eight are Catholic; six are Protestant; one is Jewish; and one is Russian Orthodox. The oldest of the theologians interviewed is Father Francis Connell, born in 1888, and the youngest is Father John Meyendorff, born in 1926.

The idea of interviewing sixteen theologians appeared deceptively simple at first. I did not anticipate that the interviews that I had planned to record on tape would require so much time and effort. However, as I got involved in the project, I realized that I had more to do than I had originally bargained for. First of all, there was a great deal of correspondence. There were the initial letters inviting the theologians to be interviewed, letters to arrange a suitable meeting place, a series of letters back and forth concerning the editing and approval of the manuscripts, and finally several letters to the publishers.

Preparation for the interviews was extensive. My "homework" consisted of reading some biographical material and whatever books and articles of these theologians that I had not yet read. I tried to immerse myself in their theology, to develop a sense of rapport, so that I would feel at home when I met them personally. From the notes that I took while reading, I prepared several pages of questions carefully organized in various categories. Armed with these, I began the interviews.

I was fortunate in being able to meet several foreign theologians during their visits to the United States. Georgetown University and the University of Notre Dame were the locale of these interviews. The others took place in Washington, New York, Denver, and New Haven.

I soon discovered that an interview is an unpredictable and fluid kind of communication. It is impossible to predetermine its course. My prepared questions often became only guidelines, and more than once they were not used at all. The conversations were free-wheeling with the result that many themes were introduced that were not fully developed. This was inevitable. The *genre* of the interview is quite different from the studied and carefully thought-out prose of the scholar. What is lacking in logical thoroughness is, it is hoped, compensated by the spontaneous, lively, and natural character of the interviews.

The interviews lasted on the average of an hour and a half, and at times, more than one session was necessary. The theologians interviewed could not have been more gracious and accommodating. I saw my role as interviewer not as a debater who has to challenge his opponent with an impressive show of erudition. Nor did I consider myself simply a partner in the fixed pattern of the traditional theological dialogue, like Augustine's Evodius, Gregory's Peter the Deacon, and Anselm's Bozo. I felt that as a creative listener my function was to ask pointed questions that would elicit direct replies. I tried to keep the conversations moving at a good pace and, while remaining in the background, to be persistent in my inquiry.

All the interviews were recorded on a Wollensak—my traveling companion on my train, plane, and bus trips. It behaved beautifully through nearly fifty hours of recording. I must confess, however, that during each interview I was haunted by the fear that some unexpected electronic failure would occur undetected, and a never-to-be-repeated conversation would be forever lost. I was invariably reassured at the end of each interview when a quick replay produced a clear, crisp reproduction. Some of the theologians became a little apprehensive when they saw the tape recorder. This fear was usually overcome when I told them that they could see the text before it was published. The low hum of the moving reels and the flashing orange light of the sound indicator made a few of them uneasy and extremely cautious at first, but after a very few minutes the recorder was soon forgotten. The conversations were friendly and relaxed. I treasure the friendly hours spent with these men talking of things theological.

Transcribing the tapes was a wearisome task. I did only a few of them, but enough to realize it takes great perseverance and energy. Most of them were done by Father Edward Markley, O.S.B., of St. Bernard's Abbey, Cullman, Alabama, and Father Arthur Wiles, of Columbus, Ohio. I am grateful to them for their diligence and willingness, as I am to the help given me by my Benedictine confreres at St. Anselm's Abbey, Dom Aidan Shea and Dom James Wiseman. I am also indebted to Miss Susanne Thibault who did most of the typing of the manuscripts and who became an expert at deciphering handwritten corrections. I would like to add a special word of appreciation to my brother, Dom David Granfield, O.S.B., for his never-flagging encouragement and valuable assistance. He followed the book through all its stages and contributed numerous suggestions.

After I received the original transcription, I set about editing it. I then sent the manuscripts to the authors for corrections, deletions, additions, and final approval. Most of the authors made only minor changes, but some did rework the whole manuscript. Father Congar, for example, sent in three single-spaced pages in French that contained thirty-three changes. Robert McAfee Brown and Markus Barth also made major corrections. I was amazed at the promptness with which the manuscripts were sent back to me. I usually received them by return mail. This reflected, I felt, the scholarly discipline of these men and helped explain why they have had such active and productive lives. Great theologians have always had a remarkable capacity for prolonged concentration (and that enviable virtue of *sitzfleisch*). They get things done and can communicate the fruit of their efforts.

II

The sixteen men interviewed in this book are working theologians. They belong to a noble profession that has produced bril-

liant personalities who have radically transformed the course of
Western culture. The names of St. Paul, St. John, St. Augustine, St.
Thomas, Luther, and Calvin come quickly to mind. The history of
theology is entwined in the history of Western civilization. Theological history is colorful and makes exciting reading. We tend to
forget, in this ecumenical age of polite disagreement, that in the past
theologians were often spirited and disputatious characters. Polemics
was not something rarely used, but an accepted form of theological
debate. Gilson once remarked that "to replace a refutation with an
accusation of heresy is good warfare." Jerome, carried away with
righteous indignation, was impetuous in his writings against Rufinus
and Helvidius. Athanasius did not disguise the fact that he was *contra
mundum* any more than Karl Barth left room for misunderstanding when he pronounced his ringing "No!" to Brunner. The followers of Bañez and Molina heatedly leveled charges of heresy at
each other in disputing the efficacy of grace. Perhaps the extreme
of religious "enthusiasm," as Ronald Knox calls it, was found
among the Circumcellions, the Donatist terrorists from Mauretania
and Upper Numidia. With clubs in hand, they hunted down their
religious opponents. With shouts of *"Deo laudes,"* they attacked and
massacred whole villages—maiming, mutilating, and torturing. The
critics of Bishop Robinson and Harvey Cox are gentle and moderate
compared with the polemicists of the past.

   Across the theological spectrum, there has been a wide variety of
personalities, ideologies, and styles of theologizing. The personal, experiential, concrete theology of the New Testament is quite different from the metaphysical and abstract theology of the early
Councils. Both dialectical theology and apologetical theology have had
their vogue. Today's ecumenical and secular theology explores with
new vitality the area where the Church meets the world. In spite of
many differences, one can detect an underlying unity in the history
of theology that cuts across the barriers of denomination and personality. Theology has to be in every instance a response to what
Latourelle calls "the first fact, the first mystery, the first category"—
the revelation of God to man. This is the basis of all theology. Once

one believes that God has spoken to man, then there arises the exigency of understanding this communication. Theology is the questing, probing, and searching of the Word of God; it is a rational effort, guided by faith, that attempts to penetrate the message of God. To do this, it uses all the means that human knowledge can supply. The description of St. Anselm is classical: "Faith seeking understanding *(Fides quaerens intellectum)*."

In theology, faith develops in a properly human way according to the laws and resources of reason. Through the centuries, these resources have been employed in various ways. In the past, art, philosophy, and history influenced the development of theology. Today, our theology must also take into account psychology, phenomenology, existentialism, sociology, and literature. The theologian must avail himself of the insights of all the various sciences if his theology is to be dynamic. This means that the theologian must wear many hats. He cannot be the "encapsulated man." He has to be a *specialist* in one field, but at the same time he has to be a *generalist,* at home in several other disciplines. Theology does not pretend to be a vast computer-like science solving the problems of other sciences. But a mature theology cannot cut itself off from the sciences if it is to speak to contemporary man and to answer the *theological* questions that modern science raises. Jacob Burckhardt has said that the man who will "forfeit his capacity for taking a general view . . . will remain ignorant in any field lying outside his own speciality and perhaps, as a man, a barbarian." Because revelation is mysterious and complex, it cannot be exhaustively categorized. It is so rich and diverse that human thought is unable to grasp it fully. The theologian, because of the essential complexity of revelation, must resort to many approaches in his efforts to understand—even partially—what God is saying to man.

Theologians have always been awed by the task they face. They realize too well that very few of their fraternity possess the enviable *habit* of theology. In theology, as in other intellectual disciplines, mediocrity has been the lot of too many of its practitioners. How rare are the great theologians, men whose judgments are sharpened by years of study and familiarity with the sources, men who can theologize with skill and ease. Theology demands a realistic blend of professional competence, unfaltering courage, and deep humility. Theology is a lifelong endeavor, a paradoxical adventure—a mélange of frustration and sublime understanding. In attempting to arrive at the core of simplicity that is God, theologians often develop elaborate constructs that are obstacles rather than aids to comprehension. Theologians, like artists, seek the uniqueness of truth. They both must avoid obscuring reality by needless fragmentation. Alfred Hitchcock noted this common fault in young movie directors. "They don't take time to learn," he said, "as Somerset Maugham learned, that true simplicity is the hardest thing to attain—the elimination of all that is unnecessary."

Feelings of inadequacy and humility are rarely absent in the theologian. The masters of theology are keenly aware of their ignorance. St. Thomas at the end of his life referred to all his writings as "so much straw." Francis Vitoria, who restored theology in Spain in the sixteenth century, was overwhelmed by the immensity of the theologian's task. Speaking to his students shortly before he died, the old professor, looking back over his forty years of labor, uttered what most theologians have, at one time or other, felt: "It used to seem to me, at the beginning of my career, that I knew a great deal; but now, to tell the truth, I see that I am still at the threshold. My age and the arduousness of the task terrify me, for I realize that in twenty or thirty years a theologian can know very little." Dominic Bañez felt that the difference between a great theologian and the ordinary believer is that "the wiser a theologian is, so much more earnestly does he acknowledge his own ignorance and infirmity." Schleiermacher even as an old man put before his signature the German title, *stud. theol.* Karl Barth, in his book, *Evangelical Theology: An Introduction,* which he wrote after his trip to the United States in 1962, reminisced about his theological career. He hoped that Americans would not look upon him as "the prophet," "the giant of theology," or "the gloomy theological gladiator." He wanted to be thought of "as a normal human being who is . . . distinguished from other men by the simple fact that he chiefly devoted his days to a special emphasis on the question of proper theology. . . ."

III

Theologians in every age must re-evaluate their function. Today's technopolitan theologian faces critical and complex issues that question the very credibility of his profession. Secular man poses trenchant questions that demand from the theologian the utmost in perception and judgment. It is not in vain to ask: What qualities must a theologian possess if his activity is to be meaningful in this last third of the twentieth century? I would suggest that the theologian above all must channel his abilities and energies according to a sense of community and a sense of tradition. I would like to comment briefly on these two qualities that guarantee the vitality of theology.

First of all, I believe that the modern theologian must be *communitarian*. He must operate *in, for,* and *through* the *koinonia*—the community of love and worship that is God's people. This is necessary because the Word of God is given to the community, the *qahal Yaweh,* the *Ekklesia*. This community is called, established, and sustained by the Word of God that is redemptive and consoling. Theology is a quest *within* the community for the genuine understanding of God's Word in all its purity and clarity. It mediates between the Church's faith and the Church's teaching or, as Barth puts it, between faith and speech. The quest for truth is at stake here. It is the concern of the whole community that is aware of its unique place in the world. The theologian is a *diakonos,* a servant of the community.

This communitarian involvement of the theologian as person-in-community is rooted in man's nature. Erich Fromm has observed that human nature necessarily moves toward communion with another person or persons. Once a theologian draws apart from the community and stands "in splendid isolation" far from its needs, he is no longer faithful to his calling. A theology that is simply an intellectual exercise remote from the real world is a dead theology. Theologians who do not relate to the world about them and meet their fellow men only in an "hypertheological" way distort the beauty and the true function of theology. What is needed is *Ebed-*Theology (the theologian as servant), which deals with personal truths, man's encounter with God, and his final destiny. "The Son of Man has not come to be served, but to serve" (*Mk.* 10:45). Theology serves the community by helping it become an accurate and vital witness to the truth. The theologian's work is an ongoing process that is never completed. However, he can feel moderately successful in his efforts if, according to Vincent of Lerins, "that which was formerly believed with difficulty be made through your interpretation, more understandable. . . ."

Through the ages, theologians have been tempted to retreat from the world and, in the quiet of their book-lined rooms, work out a theological synthesis. "Ivory tower" theology is still a very real occupational hazard. To succumb to it is to propagate an artificial and lifeless theology. Such a theology can become parasitic—an ineffectual subculture of the ecclesiastical society with its own jargon, customs, and methods that are totally unreal and unrelated to the community. Felix Lamennais described the fragmentation and irrelevance of this kind of theology in the early nineteenth century. Portrayed by Daniel-Rops as "a lean little figure . . . face yellow and wrinkled with prominent cheekbones and aquiline nose," Lamennais wrote in 1829 that the theology taught in most seminaries is a "dried-up and decadent Scholasticism whose dryness repels the students, giving them no overall picture of religion nor its marvelous relevance to all that interests man. . . ." *Ebed-*Theology, on the contrary, has a broad world-view that recognizes the corporate or societal dimension of man. It is this wider vision that establishes the proper identity of theology.

Religion and theology are primarily concerned with God, but God in relation to man. If religion is the acknowledgment and response to God as a Creator, then theology is the intellectual interpretation of who and what God is. But the *Whoness* and *Whatness* of God can be seen only in terms of humanity. Theology, call it incarnational or anthropocentric, cannot be seen apart from man. Revelation, that personal, mysterious, salvific, and God-initiated self-dis-

closure of the Almighty, is ordered to man. Biblicists agree that revelation is functional or economic. God reveals Himself to man by inter-
vening, acting, and speaking at specific times in history. God acts
and speaks *for man*. Theology reflects revelation because it too is
economic, that is, concerned with God in relation to man.

However, theology must also engage in a deeper study of God
and view Him in ontological and essential terms. Using as a source
the personal communication between God and man, the theologian
tries to grasp God who is Being Itself. But even this speculative consideration of the immanent (God in Himself) is oriented toward
the economic (God dealing with man and effecting his salvation).
Theology has to study both of these aspects. To be concerned solely
with the economic is to approach humanism, and to concentrate
only on the immanent is to ignore the real meaning of God's personal self-manifestation to man.

The twentieth-century theologian has to be, in one sense, ill at
ease, anxious, and perplexed. Although secure in his faith and grateful to the Church as the "pillar and mainstay of the truth" (*1 Tim.*
3:15), he is still a pilgrim and must contend with the pilgrim's dis-
appointments and uncertainties. If he is sensitive to his vocation and
to the world he lives in, he realizes that he must face the questions
posed by the technological revolution, urbanization, and seculariza-
tion. He is struck by his own inadequacy to speak to secular man of
God in terms that make sense to him. The secular agnostic, the scientific humanist, the atheist, the apathetic, and even the believer
within his community are forcing the theologian to rethink the
traditional answers and formulas. The "Beauty ever ancient, ever
new," must be expressed in language that speaks to contemporary
man. "Let there be growth," pleaded Vincent of Lerins and then,
as if to answer some who might question the reasonableness of his
plea, he adds: "Who is so grudging towards his fellowmen and so
full of hatred toward God as to try and prohibit it?"

The sensitive theologian who reads the signs of the times correctly cannot be complacent and comfortable. When he sees the ferment in every stratum of contemporary life, he is overwhelmed. He
knows he must act, and *do* something, but he is not sure where to

begin, so vast is his work. Yet he must not fall victim to despair or apathy. He has to provide positive direction for the confused and the doubting. Paul Tillich exemplifies this sensitivity to man in his theological approach. He explains that he starts "with man asking questions about the ultimate meaning of life." In fresh, reasonable, and comprehensible language the theologian has to address the healing Word not just to the card-carrying members of his denomination, but to the wider community of the non-Churched. A vigorous and honest theology can help all those who are looking for solid ground amid the shifting sands of change and radical doubt.

Two kinds of theologians are badly needed at this time if the needs of the community are to be served. First of all, we need the scholar who is qualified, academically and emotionally, to dedicate himself to research. Today, this kind of unspectacular but profound probing of theological issues is not a luxury but a necessity. Complex problems deserve answers that are painstakingly thought-out and supported by convincing evidence. Learned theological study of biblical and historical truth requires sheer doggedness along with intellectual acumen. It means that the theologian must not only have control of the classical theological languages—Hebrew, Greek, and Latin—but also be well versed in modern laguages. That this linguistic prerequisite is no mean achievement or that it is easily acquired can be seen from the comments of St. Jerome whom you can almost see working over his scrolls in a bare cell. He describes his study of Hebrew this way:

> What labor I spent upon this task, what difficulties I went through, how often I despaired, how often I gave up and then in my eagerness to learn commenced again, can be attested both by myself, the subject of this misery, and by those who lived with me. But I thank the Lord that from this seed of learning sown in bitterness, I now cull such sweet fruits.

Every theologian has to be something of a scholar. He has to devote much of his time to serious study and meditation. These quiet periods of reflection cannot be neglected if his theology is to be more than a superficial and unsatisfying response to the urgent problems men face. The theologian has to withdraw frequently for personal communion with God if he is to know the reality that is God in the lives of others. St. Anselm's writings were the result of many years of study. We have none of his writings before 1070, when he was already thirty-seven years old. His greatest works were written in two periods: when he was forty-five and when he was over sixty years old. In our own day, we have the Jesuit theologian, Bernard Lonergan, who went through a long preparation of intense study before he started writing. He was forty-two when he wrote his famous *Verbum* articles in *Theological Studies* and fifty-three when he published *Insight*. One of his confreres, Father F. E. Crowe, has written this about him: "Lonergan has worked almost alone. He has had no collaborators, he is almost a stranger to congresses, encyclopedic enterprises, and the like, and I really do not see how what he has done so far could have been done except in loneliness."

Besides the scholar-theologian, there is need for the prophet-theologian. For too long, prophecy has been associated with the distant past. Prophecy is an ever-present requirement. The contemporary community demands theologians who are prophets in the biblical sense of the word—men who are perceptive to both the needs of the world and the voice of God. Such men are not seers who foretell the future. Their task is to proclaim and interpret present history in a creative way. The Old Testament prophet had privileged access to Yahweh—he knew Yahweh, understood Yahweh, and was on terms of intimate friendship with Him. Yahweh revealed His plan to the prophets and they communicated it to men. Prophets today operate in a similar fashion. The prophet-theologian recognizes the intervention of God in history and interprets this for men of his age. He serves the community by working out the implications of revelation in the present situation. He tries to interpret contemporary developments in light of the salvific plan of God to call all men to a vital and loving discipleship. History has shown that prophets are not usually popular with their peers. It is inevitable that they are ignored, ridiculed, and considered as disruptive elements by many. The community does not readily accept them and may look upon

them as "false prophets" or "prophets of doom." Prophets must
prove themselves by the integrity of their lives and the honesty of
their message in spite of opposition and rejection. Theirs is a lone-
some, unrewarding, but absolutely essential task. History has shown
us that it is from the initiative and brilliance of a few that great
movements have started. Father Bernard Lonergan, describing the
"creative minority" of which he is surely a member, writes:

> Every . . . historical movement, however great, profound, and
> lasting it may be, begins with a "creative minority": it is the minor-
> ity that questions, thinks, understands, decides, and takes the lead;
> the majority are taught, persuaded, and led. Marx lived in the
> nineteenth century and was an object of ridicule; in the twentieth
> century Marxist doctrine is victorious over a large part of the world.
> The Greek philosophers were very few, the apostles of the Lord a
> little flock, the first monks not numerous; there were not many
> profound scholastics, no army of early companions for Ignatius,
> nor was Luther a mob, or Calvin, or Descartes, or Galileo, or
> Rousseau, or Kant. The essential thing is to understand the state
> of men's minds and the character of events, and discover what can
> and ought to be done. If, with the direction and help of the Lord,
> you succeed in this, you will make your own contribution to that
> greater glory which is promoted by external activity.

I V

In the last few pages I have been discussing the theologian's
function in the community. However, this is only one aspect of the
theological vocation that must be counterbalanced by another quality. The theologian of the twentieth century must situate himself in
the developing tradition. It is to this *sense of tradition* that I would
now like to address myself.

Theology is, by definition, linked to tradition. It is a continual
effort to explore, to analyze, and to understand the meaning of
God's intervention in history. Exciting, creative theology is not possible if it has no relationship to what has gone before. The theologian works with the *"traditum"*—that which has been handed down.
"The unhistorical," lamented C. S. Lewis, "are usually, without

knowing it, enslaved to a very recent past." To abandon the vast riches of theological tradition is to condemn theology to a shallow and unproductive existence. If the theologian is to answer the question, "Who am I?", he must first answer the question, "Where did I come from?" This identity crisis is solved when the theologian becomes aware of the long-developed tradition of which he is a part. Dr. Eric L. Mascall presents a realistic ideal for theologians. He says that the theologian should develop "a deliberate habit of loyal submission to Christian tradition, while at the same time bringing to bear upon it all the critical and interpretative gifts which God has given him."

What do we mean by the theological tradition? It is the common heritage of theology that includes the biblical witness, the patristic reflection, the conciliar *corpus,* the *sensus fidelium* expressed in cult and belief over the ages, the teaching of theologians, and finally, the Church's preaching of the faith. Tradition is a complex and many-faceted reality. It is both the *process* by which the revealed Word of God is passed on to man and the *truth* that is transmitted. Today's theologian in his attempt at relevancy must know his tradition according to its proper *Sitz im Leben,* its life-setting.

Let us delineate more clearly the meaning of tradition. Tradition cannot be identified with the past. To be traditional does not mean to reach into the grab bag of the past and pull out useful ideas and insights. To adopt the past simply because it is the past is archaism—a posture to be studiously avoided by thinking theologians. The Fathers, the Councils, or certain theologians have not said the last word about all the problems of theology. Every theological problem is capable of further understanding and development. Theology is more than a mere repetition of formulas and propositions. Even a dogma does not claim to solve all the aspects of the truth that it enunciates. Dogmas rather announce the beginning of fresh theological study and development. Theological tradition, then, is not a static reality, but progressive and evolving.

However, although tradition is not a mere mouthing of the past, it does deal with the past. The theologian is a man of tradition who follows the maxim of Pope Leo XIII, *Vetera novis augere et perfi-*

cere—augment and perfect the old with new things. The theologian, then, must determine what precisely are the *vetera*—the sources of his theological investigation. He must examine carefully in a rational and scientific way the *auditus fidei*—the articles of faith contained in tradition. The more the theologian knows about the *vetera,* the more he is capable of contributing the *nova*—the relevant applications to current demands. A creative return to tradition is the best guarantee of an authentic and constructive theology. The Church must have, as St. Bernard wrote, eyes backward and forward. The theologians are those eyes.

American theologians, more than their European counterparts, live in an environment inimical to an appreciation of tradition. Perhaps this explains the derivative character of much of American theology that is dependent on European scholarship and initiative. The rejection of tradition has accelerated rapidly in America since the end of World War II. The sense of continuity is fast disappearing from American life. A *Time* essay in 1966, can report that the United States "still views all kinds of tradition with more youthful irreverence than any other nation, past or present." This same restless, fluctuating spirit was noted by Jean Paul Sartre when he visited America in the forties. He wrote sadly:

> Today the American sees his city objectively; he does not dream of finding it ugly, but thinks it really old. If it were even older like ours, he could find a social past, a tradition in it. We generally live in our grand-father's houses. Our streets reflect the customs and ways of past centuries; they tend to filter out the present; none of what goes on in Rue Montorgueil of the Rue Pot-de-Fer is completely of the present. But the thirty-year old American lives in a house that was built when he was twenty.

A disturbing element in much of modern theologizing is the emergence of a new dogmatism. It aims to replace an outmoded structure by a new, up-to-date model. Unfortunately, although it is motivated by noble reasons, it easily makes the same errors that it is trying to correct. By its myopic concentration on the present, such theology becomes simplistic and unhistorical. Its aversion or avoidance of the past distorts its judgments of present issues. The only tradition is the present tradition. There is a danger that the present will be canonized and become the sole criterion for truth. This would produce an enfeebled eschatology consisting almost exclusively in a denial of the past and an overpowering concern for the present. Tradition cannot be identified with the present, because the *status quo nunc* is the product of the past and can only be understood in relationship to it.

Tradition, for the theologian, cannot be equated solely with the past or the present. It is both the past and the present and will continue into the future. St. Augustine says that sacred history continues *usque ad praesentia,* and Jean Daniélou, commenting on this, adds: "Sacred history is not restricted to the contents of the Bible: we are living in sacred history." This concept of history helps situate theology as a dynamic and developing study. Theology deals with a revelation of God given once and for all and attempts to translate the meaning of this message into contemporary language. "The crucial problem of all theology," writes the Orthodox theologian P. Evdokimov, "is the link between the fact of revelation and its actualization here and now." Thomas Merton brings out the same point when he writes: "The biggest paradox about the Church is that she is at the same time essentially traditional and essentially revolutionary."

Theological tradition is a tradition of growth, and the theologian stands at the outer periphery of the "growing edge" of tradition. He must study theology in terms of the evolutionary development of doctrine that is a sober evaluation of the past and the present. This is historical orthodoxy and relevant theology at its best. It regards theology as open-ended and capable of growth. While admitting the objective substance of doctrine, it allows for its organic development. Pope John XXIII described this type of theologizing when he opened the Second Vatican Council. "The idea is one thing," he said, "and its concrete expression in words is another. While still faithfully preserving pure doctrine, it can be expressed with varying and diverse concepts according to the mentality and language of the people."

The sixteen theologians interviewed combine an acute appreciation of the past with a sympathetic recognition of present problems. The communitarian and traditional perspective of their theology is profound and purposefully orientated. It is my hope that the comments and observations in the interviews that follow are as informative and stimulating to others as they were to me, the first to hear them.

Robert McAfee Brown

O*n the twenty-second floor of the Brown Palace Hotel in Denver, I interview Robert McAfee Brown. With his wife and children, he is* en route *to Massachusetts from California where he teaches at Stanford University. He is stopping in Denver to address the annual meeting of The Catholic Theological Society of America.*

Punctual to the minute and conservatively dressed in a dark green suit, Dr. Brown has the air of a prosperous young executive. His glasses and prematurely gray hair give him a scholarly look, but it is combined with a vitality and intensity that is not usually associated with the stereotype of a professional theologian. His speech is crisp, almost clipped, and as the excitement of the conversation develops, it becomes more and more rapid and is accompanied by vigorous gestures. An occasional wry remark or amusing aside gives only a fleeting glimpse of the creative humor that produced that minor classic of hagiography, The Collected Writings of St. Hereticus.

INTERVIEWER: You wrote on the crucial problem of doctrinal authority in Protestantism in *The Commonweal* (Oct. 9, 1964). Your views were criticized in a later issue by a fellow Protestant who argued that Protestantism was losing its sense of authority. Would you please comment on this.

DR. BROWN: My critic, as I recall, felt that the further Protestantism drifts away from a kind of fundamentalist interpretation of the authority of Scripture, the more vapid it becomes. He also felt that ecumenical Protestantism, in trying to please everybody, gets further

I

and further away from the *kerygma,* the New Testament proclamation, and waters it down more and more.

INTERVIEWER: What are your feelings on this point?

DR. BROWN: I feel very strongly, on the contrary, that as the ecumenical era has drawn Protestant churches closer together in their theological life, through the World Council of Churches, for example, what has emerged has not been a least-common-denominator theology, but an increasingly deeper and richer theological articulation. This can be symbolized by the contrast between the initial basis for membership in the World Council, formulated in Amsterdam in 1948, which was simply acceptance of Jesus Christ as God and Savior, and the amplified basis approved by the World Council in 1961 in New Delhi. The latter assembly placed the Christological affirmation in the context of a Trinitarian affirmation and put both affirmations in the context of the authority of Scripture. While this is not yet the fullness of the Catholic Faith, the point is that the years of ecumenical exchange from 1948-1961 have led us to a deeper theological affirmation rather than a thinner one. It is my expectation that this process will continue as the churches in the World Council continue their ecumenical explorations together.

Of course, there is another factor that has entered the scene since 1961, and this is the possibility of increasingly open exchange between Catholics and Protestants. I am personally not fearful that we are going to sell our respective heritages downstream in an effort to be ecumenically polite to one another. Rather, to the extent that these encounters are real encounters, each of us must attempt to articulate his own tradition with as much authenticity and vigor as possible, so that out of this new exchange a more creative and enriched theological affirmation will become possible for all of us.

INTERVIEWER: Ecumenical encounters, however, often bog down because of a mutual misunderstanding of terminology. For example, Protestants and Catholics mean something different by the "church tradition."

DR. BROWN: It is true that there are great differences between the Catholic and Protestant understanding of this term, but this is an area where we are moving toward a greater area of shared conviction. Catholic recognition of Scripture as the source of all theology is much stronger today than it was twenty or twenty-five years ago. Similarly, when Protestants talk about *Sola Scriptura,* we discover that this is not just Scripture-by-itself, but Scripture as it has been interpreted within the life of the church. We are recognizably closer to one another on the issue of Scripture and tradition than we were when the ecumenical age began to dawn. My hope is that we will be drawn even closer as Catholics take more seriously what Father Geiselmann and others have called "the sufficiency of Scripture" for doctrinal statements. I see problems, of course, for Catholics as this is done, particularly in regard to the Mariological doctrines, and in certain other areas where the Catholic has to ask himself honestly if some things in tradition have not become disproportionate in terms of what the scriptural witness emphasizes. We Protestants, for our part, have to go beyond a kind of phony *Sola Scriptura,* as though we could leapfrog over nineteen centuries, and come to terms much more seriously with what we mean when we talk about tradition. This cannot be simply picking out what we like from the Fathers. Our task is to take the *whole* heritage into account and to ask ourselves if there are not some points on which we may have short-changed tradition.

INTERVIEWER: What Catholic authors are most popular with Protestants?

DR. BROWN: I think the Catholic theologian who strikes the most responsive note with Protestants is Hans Küng. I do not say this to give him the kiss of death by implying that I think he is really a "Protestant at heart" or anything of the sort. But Küng's theological life at Tübingen is lived within the context of not only a Catholic but also a Protestant theological faculty. Thus he does his thinking in relation to the problems that Protestant questions thrust upon Catholic theology, and his Catholic answers force Protestants into new areas of concern. Küng thus speaks out of a framework with which a Protestant finds a sense of great *rapport.* This is true not only of Küng's more popular works, but even more of things like his *Structures of the Church* and *Justification.*

Protestants also read theologians like Karl Rahner and Yves

Congar with great profit—and of course in the field of biblical scholarship we make continual use of Catholic writers. A theologian like Father Congar is every inch a Catholic, and yet he writes out of a knowledge of Protestantism, and thus communicates the Catholic Faith to us in ways not possible to a Catholic theologian who has never bothered to read what Protestants write.

INTERVIEWER: One seems to detect the influence of Karl Rahner in your writings, especially in your frequent references to Christianity as the religion of the remnant.

DR. BROWN: Father Rahner still writes faster than I can read, and there is much of his work with which I am not yet acquainted, but I find him a *creative* thinker willing to rethink how the Faith can best be communicated in our day. The notion that Christianity in our day is the religion of the remnant is of course original neither to me nor to Rahner. But as I think about its meaning, I am immensely fortified to discover that Rahner is working with much the same concept. Rahner describes the Church as entering into a period of *diaspora*—of being scattered abroad in the world. We no longer live in the age of "Christendom," and we are not going to return to it. Rather than bemoaning this, we should accept it as the way God intends us to live in our new situation, and then see what this means in terms of new forms or structures for the life of the Church. I am indebted to Karl Rahner for giving me some help and encouragement in facing a problem I must try to think through in ecumenical terms.

INTERVIEWER: Would you agree that one of the vital areas for discussion in the present ecumenical dialogue is the development of doctrine?

DR. BROWN: I fully agree. Until quite recently, it seemed to Protestants that everything in Catholic thought came to a halt in 1870. Formulas were fixed. Viewpoints were frozen. If there was anything more to be said, it would take place by papal *fiat*. New doctrines might come (as the dogma of the Assumption did in 1950), but there would be no refining of old doctrines.

But that's not quite how it has worked out. The thing that is opening the door now is that more and more of the bishops at the

Council have appealed to this notion of doctrinal development. It is not just the *avant garde* theologian who is saying this. The door is open, and it must be kept open. There is a problem remaining, of course, in any attempt to engage in the purification of "irreformable" decrees. But many theologians are working on that problem and asserting, as Küng has done so forcefully, that even in the area of irreformable dogma there are always better ways in which a fuller comprehension of the truth can be articulated by the Church. Thus even though the dogma of the Assumption has been "defined," I do not think many Catholics would yet claim to know just what the dogma "means," and here I hope that the ecumenical encounter can help to keep the "meaning" of the dogma from developing in a theologically distorted and ecumenically divisive way.

INTERVIEWER: Is there any parallel interest in Protestant theology concerning the question of development of doctrine?

DR. BROWN: One might say that the liberal Protestant theology of twenty years ago represented a sort of unbridled expression of the theme of development of doctrine. Doctrine developed all over the place without any disciplined sense of where the limitations were. In the early twentieth century Protestantism was in danger of doing no more than spinning out a reflection of the cultural milieu and losing all anchorage in the past.

What happened to Protestant theology subsequently has been almost the reverse of what took place in Catholic theology. Our need has been to recover a sense of rootage, of heritage. In our recovery of Scripture, we have attempted to rethink for our day what the Reformers were trying to do in their day, which was not to invent new ideas nor to let individualism run rampant, but to try to recover the *kerygma.*

The best Catholic historians are now affirming this quite clearly: Lortz in his two volumes on the Reformation, John Todd in his recent book on Luther, Father Dolan in his large work on Reformation interpretation. Others are indicating that at least in intention the Reformation was an attempt to purify something that was in serious jeopardy in the late medieval period. The issue was not innovation, but quite literally *re*formation.

The recovery of biblical theology and the new concern for tradition of which we were speaking earlier are Protestant counterparts of the Catholic concern for the development of doctrine. We have been attempting to understand the present in the light of the past, whereas it seems to me that you have been attempting to understand the past in the light of the present. The Catholic has now been emancipated, it seems to me, from a kind of imprisonment; not an imprisonment in the teachings of the past, but in the notion that the only way to talk about this teaching was in exactly the same way it was talked about in the past.

INTERVIEWER: What do you feel has been the most significant factor in Catholic ecumenical theology over the past few years?

DR. BROWN: I would describe it as the willingness of many Catholic theologians, reflected I believe in some of the Council statements, to accept the principle, *Ecclesia semper reformanda.* They are willing to urge openly that the Church—the Roman Catholic Church—stands always in need of reform, and that this is a loyal and not a disloyal concern for a Catholic to have. The Church must always be under the purging, purifying influence of the Holy Spirit. When this is being honestly articulated, as I think it now is in many quarters of the Catholic Church, then *in principle* there is nothing that can finally be a barrier to the possibility of eventual reunion. There are, of course, many awesome barriers that are not going to disintegrate easily. But as long as we can affirm the notion of *Ecclesia semper reformanda,* then we can put no straight jacket on the Holy Spirit and on what He can do with this new situation. To be sure we don't mean exactly the same thing when we use this principle, and yet it is a helpful point from which we can begin to grow toward one another. Some of our Protestant notions of reform can become more disciplined and chastened, while the narrower arena of possible Catholic reform may be widened in time from the Catholic side. It is a cause of great encouragement to me that the topic chosen for the Catholic-Presbyterian theological consultations is "reform and renewal as an ongoing process in the life of the church."

INTERVIEWER: Does the fact that reunion is not imminent have a debilitating effect on the ecumenical exchange?

DR. BROWN: I don't think that we have to be discouraged by the fact that organic reunion is not just around the corner. If anything, that should make us *more* concerned to speed the day. In the meantime, all kinds of *levels* of reunion can be manifested. For instance, it is very encouraging that the Vatican Council *Decree On Ecumenism* sets a whole new tone for the Catholic understanding of the Church, with its recognition that Protestants are not just individuals upon whom a little grace has mysteriously rubbed off. It is there acknowledged that in our corporate life the *ecclesia* is somehow present. This means that there is a whole new framework for the ecumenical encounter. We can start off from the fact that on some very fundamental level we are already one in Christ. When we start from that point we are in a much better position than if we consider Catholics and Protestants as two totally separated entities who share nothing in common. Even the more conservative *Constitution De Ecclesia* stresses that baptism incorporates all who receive it within the Body of Christ, which, of course, includes non-Roman Catholics as well. Also of immense importance is the realization that we share a common Scripture, and that the gifts of the Spirit have been given to the "churches and ecclesiastical communities" of Protestantism and not just to individuals. It is upon such things that we can build creatively toward deeper and deeper levels of sharing. While Vatican II insists that the *fullness* of catholic faith is found only in the Roman Catholic Church, it does not insist that gifts of the Spirit have been denied to non-Catholic churches. This does not solve all the ecumenical problems, but it does create the possibility of a context of discussion in which they can be approached creatively rather than polemically.

INTERVIEWER: Do you think that most of the priests and ministers in the parishes are fully convinced of the value of the ecumenical dialogue?

DR. BROWN: It depends where they are. From the Catholic side it depends very much on the degree of openness of the bishop and how much ecumenical encounter he will permit. It's no secret that there is more ecumenical activity in St. Louis than in Los Angeles. Structurally, this is simply one of the facts of ecumenical life, and we have to hope for greater openness on the part of more and more bishops so that things can be done without fear.

I know some Protestants who feel threatened by the new Catholic openness. They think it is some kind of Catholic trick, a kind of soft sell, designed only to get everybody to return to Rome with a little less pain. There are also Catholics who feel that the ecumenical dialogue is jeopardizing the distinctiveness of the Catholic Faith because so many nice things are now being said about Martin Luther or Karl Barth. Others feel that the liturgical reforms of the Mass give it too much of a "Protestant look." There are many such residual fears to be overcome. But so much has happened that even if ecumenism were slowed down, it would be impossible to stop it. "The genie is out of the bottle," as one of our Protestant observers remarked at the Council, "and no one is going to get it back in."

INTERVIEWER: What role will the liturgy play in future ecumenical encounters?

DR. BROWN: One of the most creative areas for further experimentation is going to be the sharing of a common liturgical life. I know that many Catholics are greatly concerned about this; they worry that the distinctiveness of the Mass will diminish if Protestants are welcome to attend Catholic services and Catholics are free to attend Protestant services. Catholic authorities are being very cautious in this area. But in the long run, it may well be that one of the most fundamental things the Council did was to encourage the extension of *communicatio in sacris,* for this begins to make it possible for us to know each other at the point of our deepest convictions. To me one of the most important things about being at the Council was the chance to be present each day for Mass. After ten weeks of five days a week, I began to understand something of what the Mass must mean to the Catholic and why it is so central for him. But it is also important for the Catholic to share in common worship with Protestants—to share as far as his conscience will permit in the singing of hymns, the hearing of Scripture, and the corporate prayers that are part of Protestant worship. Such experiences will make clearer to the Catholic than any book could ever do that Protestantism is not just individualism run rampant, but that there is within it a corporate discipline that gives great stress to an historical continuity with the liturgy of the ages.

INTERVIEWER: What do you consider the most pressing task facing the Catholic Church today in its desire to foster the genuine spirit of ecumenism?

DR. BROWN: The consolidation and development of the *Constitution De Ecclesia* is fundamental, and the degree of implementation of the principle of the collegiality of bishops will indicate how serious the Church really is about reform and renewal.

INTERVIEWER: What of the whole problem of the Church in the modern world?

DR. BROWN: We are beginning to see that the Church can affirm the creative possibilities of the *diaspora* situation. The Church does not need to yearn for a situation in which it is the dominant factor in the life of society. It does not have to look back fondly to the thirteenth century as if that were the ideal situation. It can move out into the modern world as a kind of partner in the human venture. It must be a partner even with those who do not share all its presuppositions. This, I believe, is only beginning to happen, and it must happen at an increasingly accelerated rate. The Church must involve itself in the civic order, not to bring the civic order under the domination of the Church, but to embrace the civic order as the arena of man's humanity where Catholic, Protestant, Jew, and humanist all have common concerns and common problems. We must work *together* on the common problems that face mankind, whether these are questions of nuclear warfare, the population explosion, the war on poverty, or politics. A good symbol of this new kind of concern is the fact that the involvement of the Church in the area of civil rights has finally occurred. The presence of priests and nuns at Selma is an important symbol of this new attitude. It is not enough, of course, to have nuns and priests go bail for Catholic laymen in the world. But the very fact that priests and nuns can occasionally be found on picket lines indicates a new posture that is an important one.

INTERVIEWER: Let us now turn to the Protestant Church. What would you say is the central ecumenical task facing the Protestant Church today?

DR. BROWN: I think that our main intramural responsibility now is to put our own house in order, and on the ecumenical front this means overcoming the divisiveness of denominationalism. I don't think that Catholics realize to what degree actual, organic reunions are taking place within the Protestant world. Even though there is an inordinate amount of talk about getting rid of denominational barriers that never gets beyond talk, there is also more than just talk. There have been something like fifty actual reunions of formerly divided Protestant denominations within the last two decades. A move like the "Blake Proposal" (now the Consultation on Church Union), which would draw together six or even nine denominations into one, is very important. It is a long and wearisome process to bring groups together that have been divided for over four hundred years, but it is a necessary next step for us. At the very least, we have become aware that our own internal divisions are scandalous, and we can no longer remain complacent in the light of that fact. So the actual overcoming of our division must have a high priority.

INTERVIEWER: Would this be a *sine qua non* condition for eventual reunion?

DR. BROWN: We have certainly got to offer the Catholic Church a more united front than we now possess. We are not going to dispel all Protestant divisions within a few years or over a few decades; the main Protestant groups realize that the smaller sects and Pentecostal groups are not exactly enamored of all this ecumenical business. Those who are in any way committed to the ecumenical venture know that one arm of ecumenical activity must be tireless work for the reunification of divided Protestantism. This is something that has to proceed at the same time that the Catholic-Protestant dialogue is going on.

INTERVIEWER: Doesn't the Protestant church also face the need to relate itself to the modern world?

DR. BROWN: Yes, both churches must be committed to this. Many people are now discovering, as I did when I began teaching within a secular university, that all the talk about "reunion" is of interest only to a handful of people. And reunion, no matter how theologically proper, is not really going to count for very much unless the reunited churches express in a corporate way their concern for the world. We can be reunited among ourselves in a wonderfully irrelevant fashion and congratulate ourselves on the overcoming of our divisions. But we need to remember that Jesus' prayer that we are always quoting goes on, "...that all may be one,...*that the world may believe.*"

INTERVIEWER: What contribution has the history of Protestant ecumenism made here?

DR. BROWN: From 1910 on, there has been a double stress, and ecumenicity has meant both concern for *unity* and concern for *mission.* It is the latter area that sometimes gets lost sight of when we talk about the contemporary ecumenical movement. It is important to remember that in Protestantism the ecumenical movement started on the mission field. The nineteenth-century Protestant missionaries went out and discovered that they were exporting Western Christian *divisions* to India, China, and Japan. Consequently, it was a recognition of the scandal of division in the missionary activity of the church that led to the first really ecumenical conference at Edinburgh in 1910. There an initial attempt was made to cope with the problem of division and find ways of working co-operatively on the mission field. What could be more devisive than converting an inhabitant of Hong Kong to the Canadian Baptist church?

In recent years it is significant that the impulse toward unity has come from the so-called "younger churches" in Protestantism. The most significant union of Protestant groups thus far took place in South India in 1947. Christian unity and the missionary outreach of the Church into the world are really two sides of the same coin.

INTERVIEWER: Let us turn for a moment to another subject. In an article in *The Christian Century* (May 5th, 1965) you wrote: "I continue to believe that only he who can affirm as well as deny has claim to the title of 'theologian.'"

DR. BROWN: The statement was in the context of some comments on the so-called "death of God" school of thought. There is a great deal of this making the rounds in contemporary Protestantism, and a number of theologians are glorying in acts of negation. It seems to me that this position works itself into a *cul-de-sac* from which there is no escape. The desire of the group is to whittle away from Christianity what they consider to be unnecessary accretions. In doing this, however, they appear to have no criteria by means of which to arrest the process, and it is hard to see how they can end up with anything save a kind of exalted humanism. If one can affirm no more than the latter, then he must be honest and do precisely that, but I fail to see how his statements qualify as statements of Christian theology. The theologian (I was trying to suggest in the statement you quoted) cannot simply negate certain things that in the past might have made it hard for men to believe. For the faith he is called upon to explicate is a series of affirmations rather than negotiations. The theologian must make them relevant, but he has not been faithful to his calling if he simply transforms Christianity into what Ronald Knox once called "those things that Jones can be persuaded to swallow."

INTERVIEWER: But what is the precise function of doubt in the theological quest?

DR. BROWN: I believe there is an important place for doubt in theology, in the sense that doubt is a kind of catalyst to a living faith. The theologian who has no more questions left to plague him, no more burning problems that he has not resolved to his total satisfaction, cannot be called a genuine theologian. He has simply became a repeater of words. He has developed a compact, all-inclusive system that may be consistent, but fails to be truly descriptive. He is guilty of what Pope Paul, in his address to the Protestant observers at the Council, called "theological immobilism." Cardinal Leger, and others at the Council, frequently stated that in principle there is always a better way to state one's understanding of the Christian Faith. No theological affirmation is finally exhaustive and totally inclusive. If it were, we would be God and not men. We must always be willing to question the way that something has been said. This is an important part of the growing edge of any theological endeavor.

INTERVIEWER: In the above-mentioned article you wrote: "Faith without doubt is dead." Isn't this a contradiction?

DR. BROWN: That may have been a little flip, but I would stand by it in reflection. The very notion that faith continually seeks understanding (which is what I take it Anselm was talking about) means that one is never in total possession of what faith is. Our difficulty may lie in the fact that we mean different things when we speak of the act of faith. Perhaps a Catholic cannot really say, as I must say, that to be a believing Christian always involves an element of risk. Faith is not such a "sure thing" that it is beyond the possibility of challenge. I have elsewhere referred to this as the "Protestant risk," and I think it may be one of our contributions to the total ecumenical venture to keep suggesting that we must be willing to embrace the life of doubt as something that exists within the life of faith. This may be a necessary counterbalance to a certain type of Catholic *securitas* that feels it would be disloyal ever to intimate, even to oneself, that faith is hard.

Having said that, let me also say that I have come to the point where the life of doubt is not as seriously threatening as it once was. I think that my faith is such that it can encompass the doubt, but not in a way that totally extinguishes it. In this latter admission I am a "modern man" as well as a Christian. I would like to believe that one can be both a modern man and a Christian, and I am not at all sure that a person is called to be one to the total extinction of the other.

INTERVIEWER: Even though we live in a nondefinitional age, it might help our present discussion if you would define what you mean by faith.

DR. BROWN: I would define faith more as trust or commitment than as an assent made with complete certitude. Faith, then, is the act of commitment and trust of the whole person out of which the explication of this in terms of "assent" must come. This is what *fides quaerens intellectum* means to me. In faith I commit my total being to God as the reality who is all-encompassing for the meaning of my life. It is then my task as a theologian to give as much clarity as I can to what it means to have done this. Theology is loving God with the mind; and that is all very well, so long as we remember that we are called upon to love God with heart, soul, and strength as well.

INTERVIEWER: You would find no difficulty, then, in reconciling the Protestant concept of faith with the traditional Catholic teaching?

DR. BROWN: It doesn't seem to me that what I have been trying to state is as different from the concern of the Catholic theologian as I once thought it was. I suppose it depends largely on which Catholic theologians one reads. The people I read make room for the recognition that theological understanding must always be open to re-examination and clarification. The Catholic theologian, of course, is confronted by the area of infallible, irreformable truth that is not subject to the kind of doubt I have been trying to describe. But even here I discover a real sense in which the so-called "irreformable" doctrines are still subject to further development and fresh interpretation. In view of the fact that Vatican II is making a legitimate place for development of doctrine in the Catholic Church, I don't feel nearly the hiatus between the Catholic and Protestant understanding of the theological task that I once felt.

INTERVIEWER: Has your teaching experience in a secular university influenced your theological thinking in any significant way?

DR. BROWN: I think to a considerable degree it has. I had been teaching for ten years in a Protestant seminary, and the decision to move into undergraduate teaching on a secular campus was a hard one to make. I realized that it was a real vocational shift, but it has been very important in redefining my approach to the theological task. It means that I now have to be a theologian within the atmosphere of an academic community that by and large couldn't care less about theology. If the theological venture is an authentic one, then it has to be able to authenticate itself within the nonsupportive atmosphere of the secular university as well as within the supportive atmosphere of the seminary. The change is part of my concern to be engaged in dialogue with the world as well as participating in the internal dialogue within the life of the Church. I must do my thinking in close proximity to the world of doubt and the secular world, indeed as a partial citizen of both of those worlds. After three years at Stanford, I am increasingly sure that the secular world must be affirmed by the Christian on its own terms. We are not interested in the secular world only to convert it and make it Christian. We must enter into a kind of partnership with this vast hoard of people who are not Christians, and who are not in any conceivable future about to become Christians. We share many basic human concerns with them and we have to make common cause with them in combating human ills. So I am more concerned now than I once was to affirm that which is best in the secular world.

INTERVIEWER: Do you think that seminaries, both Catholic and Protestant, have failed to prepare students adequately for this confrontation with the modern world?

DR. BROWN: I think there could certainly be more of this confrontation in Protestant seminaries, and from what I have heard about Catholic seminaries, I feel sure the same thing would apply there also. Indeed, after three years at Stanford, I sometimes wish that the Protestant seminarian could have his seminary education within the context of the secular university. I see no reason why that would not also be desirable in Catholic theological education. It doesn't make sense to separate the ordinand from the world to which he will later be ministering. Of course, there is a value in being drawn apart into the community of the like-minded and being nourished by a common liturgical life. But this must always be done, if it is to be creative, in a kind of dialectic of living in the world. The entrance of the lay theologian into the Catholic seminary would be immensely rewarding, but so also would be the exposure of the Catholic seminarian to the thinking of the leaders of the labor unions, civil rights groups, politicians, and so on. This should be part of his basic training, not an addendum to it. In this way, the theology he gets could be developed in the context of having had to listen to the problems and questions of modern man, rather than being spun out in splendid and irrelevant isolation.

INTERVIEWER: You once wrote that Catholic seminaries need a vital biblical theology and a greater contact with the world. Do you have anything to add to this?

Dr. Brown: That was a very broad prescription for the problem. A good symbol for what seminary life should be is contained in one of my favorite statements from Karl Barth. He says that the Christian must always read with the Bible in one hand and the morning newspaper in the other. As a seminarian reads the Scriptures, this ought to help him understand the morning newspaper, while in reading the morning newspaper, he ought to be challenged more and more to understand the human situation under God as Scripture depicts it. Each illumines the other. The whole of the Christian heritage must be related to the world in which the priest or minister is going to find himself. I am glad that Union Seminary is located right in the heart of New York City, for that fact makes it more difficult for a student to ignore the world around him, even though there are always ways to retreat within the cloister. The church is not a preserve to protect one from the ravages of the world. The church is the arena from which one must love the world, affirm it, and not simply shake a finger of scorn at it. There is much to affirm in the secular world, as I have found in my associations with the faculty and students at Stanford. I have discovered that the concerns I share as a human being about civil rights or nuclear warfare, for example, are not to be pursued simply by seeking out fellow Christians within the academic community. I have found that the lines aren't cut as neatly as I might have expected they would be.

Interviewer: Dr. Brown, would you please give me some words of advice to seminarians to help them meet realistically and effectively the current challenge?

Dr. Brown: I would hope that, in addition to absorbing the best in the creative currents in contemporary Catholic thought, they would be getting firsthand exposure to currents in Protestant and secular thought. The latter insights should not just be filtered through some Catholic sieve of interpretation. Instead of just reading a Catholic book about Martin Luther, they should read his *Treatise on Christian Liberty*. Instead of just hearing a Catholic scholar describe the World Council, they should read the documents from Evanston, Amsterdam, and New Delhi. Instead of just being told about the modern world by a priest, they should read some very tough-minded contemporary authors. Seminary education, I would hope, would involve among other things a real engagement with non-Catholic points of view.

One of the things that has been so important to me as a member of a secular university faculty is that I am now in elbow-to-elbow contact with high-minded secularists whose concerns I share, but whose motivation is not based on any discernible Christian involvement. In one sense it is very reassuring to have such people around. In another sense it is disturbing to discover that you don't have to be a Christian to do many of the important things in life. But that is the way the world is. I can know this in principle or I can read about it. But to be in living contact with it is very important to me theologically. Certainly the seminarian needs to grapple with the same sort of problem.

INTERVIEWER: What approach would you suggest to make these "high-minded secularists" aware of the Christian message?

DR. BROWN: I don't think there is any formula that applies here. I am wary of all attempts to develop Six Handy Rules for Dealing with Secularists. I think that we have to relate to each of these persons first of all in terms of the humanity we both share. That is our basic point of association. We can then begin to build on this and discover that with whatever different motivations, we have common goals, common causes, common concerns to share. Thus, we get to know each other and in time can explore each other's motivations. If we share a concern for civil rights, he may legitimately wonder just what my Christianity has to do with the question, since all he has seen organized Christianity do is block genuine progress in civil rights. He may feel that social conservatism in the churches is widespread and that racism receives a theological vindication in many Protestant pulpits. So he may press me on just how there is any connection between being a Christian and being concerned over civil rights.

INTERVIEWER: How, then, would you answer him?

DR. BROWN: It may become possible for me to ask what his motivations are, and we may be able to pursue the interesting fact that the noble humanist lives by what I would call a sublime inconsistency: he cannot affirm the *ultimate* worth of a man, and yet he is willing, if need be, to lay down his life for the *provisional* worth of the human being.

Albert Camus represents a genuine option to the Christian Faith. He doesn't try to make life rosy, and he will not invest it with ultimate meaning. Yet somehow (in a way that finally escapes me), he is able to make the jump from the absurdity of the human situation to compassion for human beings. I would like the secularists to explore the nature of that jump and how it is that one can move from absurdity to compassion. It may be that they are importing other factors, some of which might even be rooted in the Judaeo-Christian tradition.

INTERVIEWER: What are the obstacles to this type of approach?

DR. BROWN: For the Christian, the main obstacle is probably that he is not *really* willing to listen. Mutual exchange must be kept up. *Both* have to be willing to listen. It isn't the job of the Christian to be giving answers to questions that have not yet been asked. When eager Christian students are talking to me about this kind of problem and want to know how to deal with an agnostic roommate, for example, my first concern is that they be willing to listen. Too often they already know the answer they want to give: "Christ is the answer." But it is not enough to affirm Christ as the answer until this can be affirmed in terms of a response to a question that is really being asked. And sometimes we must be very patient in waiting for the questions to emerge.

INTERVIEWER: In your various writings, especially the more recent, I seem to detect a certain unrest or *malaise* in your attitude toward the Protestant Church.

DR. BROWN: What may sound like uneasiness to the Catholic is simply my attempt to be faithful to the dictum *Ecclesia semper reformanda*—the church always in process of being reformed. It is my feeling that part of the job of a Protestant is to be rigorously critical of Protestantism. The critique proceeds out of love rather than disaffection. My criticisms of Protestantism are based on the criteria of what the church ought to be and is not, but can become.

My task is to try to see that the household of the faith within which I have been placed by God becomes as true to its heritage as it can. If the Catholic takes seriously what it means to be a Catholic, then he too will surely be making a similar kind of critique of *his* household of faith, and of course some Catholic theologians have long been doing this. De Lubac, for example, has a chapter in *The Splendor of the Church* in which he insists that criticism must always be done in the framework of affirming one's belief in the Church. So what you describe as "unrest," I would rather describe as a Protestant counterpart of concern for *aggiornamento*.

INTERVIEWER: How can such criticism avoid the extreme of negativism and remain a positive, creative force in the church? Might not your criticisms finally force you to leave Protestantism?

DR. BROWN: I am a Protestant, first of all, because here is where God has placed me. In terms of the whole ecumenical task of establishing "the catholic church" (in the broadest sense), my contribution is to try to work in such a way that the Protestant church, and more specifically the Presbyterian church, becomes a more authentic vehicle of transmission of the *kerygma* to the world today. This means being critical, but being critical out of love. The critique must be an expression of loyalty. To criticize Protestantism is not to have entered a halfway house on the way to Roman Catholicism. Wherever a Christian finds himself within the family of Christendom, it is his job to stay there unless it becomes clear to him that it would be positively sinful for him to do so. It is much too easy, particularly for Protestants, to do a lot of denominational jumping around. My task in terms of the coming great church is not to jump over into the Catholic Church or into another Protestant denomination, nor do I really want "progressive" Catholics to become Protestants. I want them to work for reform and renewal *within* the Catholic Church. Each of us must see that the stream of Christendom in which we have been placed becomes a more faithful transmitter of the Gospel. If we all do this, wherever we now are, then I firmly believe that we will all, in the process, be drawn closer and closer to one another. Whatever works for reform and renewal in one area of Christendom is advantageous to all the rest. This is why I believe that ecumenism and conversion can be two different things.

INTERVIEWER: What do Protestants consider the greatest obstacle to reunion in Roman Catholicism?

DR. BROWN: The basic stumbling block for Protestants is of course the issue of infallibility. I sometimes think that if there had not been a Vatican I, the whole ecumenical situation would be a very different one, since there would be *in principle* no barrier to cut us off so absolutely from one another. For the Protestant, infallibility seems to say that men can speak with the untainted accents of the Holy Ghost, and this for the Protestant is an insupportable position. In bluntest terms, it appears as the epitome of spiritual pride in ecclesiastical life, a kind of denial that judgment must always begin at the house of God. Here is the point at which for me to become a Catholic would mean a denial of an important Biblical insight into the nature of the church. However, as the "development of doctrine" continues and the dogma of infallibility is refined in the ecumenical dialogue, it may conceivably come to have a meaning in the future where it would not be quite the barrier it is now. One must always leave that possibility open. Perhaps it is the Protestant task to keep affirming as vigorously as possible the nature of this ultimate ecumenical hurdle.

INTERVIEWER: To conclude our interview, Dr. Brown, would you please describe the attitude that Christians must foster if the ecumenical dialogue is to succeed?

DR. BROWN: Another remark from Karl Barth might be appropriate here, both in terms of ecumenical dialogue and dialogue with the non-Christian. He says that the Christian is not the one who out of the *largesse* of his bounty "stoops down" to the other (whether separated brother or non-Christian) to offer part of what he has. Barth says on the contrary that the Christian is the one who *stands beside* his fellow human being and affirms that the One Who "stoops down" is God, Who has humbled Himself to become man and to reach out to Christian, non-Christian, Protestant, Catholic. God became man to redeem the cosmos not just for Christians, not just for the church, but for all mankind. Therefore, the true Christian is the one who stands beside his brother, recognizing that *both* are the recipients of a gift. The only advantage one has over the other is that he knows the true nature of the human situation, which is that God has redeemed His people.

Something of that attitude, it seems to me, must come to characterize all of our dealings with one another. We have received a gift. Let us share that gift and let God do what He will with our act of sharing.

✻✻

ROBERT McAFEE BROWN was born in Carthage, Illinois, on May 28th, 1920. A philosophy major at Amherst College, he received his B.A. in 1943 and his B.D. from Union Theological Seminary in 1945. An ordained Presbyterian minister, he served as a United States Navy Chaplain from 1945 to 1946. After the war, he spent two years as an Assistant Chaplain at Amherst. Dr. Brown received his Ph.D. from Columbia University in 1951 and has also studied at Mansfield College, Oxford, and St. Mary's College, St. Andrew's University, Edinburgh, Scotland. He was Professor of Religion at Macalester College from 1951 to 1953 and returned to Union Theological Seminary in 1953 as the Auburn Professor of Systematic Theology. In 1962, he became Professor of Religion in the Special Programs in Humanities at Stanford University. He is married and the father of four children.

Dr. Brown was a Protestant observer at the Second Vatican Council and is a member of the editorial boards of *Christianity and Crisis*, *Theology Today*, and *Journal of Ecumenical Studies*. He is general editor of the twelve-volume *Layman's Theological Library*, and his several books include: *P. T. Forsyth: Prophet for Today*; *The Bible Speaks to You*; *The Significance of the Church*; *An American Dialogue* (with Gustave Weigel, S. J.); and *Observer at Rome*.

Johannes Quasten

Curley Hall is a graystone residence for priests on the northwestern fringe of the Catholic University campus. Father Quasten lives on the second floor, in Room 215. The room reflects its scholarly occupant: well-ordered and functional. Books line the walls from floor to ceiling—a rich collection of patristic writings in several languages. His desk is clear except for a few papers and one book. Close by is his typewriter. A small table next to his desk is covered with two or three foreign periodicals and a number of opened letters. There is no television, but a radio is visible in the adjoining bedroom.

He welcomes me heartily and motions for me to sit in a low, red leather chair. He puts down the German periodical he was reading, and we chat for several minutes. He is a large-framed man, friendly and confident. His strong features reflect a subtle mind, disciplined by years of intense scholarship. Talking with him, if only for a few moments, reveals his enthusiasm and love of the Fathers.

INTERVIEWER: You have spent your life working in the field of patrology. Could you begin by telling us something about the nature of patrology.

FATHER QUASTEN: Patrology may be formally defined as the science of the Fathers of the Church. It deals with the theological writers of Christian antiquity, but it is much more than simply biographical studies of these authors. It includes a thorough study of their writings and an analysis of the doctrines they proposed. Patrologists of the twentieth century are interested in the history of the ideas, concepts, and terms that are found in ancient Christian literature. Of great importance now is the question of the development of doctrine —the gradual, organic progress that has been made in Christian thought through the ages. To understand this development, one must know what the Christian writers of the early Church taught.

INTERVIEWER: What are the limits of the patristic period?

FATHER QUASTEN: Traditionally, the patristic period starts with the beginning of theological literature in the middle of the second century. It extends in the West up to Gregory the Great (d. 604) or Isidore of Seville (d. 636) and in the East up to St. John Damascene (d. 749). However, not all the authors that are studied in patrology are technically "Fathers" of the Church. The term "Father" is somewhat ambiguous. In ancient times, the title simply referred to a Christian teacher. Later, it was applied to the bishop, since he was the official teacher in the Church. In the fourth century, during the doctrinal controversies, the term "Father" was extended to refer to all ecclesiastical writers as long as they were accepted as teachers who were faithful to the Christian tradition. Today, we call those authors "Fathers of the Church" who possess the following qualifications: orthodoxy of doctrine, holiness of life, ecclesiastical approval, and antiquity. All other theological writers are called "ecclesiastical writers." In the second category, we have such great men as Origen and Tertullian who have contributed so much to the development of Christian doctrine. It was with this distinction in mind that we called our series of patristic writings *Ancient Christian Writers*.

INTERVIEWER: How is patrology related to theology?

FATHER QUASTEN: Theology began in the patristic period. There is no theology, in the formal sense, in the New Testament. In the second century, you find Christians who were called upon to explain their faith to the world around them. They had the faith, but they used reason in attempting to explain it to others. It was simply reason applied to faith. This is how theology began. Today, patrology is sometimes called historical theology, since it deals with the early sources of theological thought.

INTERVIEWER: What was it in the study of patrology that first attracted your attention?

FATHER QUASTEN: I found that one of the most challenging points of view in early Christian literature was the confrontation of the pagan world with the Christian faith. The Hellenistic world faced the Christian world—the old struggled with the new. This fascinated me. The relationships between these two worlds resulted in an exchange of influences. You see this clearly on a doctrinal level. It is not without reason that the first ecumenical councils were held in the East. Hellenistic philosophy and Christian theology met. The various Christological and Trinitarian controversies and the use of highly technical and abstract terminology are rooted in Hellenistic philosophical thought. These subjects were more widely discussed in the East than in the West.

INTERVIEWER: Would you also say that the early Church adopted many customs from the pagan world?

FATHER QUASTEN: Certainly. The first Christian missionaries followed a plan of accommodation that let them adopt whatever could be used by the Church. Many simple customs of the people fit perfectly into a Christian liturgical celebration. This was true especially in the ceremony of baptism. The use of salt and holy water would be two examples. The same is true of the cult of the dead. Symbols, too, were often borrowed from paganism. My dear friend and professor, F. J. Dölger, has shown in his great work of five volumes that the symbol of the fish was popular in pre-Christian times in the Hellenistic period. It was used as a symbol of life and in some cults it was the symbol of sacrificial food. The Christians took this symbol and transformed it. It became a symbol of Our Lord and is found in many of the catacombs. The Greek word for fish is *ichthus* and this became an acrostic, since it contains the initials of the Greek for "Jesus Christ, Son of God, Saviour."

INTERVIEWER: What other pagan customs were introduced into the rite of baptism?

FATHER QUASTEN: I would like to mention one in particular—the custom of giving the newly baptized a drink of milk and honey. The pagan or secular custom is mentioned in a handbook for nurses, a kind of instruction book for midwives written by the Roman physician, Soranus. In his book, he says that the newly born infant should drink honey mixed with milk as his first food. The Church adopted this and gave such a drink to the newly baptized during the eucharistic service that took place after the baptism. It was a custom that was followed for centuries by the Christians in Rome, Africa, and the East. In fact it became so popular that a Council of Carthage had to warn the faithful that they should not put it on the same level as the Eucharist. Yet this was a good symbol not only as the fulfillment of the prophecy of the chosen people being led into a land flowing with milk and honey, but also as a symbol of rebirth.

INTERVIEWER: Isn't the celebration of Christmas on December 25th another good example of the early Church's adaptation?

FATHER QUASTEN: Yes it is. The entire liturgy of Christmas shows the great influence of the theology of light and shows the intimate connection with the date of December 25th that the pagans celebrated as the *dies natalis,* the birthday of the *sol invictus,* Mithra, the god of the sun. In the fourth century, Christians changed the celebration of Christ's birth from January 6th to December 25th and built up an entire theology of light.

INTERVIEWER: Do you think that patrology can serve the cause of ecumenism?

FATHER QUASTEN: Definitely. We must remember that in the patristic period Christianity was united. A serious study of the Fathers of the Church will certainly emphasize what Christians have in common. The theology of baptism, for example, has not received the attention that it deserves from Catholics. Today, in the ecumenical movement, there is a decided return to the meaning of baptism. After all, Christians do believe that it is necessary to be baptized in Christ. If the Fathers, especially the Greek Fathers, are studied diligently, I am convinced it would be to the advantage of the ecumenical movement.

INTERVIEWER: Does your own background lend itself to an ecumenical interest?

FATHER QUASTEN: I would say so. I came from that part of Germany where Catholicism was definitely in a diaspora situation. I attended a gymnasium in Moers which was Protestant in character. I went to school with Protestants, and many of my neighborhood friends were Protestant. That explains why there were so many Protestants at my first Mass. As a student, I was always in the midst of some controversy with my friends. We had wonderful discussions about Scripture, the meaning of faith, and the nature of the Church. There were very few Catholics in the school I attended. I remember very well one of my Latin teachers, Professor Hofius, who would frequently ask me questions about Catholicism. He would talk about St. Peter, for example, and then ask the Catholic and the Protestant students what they thought about him. I remember one day he called on me. "Quasten," he said, "was Peter really a pope? Wasn't that name given to the Bishop of Rome much later?" I would go home and that afternoon pay a visit to our parish priest who was a very scholarly man. The two of us would spend the afternoon checking on the various sources and talking over this problem. Then the next morning I would come to class and report on it. Another time Professor Hofius asked me about the Catholic custom of having a light burning in church. He thought it was the same symbolism as the fire that burned in the Temple of the Vestal Virgins in Rome. The symbolism was quite different. The flame that was before the Temple of the Vestal Virgins was a symbol of the domestic virtues— it was a hearth fire, a cooking fire.

INTERVIEWER: Did you know Werner Jaeger in Germany?

FATHER QUASTEN: Werner Jaeger was born about fifteen miles from my home town. He, too, had early ecumenical interests. He was a Protestant, but he attended a Catholic gymnasium. He once made the remark at a lecture he gave at Marquette that he inherited his love of the Church Fathers from the classes at the gymnasium. Although he had taught classics in Berlin, he returned to the Fathers and produced that great edition of Gregory of Nyssa.

INTERVIEWER: Can you recall any other influences in your student days that instilled in you a love of the Fathers?

FATHER QUASTEN: The greatest influence in my academic life came from Professor Dölger of the University of Münster. He taught early church history, and when I arrived at Münster, he noticed my deep interest in that period. He gave me special permission to attend his seminar in advanced problems even though ordinarily one had first to finish several semesters' work. It was he who gave me a thorough training in patrology and a great love for the Fathers.

Through Dölger I also became interested in the work the Benedictines of Maria Laach were doing. At that time, I became acquainted with Odo Casel who shared with me an interest in the confrontation of Christianity with the Hellenistic world. Casel was a theologian of the liturgy; he had all the necessary equipment of a classical scholar. He had a good command of pagan as well as Christian sources. I publish the series *Liturgiewissenschaftliche Quellen und Forschungen* with the Benedictines of Maria Laach.

INTERVIEWER: Along with your studies in patrology you have maintained an interest in archaeology.

FATHER QUASTEN: Yes, I studied archaeology in Rome at the Institute of Christian Archaeology, which was established by Pius XI near the church of Santa Maria Maggiore. John Peter Kirsh was the director of the Institute, and I was one of the first students. During that time, I made many visits to various excavations in Rome and in North Africa. Archaeology is very important in the work I am doing. Whereas the Fathers very often give you the thinking of the theologians, archaeological monuments give you the thinking of the people. It is absolutely necessary to know the popular mentality as compared with the theological speculation. Often, there is complete agreement, but occasionally there are differences. Most frequently, it is the approach that is different.

One of my favorite archaeological monuments is the inscription of Abercius, which is called the queen of early Christian inscriptions because of its antiquity. It is a tombstone that dates from about 180 or 190. The author is Abercius, Bishop of Hieropolis, who at the age of seventy-two made a trip to Rome. It is rich in doctrine; he says that wherever he met fellow Christians, he was given the Eucharist under the species of bread and wine. It is the oldest stone monument we have that mentions the Eucharist.

INTERVIEWER: The field of patristic studies has been dominated by European scholars. Is there an American patristic tradition?

FATHER QUASTEN: Of course, there are many outstanding patrologists in this country, but I don't think there is really an American patristic tradition. American theologians on the Catholic side have been more interested in speculative and moral theology. However, Harvard University has been remarkable in fostering interest in patrology. Werner Jaeger, whom we mentioned earlier, established an institute of studies of Gregory of Nyssa at Harvard. The new edition of his works that they published is known all over the world and has become a model of patristic publishing.

INTERVIEWER.: What is the present state of European patristic studies?

FATHER QUASTEN: It is not what it was before the war. The classical times of patrology, with Harnack representing the Protestants and Bardenhewer the Catholics, have not returned. All scholarship suffered because of the war. However, there are some signs of recovery. One of the most encouraging things is the patristic conferences established by Professor Cross at Oxford. The conferences take place every four years and attract scholars from all over the world. We can look with optimism to the future of patrology, because such meetings are able to organize patristic scholars throughout the world to work on special projects. In Germany, W. Schneemelcher edits *Bibliographia Patristica,* which appears annually and is very useful for patristic scholars. In England, G. L. Prestige and J. N. D. Kelly are doing excellent work. The Vienna Academy has resumed publication of the *Corpus scriptorum ecclesiasticorum latinorum.* That project started in 1866, and they have published almost eighty volumes so far. The Academy of Berlin has also continued to publish its excellent editions of patristic texts. Then, we must not forget the Benedictines of Belgium who have started a very ambitious project, the *Corpus Christianorum.* They plan to publish, besides the Greek and Latin Fathers, all Christian inscriptions and all the *Acta* of the ecumenical councils. It will be an enormous and difficult task to continue for so many years. It might take a century.

INTERVIEWER: Do you think that patristic studies have directly influenced the Second Vatican Council?

FATHER QUASTEN: Yes, especially in ecclesiology where the Council frequently turned to the Fathers. And the Fathers they used were very often from the East. In recent years, there has been a renewed interest in Eastern patristic sources. Now, in Vatican II, both the Eastern and Western traditions are represented. The title "People of God" is taken from the patristic period. It meant the Christian congregation, the entire Church, the Mystical Body of Christ. It also referred to the group assembled for the liturgy.

Another title that is used in the Council is *"Mater Ecclesia."* This came from the East. It is in Clement of Alexandria and Origen, and later, at the time of Damasus, Rome adopted it. However, this title was more in accord with the Eastern theology of the Church. The West was more interested in legal and juridical terms.

INTERVIEWER: What of the liturgical documents of Vatican II?

FATHER QUASTEN: I was a member of the Preparatory Commission that worked on the Constitution on the Liturgy, and in our meetings, I noticed that the basis for all our discussions was patristic. The members of the commission tried to renew the liturgy in terms of sound theology. If we change our ceremonies and rubrics, but do not teach the theology of the liturgy, then we are wasting our time. For the theology of the liturgy, we have to use the Fathers. In the marvelous catechetical instructions given by Cyril of Jerusalem, you have a good example of what we should be trying to do.

INTERVIEWER: Can you trace any of the recent liturgical changes back to early Christian times?

FATHER QUASTEN: The present ritual of distributing Communion is definitely a return to the early Christian practice. The priest says "The Body of Christ," and the person answers, "Amen." Similarly, Hippolytus of Rome said that the priest, in giving Communion, says: *"Panis caelestis in Christo Jesu,"* and the recipient answers *"Amen."* At one time, it was the custom to have the deacon turn to the people at Communion time and say: *"Sancta sanctis."* In the early Church, the deacon was the herald of the liturgy—a kind of commentator. As the Canon approached, he would say *"Sursum corda."* We also know that the words, *"mysterium fidei,"* inserted in the words of consecration, were originally part of an explanation made by the deacon. It was also the deacon who announced at the end of Mass with the words, *"Ite Missa est."*

INTERVIEWER: When did the problem of a vernacular liturgy first arise?

FATHER QUASTEN: This problem first appears about the middle of the fourth century. We hear of difficulties in Jerusalem, Rome, and Egypt. In Egypt, they had interpreters, which office they counted as one of the minor orders. Their job was to translate and explain in Coptic what the priest celebrating the Eucharist was saying in Greek. The same was done in Jerusalem. The description by Aetheria in 380 reveals that, although the Bishop of Jerusalem knew Greek as well as Syriac, he was permitted to celebrate the liturgy only in Greek. During the service, a priest translated it into Syriac. It is interesting that at this time the church of Rome was the most progressive. The earliest liturgy was in Aramaic, and this was replaced by Greek. This change was gradual. By 250 A.D., the official language of the Church was Latin. We know this because the letters of the popes ceased to be exclusively Greek. Pope Cornelius wrote several letters in Latin to Cyprian, and Pope Stephen wrote one. However, it was not until the pontificate of Pope Damasus (366-384) that the liturgy was celebrated in Latin. The Eastern churches followed the example of Rome, and so Coptic and Syriac were later used for the liturgy.

INTERVIEWER: Over the years, Father Quasten, you have published a great amount. Would you tell us something about the projects you have begun.

FATHER QUASTEN: I came to Catholic University in 1938 to teach patrology, ancient church history, and ancient Christian sources. In 1941, I started the series, *Studies in Christian Antiquity,* which is published by The Catholic University of America Press. It contains some of the dissertations that I have directed in patrology. The first of the fifteen volumes that have so far been published is the work by Father Alfred Rush, *Death and Burial in Christian Antiquity.* In 1946, I began with the late Father Plumpe the series *Ancient Christian Writers*—translations of the Fathers—of which thirty-five volumes have appeared. About two volumes appear each year.

INTERVIEWER: Will this series of patristic texts cover the entire patristic period?

FATHER QUASTEN: It will cover the whole period, but not exhaustively. We don't intend to bring out translations of every single text. We chose texts that are of interest today and especially those which have never been translated before.

INTERVIEWER: When did you begin your famous *Patrology* series?

FATHER QUASTEN: The first volume appeared in 1950. I started this work because I felt strongly that there should be a patrology book that emphasized the development of Christian dogma and at the same time presented some of the actual texts of the Fathers. In these volumes, I analyze the writings of the Fathers, but I always give lengthy quotations from their works. There is no substitute for this immediate contact with the text, even if it is in translation. My interest in writing such a work goes back to the time I was teaching at the University of Münster. I felt even then that it was not enough simply to give a description of a text, the pertinent biographical data, etc., about each of the Fathers. More was needed on the *content* of the sources. I started collecting material then and kept a growing list of references. So far I have spent nearly thirty years working on it. Three volumes have been published in English, French, and Spanish, although in the Spanish edition the three volumes have been made into two. The Italian edition is coming out soon. There will be five volumes when the series is completed. Volume four is finished, and I am working on volume five.

INTERVIEWER: Do you have any special work habits or methods that helped you to write such a monumental work?

FATHER QUASTEN: No, not any unusual method—just perseverance and hard work. One thing that helps me is the hour or more of source reading that I have been doing since I was a student. This is a cardinal rule for me. I have found that by continuous reading of the Fathers you find hidden treasures that have often been overlooked. I read them in the original and then make extracts.

INTERVIEWER: How many hours do you work each day?

FATHER QUASTEN: That's difficult to say. I usually begin working at six in the morning and get an hour in before breakfast. After breakfast, apart from the hours I spend teaching and a short afternoon siesta, I work through the day. I have never been able to do any creative work in the evening after dinner. I found that I got so involved in what I was doing that I was unable to sleep well. Harnack had the same experience. He once told me that the evening meal is a natural break and that the evening was no time to do any scholarly work. He would spend the time with his family. I usually spend my evenings working on bibliographies, reading, or correspondence.

INTERVIEWER: Do you have any assistants who help you with your *Patrology?*

FATHER QUASTEN: No, I've had no assistance whatsoever. In this country, it is impossible to get assistants among your students. The students are sent to the university for a certain period of time, and they are under great pressure to finish their degree as quickly as possible. In Germany, graduate students often spend a year or two with their major professor after they have earned their degree. They stay with the professor as assistants, and they receive further training in research and teaching. It is a kind of apprenticeship. I usually write out the actual text of my book in longhand, correct it, and then type it up in a final form.

INTERVIEWER: Scholarly reviews of your *Patrology* have frequently mentioned the excellent bibliographies and indices. How do you manage to keep them up to date?

FATHER QUASTEN: As you can see, I have a large library. I subscribe to a great number of periodicals in patristics, classical studies, and in theology. Whenever I come across an appropriate article, I read it and make a card for it in my files. These files are always growing. When the French edition was published, I added 1,500 new references. Another 1,500 were added to the Spanish edition, and the same number to the Italian edition. I am also very particular about the indices, because this increases the value of the book. I do the index myself, because I feel that the author is the best interpreter of his own work and only he can make a satisfactory index.

INTERVIEWER: You have been working in patristics for over thirty years, and yet you still have remarkable enthusiasm for your work. How do you explain it?

FATHER QUASTEN: Newman once said: "The reading of the Fathers has always been for me a paradise of delight." That is how I feel. When you read the Fathers, you have something genuinely inspiring —a magnificent combination of theology and spirituality. At present, there is a division between these two, with the result that both suffer. But if you read the New Testament, the Apostolic Fathers, and other early writers, you see that there is a wonderful blend of theology and spirituality. Today, some theologians are making their theology more spiritual. I think Bouyer, Daniélou, and de Lubac are good examples.

❖❖

JOHANNES QUASTEN was born in Homberg, Germany, on May 3rd, 1900. He took his theological and philological studies at the University of Münster. He was ordained to the priesthood in 1926 and the following year received his doctorate in theology. He also studied at the Institute of Christian Archaeology in Rome and at the University of Berlin. In 1931, he began teaching at the University of Münster. He came to the United States in 1938 to teach Ancient Church History and Christian Archaeology at The Catholic University of America in Washington. In 1941, he was named the Eugene Kelly Professor of Ecclesiastical History. He is former dean of the School of Sacred Theology at Catholic University and since 1951, Vice President of the Henry Bradshaw Society, London. He was a member of the Preparatory Commission on the Liturgy at the Second Vatican Council and in 1965 was named a Consultor to Concilium, a group of liturgical experts who meet regularly in Rome to discuss the implementation of the *Constitution on the Liturgy*.

Father Quasten has contributed over one hundred articles to scholarly journals and encyclopedias both in this country and in Europe. Among his books are: *Musik und Gesang in den Kulten der heidnischen Antike und christlichen Frühzeit; Monumenta Eucharistica et liturgica vetustissima; Expositio antiquae liturgicae Gallicanae Germano Parisiensi ascripta;* and *Patrology*—four volumes translated into French, Spanish, and Italian. He is the founder

and editor of *Studies in Christian Antiquity* and co-editor of the
following: *Ancient Christian Writers; Stromata Patristica et Medie-
valia; Liturgiewissenschaftliche Quellen und Forschungen; Vom
christlichen mysterium* (Festschrift O. Casel); *Volkskundliche Quellen;* and *Guide to the Fathers of the Church.*

Karl Rahner

This interview of several hours—and all in Latin—takes place in Father Rahner's quarters at Georgetown University where he is delivering a series of lectures. Several maps, a beret, and a few packs of cigarettes are on the window ledge. He smokes continuously as we talk, seemingly oblivious of the hum of the tape recorder. A small, solidly built man, Father Rahner immediately grasps one's attention with his piercing eyes that, despite his fundamentally gentle nature, give him an intense and somewhat fearsome look. He is serious and scholarly in conversation, but possesses a subtle sense of humor. Since even his extemporaneous remarks reflect the logical organization of his written works, any light touch, though in a deep and rumbling voice, paradoxically lends greater conviction to his words. Our conversation is interrupted a few times by the telephone, which he answers with a rather frightening "Hier Rahner."

INTERVIEWER: Father Rahner, you have often been called the "theologian of liberty" because of your frequent writings on that subject. Do you consider this your greatest contribution to theology?

FATHER RAHNER: By no means. It is true that I have written on the theological dimensions of liberty, but I have also written on many, many other subjects. I must say in all modesty that some of my other writings have greater value for theology than my work on freedom.

INTERVIEWER: What would you consider your most important writings?

FATHER RAHNER: I have written on the Trinity, Christology, and many other questions dealing intimately with almost every aspect of dogmatic theology. So far I have not written a complete dogmatic treatise for seminaries, except for the notes that I use in my courses of dogmatic theology that I teach at Innsbruck. Nearly all the things I have written are shorter commentaries or essays on specific points of dogmatic theology. Yet all of these are of equal if not of greater value than my work dealing precisely with religious liberty.

I am also editor of *Lexikon für Theologie und Kirche* along with Josef Höfer. The new edition of this theological encyclopedia will consist of ten large volumes, and I have written many of the articles on dogmatic problems. I have also written *Kleines theologishches Wörterbuch,* in which I presented in a condensed version the whole field of dogmatic theology. Then there is my work, *Hoerer des Wortes,* which presents the necessary speculative background for fundamental theology. There I discuss the transcendental structure of man himself in so far as his internal spiritual nature is open to divine revelation. I have also written a book on the theory of knowledge according to St. Thomas. All of these works are much more important than my writings on religious liberty.

INTERVIEWER: You have written over three hundred articles and several books. Do you have any special system or method that enables you to produce so much?

FATHER RAHNER: I have not written so much when you consider the works of St. Thomas, Suarez, and others. I have no special method. I just sit down and write. Some days I write nothing.

INTERVIEWER: *Geist in Welt* was your first book and perhaps your most controversial one. Could you tell us how you came to write it?

FATHER RAHNER: *Geist in Welt* is a study of St. Thomas' ontology of knowledge. Originally, it was conceived as a doctoral dissertation at Freiburg. However, at that time the Nazis were in power and, for reasons too complicated to explain here, I was unable to do my thesis under Heidegger. Instead, I worked under the Catholic Professor M. Honecker who was teaching philosophy at the state university at Freiburg. Professor Honecker rejected the thesis, because he felt that I had incorrectly interpreted the doctrine of St. Thomas too much according to modern philosophy (Heidegger's ideas in particular) and the fundamental tenets of German Idealism. But I am convinced that my interpretation is correct. If one analyzes St. Thomas in proper perspective, it is quite clear that he is a *penseur moderne*. There is certainly a conformity, affinity, and correspondence between the modern method of proceeding and that problem which may be called transcendental. Even in the work of St. Thomas this can be found. To grasp that fact is very important for any genuine, mutual understanding of the modern concept of man and the Thomistic concept of man.

INTERVIEWER: *Geist in Welt* has been the subject of much discussion over the years. Father C. Ernst, O.P., who translated Volume I of your *Theological Investigations,* questions the foundational principle of your theory, namely: "Knowledge is the being-present-to-itself of Being, and this being-present-to-itself is the *Being* of any entity." This, he feels, is unacceptable in terms of the Thomistic thesis that our ontological knowledge of reality is derived from our experience of the world. How would you answer this objection?

FATHER RAHNER: First of all, I would like to say that Father Ernst is a good friend of mine. In fact, he has just recently agreed to be the English co-editor of *Sacramentum Mundi,* a Catholic theological lexicon that has not yet been published. (The other English co-editor is a young Dominican Father Kerr.) So there is no question here about an attack on my theological or philosophical ideas.

Now about the objection. I think that the ideas expressed in *Geist in Welt* are truly Thomistic. But certainly this question has been freely discussed among Catholic theologians. The interpretation I have given is not mine alone; the whole school of recent German philosophical thought holds this. For example, Max Müller, Father Lotz, the late Gustav Siewerth, and other scholars find no difficulty in this opinion. Of course, it has to be correctly understood. We are not *tò esse.* We are a composite, a mixture of act and potency, if we want to use the classic terms. *Beisichsein* (being-present-to-itself) has, even in us, some element of potentiality. Every being, inasmuch as it is in act, is present-to-itself. Inasmuch as *I am,* I am present-to-myself. This thesis is certainly Thomistic; it is a metaphysical thesis that is not immediately experiential. If Father Ernst says that knowledge in the Thomistic view must be understood as an *a posteriori* knowledge, then I would say with St. Thomas that while I receive individual species from things coming to me in an *a posteriori* way, I also have a light of the *intellectus agens*. And if we try to interpret metaphysically the image of the light of the *intellectus agens* then it appears as nothing other than a dynamic, transcendental, and intellectual element in being itself.

INTERVIEWER: It is well known that Heidegger influenced you greatly. What was the precise form of this influence?

FATHER RAHNER: For two years after my ordination I studied philosophy under Martin Heidegger at the University of Freiburg. I attended his lectures and his philosophical seminars. We still see each other occasionally. However, it was thirty years ago when I was a student. One may perhaps say that it is not specific doctrines that I have taken from Heidegger, but rather a style of thinking and of investigating which has proved most valuable. This may be described as a method or approach by which one does not examine dogmatic truths *merely* as evidence derived from the positive sources, but one seeks to construct a synthesis. One takes the various dogmatic propositions and reduces them to certain fundamental principles. In that way an internal, coherent body of dogmatic truth is established. Modern man is thus able to perceive the order and harmony in the mysterious truths of the Church and Christianity. Modern man no longer is satisfied with taking a collection of the truths and various opinions that are proven in Denzinger and thinking no more about it. Rather, he looks for some synthetic idea, even though it might be quite simple, to organize the immense material of Christian dogma. Once this is achieved, he is able to understand other specific truths as obvious and necessary consequences of the principal idea.

INTERVIEWER: What other philosophers influenced you?

FATHER RAHNER: I must mention Père Rousselot and Joseph Maréchal of Louvain, for both of them exercised a great influence on my philosophy.

Certainly, while Maréchal influenced me, it cannot be said that my philosophical ideas were completely and adequately determined by

him. There were many other profound influences that help elaborate
and at times transform what Maréchal said. But the initial, truly
philosophical insight was given to me by Maréchal. His book, *Le
point de départ de metaphysique,* especially *Cahier V,* influenced
me greatly when I was younger.

One must not forget Father Erich Przywara. For the Catholics of
Germany in the twenties, thirties, and forties he was considered one
of the greatest minds. He had a great influence on all of us when we
were younger. He is now seventy-five, but is quite sick and can
barely write.

INTERVIEWER: What of Blondel?

FATHER RAHNER: His influence was more indirect than the others.
Every man lives in a specific intellectual atmosphere and is influenced by many things without actually realizing it. I can say that I
was not a dedicated reader of Blondel, even though I do accept some
of his opinions. Robert Scherer, a friend of mine who lives at Freiburg, translated the works of Blondel into German. But objectively
I am not able to say that Blondel exercised any great, direct, and
immediate influence on me that I am aware of.

INTERVIEWER: Contemporary European theology is characterized by
its involvement in modern philosophy. What is the origin of this
new approach?

FATHER RAHNER: The mutual relationship between modern philosophy and Thomistic thought was initiated by Blondel, Maréchal,
Sertillanges, Rousselot, and Hans Urs von Balthasar. One might also
mention Heidegger, Max Scheler, Siewerth, and Müller. These men
do not form a school in the proper sense of the word, since they
profess widely differing views. However, they do share one thing in
common. They agree that we must be receptive to modern philosophy without considering it absurd or as something to be opposed
and criticized. What is needed is a trusting colloquium between
traditional scholastic philosophy and modern philosophy. This is
necessary if, on the one hand, we are to be men of our time and
speak the language that men today must speak if they are to understand themselves and others. On the other hand, we do not want to
lose the true riches of tradition.

Max Müller, Gustav Siewerth, Father Lotz, and myself have all written on St. Thomas. We four were disciples of Heidegger, and yet it is clear from our writings that we have a great admiration for St. Thomas. If someone would accuse us of not being Thomists, I would reply that I know of no one who can state precisely who is a Thomist and who is not. I am not being indiscreet when I say that the young Dominican priests at Walberberg esteem my writings very highly. In fact, there is a Dominican priest from Walberberg who is studying under me at Munich. Afterwards he will be a professor at the Dominican college at Walberberg. The sterile and narrow brand of traditional Thomistic philosophy is found practically nowhere in Germany or in France.

INTERVIEWER: Do you think that is true in America also?

FATHER RAHNER: I do not know. I am not qualified to judge. Yet, I would say that the tendency is certainly along these same lines.

INTERVIEWER: Throughout the history of Christian theology there have appeared various schools of thought. What value do these have for contemporary man?

FATHER RAHNER: The Suarezian, Thomistic, and Scotistic schools are traditional. They have their great riches, but they also have their lacunae. Today they are no longer living or life-giving. For that reason they belong to history, not to the present. Our contemporary needs are different. There is no reason to establish determined schools of thought, closed systems that are carefully distinct from one another. Such schools are not needed now, nor will they be in the future. There will always be various tendencies, preoccupations, and stimuli that develop from the different aspects of the intellectual world. Thus, some will be influenced by orthodox existentialism, others will proceed according to the Thomistic method, and still others will attempt to construct a new system, as for example, Father Lonergan and Father de Finance at the Gregorian University in Rome.

INTERVIEWER: You have written somewhere that the renewal of Christian thought began with the philosophers.

FATHER RAHNER: Yes, the revitalization of Christian thought began in philosophy rather than in theology. From the time of Modernism to the present, there has been a slow but steady progress in philosophy, but the same is not true in theology. But now there are signs that progress in fundamental theology as well as in dogmatic theology is beginning. I am not talking here about the development in biblical and patristic theology that has made such great strides. I think that today speculative theology must and can be renewed. It is not a question of mere speculation, but of what answer we are to give to modern man. For example, we say that the foundation of our faith can be summarized in the phrase: *Verbum caro factum est.* Now how can we present this to modern, technical, and scientific man so that he may believe it? This is a difficult task, but, above all, a possible task.

INTERVIEWER: What is being done in Germany to facilitate the renewal of speculative theology?

FATHER RAHNER: Permit me to name two theologians who are representative of this new spirit in Germany. One is my friend Bernhard Welte who is Professor of Religion in the theological faculty at the Catholic University at Freiburg-im-Breisgau. The other is my former student and friend, Johannes-Baptist Metz who is Professor of Fundamental Theology at Münster. These men are representative of, I will not say, a school, but of a mentality that is becoming quite common in Germany. It is not universal in Germany, since there are some who follow the more traditional way of teaching dogmatic theology. We must approach the modern mentality with a simple trust and reason philosophically and theologically in such a way that it means something for the men of our age. We belong to this generation, too, and so should avoid any Catholic intellectual ghetto. It is our duty to speak with scientists, Marxists, non-Christian philosophers, existentialists, and those in America and England who may be called logical positivists. For too long we have been negligent in this area. I believe that philosophy and Christian theology must do more than has been done even in Germany in establishing a sincere and open dialogue with others. There is an immense field of work ahead for us; for too long we have remained secure in our home, and we were wrong in doing so. There is more to do than simply to keep our Catholics simple and pious as they were in kindergarten and in primary school. We have to enter into battle, or rather into an open and honest dialogue with non-Christians. An outstanding example of this has been done in Germany at the Paulus Gesellschaft, where annually about two hundred professors of science, philosophy, and theology meet and discuss common problems.

INTERVIEWER: In view of the contemporary movement to establish a rapport between theology and modern philosophical thought, can we still correctly speak of theology as a deductive science?

FATHER RAHNER: There is no doubt that St. Thomas developed a theology according to a notion of science that is not completely accepted today. Personally, I have a great aversion to dogmatic positivism that flourished in Catholic schools during the last century. For example, if you wanted a course on the seven sacraments, you were told to use your Denzinger. This was a disease that theology had contracted. Yet, while I detest dogmatic positivism, I am a great lover of speculative theology, which, if you wish, you may call deductive theology. But that is not a good word to use, since it poorly describes its function.

Theology necessarily desires to arrive at some knowledge of the intimate connection between all truth revealed by God. Single propositions cannot be correctly understood unless seen in the context of the whole. I think an example will illustrate what I mean. The infallibility of the *Magisterium* can only be understood according to Christian eschatology. What answer do you give when one asks if there was an infallible *Magisterium* in the Old Testament? Why did not God, for the salvation of the Israelites, institute some supreme authority or perhaps a special assembly of rabbis? This would have been most useful and almost necessary, since Vatican I teaches that God must reveal Himself if we are to know Him and natural truths as well without any error. Yet we know for a fact that there was no infallible *Magisterium* in the Old Testament. If we tell modern man that what God did not do in the Old Testament he did in the New Testament by His grace, he will ridicule us. What we must do is explain *why* we now have an infallible *Magisterium*. I have not the time now to explain fully, but what we must do is to show how this doctrine belongs to the history of salvation and the eschatological situation. This will be of great importance to explain even to Protestants why God instituted an infallible *Magisterium* in the New Testament. Protestants don't believe this and it is not enough to cite text after text, because other exegetes come along and say that these texts can be interpreted in a different way. Therefore, you must explain a specific point of dogma, whatever this may be, from the coherence and totality of the Christian message. This kind of theology is not the formal, deductive kind that follows Aristotelian logic. Yet it is speculative theology that seeks a simple internal principle and through it sees the unity of all dogmatic thought. This is the work that today demands our attention.

INTERVIEWER: Granted that theology must avoid an exaggerated positivistic approach, can we say that the primary end of theology is contemplation of truth?

FATHER RAHNER: No. The salvation of man is the primary end. Truth is the intrinsic constitutive element of this salvation; the possession and contemplation of truth are so close that we should not separate them. Christ and the Church preach the good news of the Gospel to men. This preaching that God wants men to receive is not complete unless some reflection accompanies it. There has to be some systematic reflection of that Word in which man hears from God, about God, and even about himself. Because there is a *kerygma,* then there must be a reflection about the *kerygma,* and that we call theology. The *kerygma* differs from theology, but there is a mutual relationship involved. Thus, theology can be considered a reflective science, as something secondary that is derived from the kerygmatic words of God, of the Church, and of Christ. Theology can be distinguished from the *kerygma,* but it must serve the *kerygma.* The same thing can be said of attempting to define love and charity. One must give great attention to his own practice of love and charity. Subtle contemplation is not necessarily loving contemplation. The ancient debates on the primacy of the intellect, and the primacy of the will seem to me to be foolish and obsolete. In the last analysis, we cannot truly know God unless we know Him as the One Who speaks the Word and Who breathes Love, the Holy Spirit. Likewise, man cannot be known except through this mutual compenetration of love and knowledge. Both demand each other. As long as a man is a *viator* then he must seek that truth that leads to his salvation. Here on earth all reflective knowledge of God's truth that we call theology must be directed toward the salvation of man and nothing else.

INTERVIEWER: You once wrote that "the strictest theology . . . is itself in the long run the most kerygmatic." Would you please comment on this?

FATHER RAHNER: Father Lakner and others at Innsbruck attempted to establish a theology called kerygmatic that would exist side by side with that theology that we call scientific, university, and academic. This I do not agree with. I believe that this attempt, while done in all good will, was false. The most scientific theology is the most kerygmatic and vice versa. If we really want to make certain elements and truths of our faith relevant to modern man so that he may understand them, then, above all, we have to ask highly scientific and profound dogmatic questions.

INTERVIEWER: Do you agree with those who call your theological approach anthropocentric?

FATHER RAHNER: I suppose one could characterize my theology that way. However, to call my theology anthropocentric can easily be misunderstood by those who say that this is in opposition to theocentric theology. Such an interpretation is foolish. There is in modern philosophy a valid development from a cosmic philosophy to a more anthropological philosophy. My friend and student, Johannes-Baptist Metz, has written a small book, *Christliche Anthropozentrik*, in which he explains the metaphysical speculative anthropocentrism of St. Thomas. He considers St. Thomas and not Descartes, the first modern anthropocentric philosopher.

If man in his concrete and historical essence cannot be described unless we say that he is that being to whom God, as uncreated grace, communicates existence, then we cannot speak of man without speaking also of God. We are not able to understand what God is except by referring to the infinite transcendentality of man himself. God is not like other beings, but the inscrutable principle of being. It is not possible to go into the whole philosophy of this now, but I must insist that the true understanding of the nature and existence of God cannot be properly grasped by us unless we develop a transcendental, categorical philosophy. This transcendental philosophy is at the same time a description of man insofar as he is a spiritual being. What is a spiritual being? I would say that it is that being that, by tending to God and transcending all limits of determined being, possesses itself. Thus you see that in the last analysis, philosophically and theologically, anthropocentrism and theocentrism are the same. How can a Christian speak adequately of God unless he speaks also of man? The Word made flesh is and remains the eternal and infinite man so that you cannot know God as He is unless you think of Him at the same time as God made man. Thus, you cannot have a full theology unless you consider its anthropological aspects. If you wish to speak accurately of God, then you must speak of man. Likewise, you cannot investigate the depths of man's nature, unless you say that he is that being whom God has created and conserves in existence.

INTERVIEWER: One could, then, correctly call your theology incarnational?

FATHER RAHNER: Yes. Certainly. Christology, theology, and anthropology are so intimately connected that it would help bring out the true idea of anthropocentric theology to call it incarnational.

INTERVIEWER: Père Congar seems to insist that theology belongs to priests. Thus, he writes: "The laity, . . . can bring a wealth to the Church. . . . But they never handle theology like priests, they have never quite the same contact with the Church's tradition. . . . Theology properly so called is preeminently a clerical, priestly, learning." Do you agree with this?

FATHER RAHNER: I do not know the full context of Père Congar's remarks, but if I must judge by what you have quoted, I would say that it cannot be true. The layman must save his soul also. Why must we say that he is less intelligent than we priests? Today's layman is looking for a relationship between his faith and his whole intellectual life. In many cases, perhaps in most, he needs more theology than the simple pastor or chaplain who teaches children. If Einstein were a Catholic you could not say that he would be like any ordinary layman or pious housewife. Certainly not! That would be impossible, since he would have established a dialogue between his Christian faith on the one hand and his scientific knowledge on the other. If he had done that he would have contributed a profound understanding to theology. In the end, he would have known more theology than is generally given to our seminarians. It is true that the priest, by reason of his office, is necessarily directed to theology. But the layman, for other reasons, practically might have the same interest. Both should be equally interested in theology.

INTERVIEWER: Your influence in the Second Vatican Council was considerable. What do you think . . .

FATHER RAHNER: Excuse me, but I must say that I have not exercised any great influence at the Council. To say anything else is just not true. There were so many *periti* and collaborators at the Council that no one, except the Pope himself and the moderators, could be said to influence the Council in any significant way. It is true that I attended almost all of the meetings of the Theological Commission and that I collaborated with the other theologians. As you know the most important schemata of this commission were on the Church and Revelation. I was a member of certain sub-commissions that worked on these, but my contribution was not great.

INTERVIEWER: What of the schema on Religious Liberty?

FATHER RAHNER: I did not see the schema on Religious Liberty that was prepared in the Secretariat of Cardinal Bea, since I was not a member. I did discuss the matter in the beginning with some of the bishops, with Bishop de Smedt for example. Yet, in the second and third sessions of the Council, I was for the most part absent from Rome. I did not get to Rome for the third session till the end of October, and I had to leave after a short time to return to Munich for my classes. Practically, I had little to do with this schema. I heard some of the debates on this schema, I talked with some of the Spanish bishops, and I saw the *relatio* of Father De Broglie, professor at the Institut Catholique at Paris. For the most part I was a spectator. I have written some things on the subject, *Das freie Wort in der Kirche (Free Speech in the Church,* 1959*)*, and something on the concept of tolerance (*Schriften zur Theologie* II, 247–277; in

English—*Theological Investigations,* II, 235-263), but I don't think these had a great influence in the writing of the schema on Religious Liberty.

INTERVIEWER: Did you not talk to many of the bishops at the Council?

FATHER RAHNER: Occasionally, I had conferences with the German, Brazilian, and Spanish bishops. These were friendly meetings during which we discussed some of the problems connected with the various schemata. In my opinion, Msgr. Gerard Philips, Professor of Dogmatic Theology at Louvain, must be given great credit for his work as secretary of the Theological Commission. With the exception of the bishops themselves, Monsignor Philips did more than anyone else in preparing the schema on the Church. One must also mention Father Congar, Father Grillmeier, Father Otto Semmelroth and many, many others who were very active and influential in the commission meetings.

INTERVIEWER: What do you think is the greatest benefit for theology that has come from the Council?

FATHER RAHNER: The Council is the beginning, not the end. It is an inauguration of a tendency, not its completion. I think that this can be easily seen in the Council debates on the Church, the bishops, the lay apostolate, etc. I am convinced that we theologians in the next ten years have to give careful thought to these and other truths. Much more than we have so far. We must re-think the problems of the existence of God and the possibility of God realizing Himself in us. We must concentrate at making the doctrines of grace and the Incarnation something meaningful for modern man. These problems are important objectively, and also they are not without a pastoral or kerygmatic dimension. Theologians have an immense amount of work to do in the years that are ahead.

INTERVIEWER: Would you say that theologians in the past have often misunderstood their task?

FATHER RAHNER: One could say so. Not long ago I saw a list of writings put out by the Academia Mariana in Rome. I think it said that over one hundred volumes have been written on Mariology since the war. This is good—*De Maria numquam satis.* But it seems to me today that we have greater problems facing us that concern the basic preaching of Christian truth. We have not the time to spend on writing thick volumes on the minute subtleties of Mariology. I can also honestly say that I cannot understand why the Institute of Josephology was established in Canada. We don't have time for these kind of things, if we see the world as it really is. I am not sure of America, but we (in Europe) have perhaps only twenty percent of those who are Catholic in origin who really believe in God and Christ. We must do something other than discuss pious subtleties. We must find out how we can make the doctrine of the Incarnation intelligible for a person who knows only dialectic materialism. How can we make the existence of God reasonable for such a person? It is not enough to say: "Well we have the five proofs of St. Thomas. Read that and that's all you need."

INTERVIEWER: What do you think of the traditional division between fundamental theology and dogmatic theology?

FATHER RAHNER: I think that there must be a greater penetration, a greater reciprocity between the two. As it stands now we are not too successful. In traditional fundamental theology we say that we must first prove that God revealed Himself to men, but we say nothing about *what* God revealed. This should not continue. An abstract and formalistic concept of revelation should not be the object of proof. Today man wants to know some of the things God has revealed about Himself before he can make an act of faith. Modern man wants to learn from you about God so that he can determine whether revealed truth is credible and existentially acceptable. For that reason I think that there should be a fundamental, basic discipline that combines the nucleus of dogmatic truth along with the proof that these things have been revealed by God. Unless I can first give some introductory notions of God and man and show how these ideas necessarily fit into an anthropological metaphysics, then modern man will say that he can never believe that God became man. A mere a prioristic proof has no force. They are arguments that do not convince. Thus, we have the doctrine of the Protestant exegetes who argue that Jesus did not appear to be the Son of God, but that this doctrine was developed slowly, evolving from the so-called "communitarian theology."

INTERVIEWER: In conclusion, Father Rahner, would you like to give a few words of advice to students of theology.

FATHER RAHNER: Students of theology should have a holy abnegation in their study of theology. Zealously and courageously they must give themselves to theology without a false preoccupation concerning their future ministry. They must study theology as much as they can—even scholastic and abstract theology—and realize that whatever they learn can later, in some way, be used profitably. Professors of theology must study ceaselessly and teach a theology that corresponds to the inner needs of their students and of modern man. Theology must be so presented that it encourages a genuine dialogue between the best of traditional thought and the exigencies of today.

❈❈

KARL RAHNER was born in Freiburg-im-Breisgau, Germany, on March 5th, 1904. In 1922, he followed his brother Hugo into the Society of Jesus. He studied philosophy for three years at Pullach, Germany, and served as an instructor for two years at the Jesuit college at Feldkinch, Austria. He studied theology at Valkenburg, Holland, and was ordained in 1932. After his ordination, he spent two years doing graduate work in philosophy at the University of Freiburg under Martin Heidegger. In 1937, he began teaching dogmatic theology at the University of Innsbruck. In 1964, he was named Professor of Christian Thought and Philosophy of Religion at the University of Munich. He was a *peritus* at the Second Vatican Council, a member of the Theological Commission, and also a member of the subcommissions that worked on the schemata dealing with the Church and Revelation. He now holds the chair of dogmatic theology at the University of Muenster.

Geist im Welt, a study on the theory of knowledge, appeared in 1937 and was Father Rahner's first published work. It was followed by *Hörer des Wortes,* which dealt with the philosophy of religion. Five volumes of his *Schriften zur Theologie* have been published, and three of them have been translated into English as *Theological Investigations*. He has written over three hundred articles. Translations of his writings known in this country include: *The Christian Commitment; The Eternal Year; Nature and Grace; Spiritual Exercises; Theology for Renewal; Free Speech in the Church;* and *Theological Dictionary* with Herbert Vorgrimler. Since 1957, he has been co-editor with Josef Höfer of the *Lexikon für Theologie und Kirche;* with Heinrich Schlier he is co-editor of *Quaestiones Disputatae* and is an editor of *Sacramentum Mundi.* He is a member of the Executive Editorial Committee, and head of the Pastoral Theology section of *Concilium.*

Reinhold Niebuhr

The Niebuhrs' fourth floor apartment on Riverside Drive in New York has a splendid view of the Hudson River, the rugged Palisades clearly visible on the Jersey side. On the river, a Circle Line ship is heading in the direction of Bear Mountain. The living room is warm and tastefully decorated. The couches and chairs, a deep blue, fit in well with the highly polished wood floor and white walls. Over the fireplace is an impressionistic painting of their son when a boy. A large bouquet of yellow gladioli adds a cheerful note.

Dr. Neibuhr is seated at his desk. His working library is close by. He is going over the morning mail. "He's like a business tycoon," his wife explains. "The first thing he has to do is to take care of his mail." He is dressed casually in an olive-green sport coat, a blue shirt open at the neck, and gray slacks. We chat for a few moments, and I am impressed by his candor and friendliness. His wife comes in with coffee attractively served on a brass oriental tray; she returns with a glass of warm milk for her husband. In this congenial setting, we begin our interview.

INTERVIEWER: As a young man, you spent thirteen years as a pastor of a small city parish in Detroit. Did the experience of these years have a lasting influence on your theology?

DR. NIEBUHR: Yes, the years I spent in Detroit influenced me greatly. In 1915, I was assigned to a small, new parish in Detroit on West Grand Boulevard. It has been called erroneously a workingman's church, but it really had the whole spectrum of working class, middle class, and even two millionaires. At that time, my "father-in-God" was an Episcopalian bishop, the late Charles Williams, an old social-gospeller. The Protestant liberal churches were completely irrelevant to the "new industrialism" of the automobile industry. During my time in Detroit, the city grew from a population of half a million to a million and a half. My parish grew to eight hundred members. The "new industrialism" was simply the highly automated automobile manufacturing business that used semiskilled labor that the crafts unions could not organize until the CIO came along. Henry Ford with his five-dollars-a-day wage was the tin god of Detroit. Nobody except Bishop Williams knew what a fantastic creature Henry Ford really was. Ford was a curious combination of humanitarian impulses and power impulses. This was all before the New Deal, unemployment insurance, or old-age pensions. I saw the economic problems of the automobile workers in my parish, and I saw how they were cynical of Ford's methods. I would say, then, that Bishop Williams on the one hand and Henry Ford on the other persuaded me that a purely liberal Protestant ethic was irrelevant. As I used to say: It was relevant for martyrs, mothers, and saints, but not for collective relationships.

INTERVIEWER: What were the sources of your social gospel?

DR. NIEBUHR: Bishop Williams introduced me to the radical social ethic of Israel's prophets. Of course, I had studied the Old Testament before, but my experience now made it relevant. Amos and Isaiah and the eighth-century prophets talked about a radical justice rather than sacrificial love. Walter Rauschenbush was the father of the social gospel in America. His book, *A Theology for the Social Gospel, 1917,* is an exposition of the radical ethics of Amos and Isaiah and the social crisis and injustices of modern industrialism.

I was shocked by the fact that the rich Protestant churches, those which we called in Detroit, the Woodward Avenue churches, insistently talked about sacrificial love and completely neglected the need of justice as a relevant norm of collective relationship. There has to be a balance of power along with all the technical details that modern man has discovered. The Protestant ethics of the twenties had no meaning for modern man.

INTERVIEWER: Did the Catholic teaching on social justice effect your thinking in any significant way?

DR. NIEBUHR: I didn't discover the social ethics of Catholicism until much later. Gradually, I became aware of Catholicism's interest in the "social substance of human existence" that is embodied in the tradition of natural law. In my anti-Catholic moments, I figured that the natural-law tradition was too inflexible, since it is rooted in the metaphysical system of Stoicism or of Aristotelianism. Yet I marvel at the way good Catholic social teachers elaborate what both Aristotle and Thomas believed and how they make pragmatic applications of general principles. I am impressed by the social ethics of modern Catholicism. However, my appreciation of the contribution that Catholicism has made to social ethics took a rather devious path. I became a pacifist because of the social-gospel tradition that was so relevant to domestic politics, to Isaiah's pacifism, and to Jesus' Sermon on the Mount. Christ's doctrine of nonresistance has to be distinguished from nonviolent resistance to injustice. I became a pacifist because of the experience between the First World War and the Second World War. Idealistic Americans were terribly disillusioned when they saw that the Versailles Treaty, which was supposed to end all wars and "to make the world safe for democracy," ended in such a failure. This is what made me a "Christian realist," and I am convinced that it has its roots in traditional Christianity.

INTERVIEWER: Would you call St. Augustine a "Christian realist?"

DR. NIEBUHR: Definitely. I am embarrassed to tell you that I came upon Augustine rather late in my career. I studied him in my theological studies, but I hadn't really gone very deeply into the history of Christian thought. Yet Augustine was for me a wonderful introduction into realism. He had a very realistic, in my present opinion too realistic, analysis of the power realities of the *civitas terrena,* which are governed by self-love. I studied Augustine further and discovered that there was something wrong about his conception of the *Civitas Dei,* and that something wrong was his Neoplatonism. There was no place for the love of brother, because the love of God was set against the love of self, and this love of self contaminated the love of created things. I found out that Augustine availed himself, from the standpoint of the normative ethics of the *City of God*, of Stoic radicalism and equalitarianism. This is the pathos of all historical, organized religion. Gradually, as the Roman Empire disintegrated and the Church became the real tutor of Western European civilization, which was feudal, Aristotelian principles were subtly substituted for Stoic principles. Inequality took over, and justice was to "treat unequal things unequally." My conclusion, which would be heretical for a Catholic, was that the whole of medieval society, impressive as it was, had a papal overlord and that the Western Empire was only a junior partner of this great construct. Hildebrand, as Gregory VII, was the father of the medieval papacy and he simply used the Augustinian conception of the *Civitas Dei*. Augustine had some apprehensions about identifying the Church and the City of God; sometimes he affirmed it, and sometimes he denied it. But Hildebrand always affirmed it. So there developed a structure that historians of culture now call sacral politics. You have the Vicar of Chirst, first Peter and then his successors, being the supreme power in society. There was great power in this structure, but also great weakness. The weaknesses were first revealed in the thirteenth century, the Golden Age of medievalism, which St. Thomas regarded as the final structure of human society, and then it all went to pot in the fourteenth and fifteenth centuries.

INTERVIEWER: Why did liberal Protestantism oppose your views of Christian realism?

DR. NIEBUHR: Liberal Protestantism was, until very recently, what I would call utopian, and this is because there was a curious confluence of influences on our frontier in the early days. The frontier was not governed by an orthodox Reformation spirit, that of Luther or of Calvin that was excessively realistic, but by the radical Protestantism of the Anabaptists, the Baptists, and the Congregationalists. They thought not only of the kingdom of God, but they were convinced—and this is a very dangerous thing—that the kingdom of God had been established in America. Meanwhile, they merged with secular utopianism, which claimed that we were on the way to having utopian self-government. I think that the President of the United States today, and his Secretary of State, with their fantastic involvement in southeast Asia are the end-products of this combination of sectarian and secular utopianism. This brand of utopianism has given an air of sentimentality to the whole political life of America. On the whole, liberal Protestant theologians did not accept my realism. I had the curious experience that I was accepted more by the political scientists than by the theologians.

INTERVIEWER: Most of your writings are characterized by a strong polemical spirit. Do you think that there is any room for polemics today?

DR. NIEBUHR: There is no need for polemics today, and there was no need for them when I wrote. My polemics were of an impatient young man who had certain things to say and wanted to get them said clearly and forcefully. However, I learned a few things as I got older. My latest book (I hope it will not be my last one), *Man's Nature and His Communities,* 1965, included the revisions, Augustine would call them *retractations,* of all my previous remarks on that subject. I said there that I have become less polemical and that I regret my polemical attitude toward Catholicism. I was also polemical against orthodox Reformation Protestantism because of its rather fantastic and excessive devotion to secular authority. I agree with the Catholics and liberal Protestants who say that the Reformation was a catastrophe for what one might call a responsible ethic of justice. I don't reject the previous positions that I took on these questions, but I do reject my polemical attitude of the past. Yet there is always a place for honest speaking, and I hope that I have tried to be as honest as possible even in my polemical days.

INTERVIEWER: What do you think of the eventual reunion of all Christian churches?

DR. NIEBUHR: In the past, I had a typical Protestant polemical attitude against Catholicism. Now I realize that the mystery of life and the mystery of human history are so great that the Catholic approach is a valid one and might well be more valid than our approach. I don't say that my ambivalence about this is dishonest. I simply say that this is the insight of old age against the polemical attitude of youth. I remember once that my old friend Father John Courtney Murray and I were on a committee of the Center for

Democratic Institutions and we were challenged by that wonderful physical scientist, my friend Isidore Rabi, of Columbia University. He said to us, as a good secular idealist would say: "Isn't it absurd that you have a Catholic form of Christianity and a Protestant form of Christianity? Can't you ever get together?" (This was before the Vatican Council.) I said to him: "Well, I don't speak for Father Murray, but we've just had a discussion about this very problem, and on the basis of this discussion, I would say that we won't have an organic unity between Catholicism and Protestantism for a long while. Although I hope that there will be all kinds of dialogue which are not apparent now." Now they are apparent.

INTERVIEWER: Do you feel that the kind of dialogue that is taking place in the Christian world will dilute the distinctive character of Protestantism?

DR. NIEBUHR: No. Some Protestants might feel that way, but I also know that there are some Catholics who think that the ecumenical spirit of Pope John XXIII will destroy Catholicism. I think there is little basis for the fear that if we open our society and communicate with each other, we will reduce religion to what in fact it has been reduced to in many parts of America, a kind of consistent mish-mash of sentimentality. However, while I am pleased that there is such honest dialogue between Protestants and Catholics, I don't think that there will ever be an absolute union of the two.

INTERVIEWER: I suppose you are thinking of the papacy as the irremovable obstacle to reunion?

DR. NIEBUHR: That's right. The Protestants believe that papal absolutism is a horrible piece of idolatry—to have one man speak as God. Protestants believe in a variety of conflicting religious communities, which from the Catholic viewpoint would be the inevitable result of absolute liberty that is on the verge of license. I would say that there is no resolution of the devotion of Catholicism to the pope and the desire of Protestantism to remain free. Why should Catholics give up the supremacy of the papacy and Protestants their idea of liberty just because they are criticized for it? The Catholic is willing to sacrifice a certain amount of freedom for the sake of the order and peace of the universal community. I remember once

speaking to Father Murray about the warning Pius XII had given to
the faithful about French existentialists. It was about the time that
Father de Lubac, that great theologian who viewed Christian problems in a Christian existential way, was silenced. I asked Father
Murray: "How do you feel about that? Must you remain silent
when you disagree with the Pope?" Father Murray told me that it
is part of Catholic piety to maintain a reverent and patient silence
when you don't agree with the pope when he speaks for the entire
Church. I told Father Murray, and this shows my ineradicable
radicalism as a Protestant or as a Renaissance or Reformation figure,
that in such a situation I would say quite simply (pardon my irreverence), "to hell with the Pope." I say that there is no resolution of
this conflict. I think Protestants and Catholics have to follow their
different patterns of loyalty. For the Protestant, it is a loyalty to
liberty even at the expense of anarchy. For the Catholic it is a loyalty
to order and unity even at the risk of spiritual depotism.

INTERVIEWER: Do you see any value in papal absolutism?

DR. NIEBUHR: Papal absolutism is the instrument of unity in a
universal church. The Church would be foolish to sacrifice this instrument of unit, even though I have some very heretical notions
about it. Pragmatically, it is an excellent political device. Although
I believe that papal infallibility is a rather political fiction, I think
that it is absolutely inevitable when you must have one voice that
speaks for a united Church of millions of souls.

The value of papal absolutism can be seen in the history of the
Church. I have always held the thesis that Catholicism has three
times availed itself of what I call papal absolutism or papal mon-
archism. The first time was to extricate itself from the Fall of the
Roman Empire. The pope became the vice-regent of the whole
Western world, and the so-called Western Empire was nothing but
an artifact of papal power and papal prestige. The second time was
after the Protestant Reformation; the Church had to reorganize itself at the fall of medieval culture. What we call modern Catholicism is a product of the Council of Trent and the Jesuits. Inci-
dentally. I must admit that I may have an extravagant appreciation
of the Jesuits. Isn't it amazing that this society, brought into being

for the Counter Reformation, should now become the organ for adapting the Church to all modern movements? We find today Jesuits as leaders in modern science, philosophy, social problems, and theology. My pro-Catholic moments are therefore sometimes chiefly my pro-Jesuit moments. . . . But to continue, thirdly, papal absolutism again appeared to salvage a Christian perspective during the rise of modern industrialism. It had to adapt the whole corpus of what I call social ethics to a modern industrial society. The Church previously had feudal lords as its clients, now it had industrial workers. It took an admirable interest in their economic plight.

INTERVIEWER: How do you feel the present Pope has operated within the structure of papal power?

DR. NIEBUHR: The way the present Pope handles his office and speaks for the whole Church is very revealing. I know that he is not the charismatic figure that the late Pope John XXIII was, but he is holding together a Church that has a variety of national cultures. The present Church is rooted in medieval culture, but it is also related to the open societies of western Europe, America, Asia, and Africa. I think that Pope Paul, who is undoubtedly a shrewd ecclesiastical statesman, has done a splendid job of holding together this diverse Church.

INTERVIEWER: As a Protestant, do you object to the Catholic claim that the Church is the prolongation of Christ on earth?

DR. NIEBUHR: Let me put it this way and please don't think me too cynical or heretical. If you are going to have a symbol of great transcending knowledge, then you had better have a grand symbol. What grander symbol could you have than to say that the Church is the incarnation of Christ through all the ages? We Protestants have rather ungrand myths or symbols. The Baptist church is called the particular repository of biblical truth. Congregationalists are called such because they believe in a particular truth. The same is true of the Presbyterians, although they are really a Scottish church. The Lutheran church is essentially a German or Scandinavian church. Almost a half century ago my brother wrote a book, *The Social Sources of Denominationalism,* and his point was that while each denomination had its specific religious emphasis, on the whole they were socially conditioned by the nations, classes, and circumstances that created them. So in my pro-Catholic moments I would say that you have a grand myth, and we have little myths or symbols that are not as impressive.

INTERVIEWER: Earlier you mentioned the Catholic Church's inflexible use of natural law. Would you please discuss this further in terms of a specific moral issue.

DR. NIEBUHR: Throughout my life I have been concerned with moral issues. After all, I was a teacher of ethics for half a century in the context of a theological education. My point is that the same natural law that has served the Church so well in dealing with the realities of racial justice and injustice and economic justice and injustice is too inflexible. I can say this because the Church's natural law is based on metaphysical theories that demand that it be so. I don't think that anyone has fully thought through the fact that the Church gradually changed from Stoic radicalism and Augustine's equalitarianism to St. Thomas' theory that embodied the whole of Aristotle. Medieval feudal society was not equalitarian, but aristocratic. Aristotelian presuppositions were more relevant and could justify feudal inequality. My chief qualm about natural-law theories is that their proponents regard certain things as inflexible, which I know to be the products of historical movements. We have to consider historical relativities. For us non-Catholics, the primary problem of the inflexibility of natural law is the old question of birth control. My friend, Dr. Bennett, and his friend, Dr. Tatum, of the Rockefeller Institute sent me some months ago a document that was an appeal to the Pope on the issue of birth control. I think it was rather idealistic, but it was not unduly critical. I willingly signed it. What it said in effect was that we are living in an age where medical science has produced a population explosion by saving the lives of many infants that used to be fated to early death. To say that we cannot use human freedom and human intervention to regulate our births, when our deaths have already been regulated, is a vexing problem. So in Catholic countries and in non-Catholic countries like India, you have a population explosion that threatens to undo everything that we are doing to help these countries by technical assistance and so on. I think that this is a scandal, and the Catholic Church should not be so tardy doing something about it. This petition was signed by Protestants, Jews, and others, and it was delivered personally to the Pope. It stated that while all the signers had respect for the moral traditions of the Catholic Church, they felt that where there is a consensus in the whole of modern society, then the Church should not disturb this general consensus.

INTERVIEWER: Am I correct in saying that while your polemical attitude has been directed against Catholicism and Protestantism, you have been through the years consistently pro-Semitic?

DR. NIEBUHR: That is correct. I think that I became increasingly less a Protestant because I was more influenced by Jewish and Catholic thought. I suppose that this is a consequence of the pluralistic society that we live in. It is true that I have always been extremely fond of Jewish people. I like to say that I have had a long love affair with the Jewish people. It began during my early pastorate in Detroit. The mayor appointed me as the chairman of the interracial committee, and I had a Jewish vice-chairman. I remember one time I talked to him about justification by faith, and he said to me: "I don't know what the hell you mean!" And yet this man had a curious combination of compassion and cynicism—realism to the point of cynicism. He dealt with delinquent boys, Negro preachers, Protestant ministers, and Jewish rabbis. I asked him once why he always went to an Orthodox synagogue and never to the Reform temple where his brother was chairman. He said to me: "Reinie, to tell you the truth, if I'm going to take my religion, I want to take it where there is a sense of mystery. I'm not going to a temple where the sermon is just a second-rate book review." I was always impressed by his great capacity for civic righteousness and his compassion was always evident.

INTERVIEWER: What do you think Protestantism can learn from Catholicism?

DR. NIEBUHR: I have gradually become aware, especially since the Second Vatican Council, that Catholicism has something that Protestantism doesn't have. It has what I would call a comprehension of the source and substance of human existence. As I mentioned before, I have had my polemics, because I am a child of the social gospel. I argued against excessive individualism of sectarian or pietistic Protestantism—such as the Protestantism of Billy Graham. Yet I see in modern Catholicism a great lesson for all Protestants. Here we have a Church that was a product of medieval culture. As a critic of Catholicism, I would say that it couldn't extricate itself unaided from this culture. The Renaissance and Reformation had to blow medieval culture to bits. But what secularists, Protestants, and Jews don't realize is that once this Church was free, once it related itself to what we call open society and democracy, it had a greater awareness of the collective problems of justice than any Protestant, idealistic secularist, or utopian secularists ever had. Pope Leo XIII was the first to champion the rights of labor and to encourage labor to organize. We didn't arrive at that in America, although we were a proud democratic society, until the New Deal. Now why does the Church insist on collective bargaining? Because it knows that there is a social substance in human existence and that there is a collective egoism in which you have to have a balance of power. A great deal of justice depends on an equilibrium of power between organized labor and organized management. I see this as one of the greatest achievements of modern Catholicism. I am not talking about the time since John XXIII, but from the time of Leo XIII. This is a superior achievement, and it rests on many things, but particularly upon the embodiment of the whole corpus of Roman classical law as a norm for collective morality.

INTERVIEWER: How did the Protestant church in America develop its social consciousness?

DR. NIEBUHR: Absolutely irrelevant individualism in the face of the increasing injustice of modern industry finally convinced American Protestants. Because we were more individualistic than European Protestantism, we have a sectarian and evangelistic Protestantism. I make a good deal of the fact that now the Catholic Church has a better attitude toward racial justice than the Protestant church has. Why? Because the Catholic Church insists on the whole Church; it has a universalism. It isn't just a collection of middle-class white Christians like the Protestant church. One of the ironic facts of American history is that both slavery and post-slavery injustice prospered in the states that were formed by two kinds of idealism— a Jeffersonian idealism and evangelistic Protestantism. All the horrible racial cruelties that are practiced in Alabama and Mississippi are done by people who have been "converted" five, six, seven, or eight times.

INTERVIEWER: In your criticism of pietistic Protestantism a few moments ago, you mentioned Billy Graham. Do you object to his approach on theological grounds?

DR. NIEBUHR: I object to it both theologically and ethically. I ceased to support the local Council of Churches when they financed a Billy Graham crusade in order "to put Protestantism on the map." This was a fantastic procedure, since on the whole, New York is governed by an alliance of Catholics and Jews. Now while these groups have their own weaknesses, they both have the sense of collective realities, collective justice, and collective injustice. Then along comes Billy Graham for his great evangelistic meeting. He is a typically modern type of evangelist. He doesn't preach fire and brimstone. His manner is bland, and he's a great biblicist. He speaks in a convincing way, and while the choir sings softly, he tells the people to pray and to give their heart to Christ and sign the decision card. He tells them in the words of St. Paul that "if any man be in Christ, he will be a new creature." This is fantastic, because it shows the weakness of Protestantism— individualism. It deals with collective sin, particularly the race question, in purely individualistic terms. You can't overcome race prejudice by simply signing a decision card. Yet Billy Graham tells them that if they sign the decision card, they will become "color-blind." Why is it that we see no evidence of the color-blindness when these people leave the evangelistic meetings?

INTERVIEWER: Speaking of the race question, what do you think the churches must do to promote equality?

DR. NIEBUHR: They must embody in their own life something more than the coerced justice of the saved. The heavy hand of the federal government is on the white oligarchies and forcing them to recognize the Negro. The first thing that the churches must do in their congregational life is to achieve something like agape. That's not the correct word, because it is too pure. It can easily be interpreted to mean love *rather* than justice. But Pope John said let love be the motive and justice the instrument. That is perfectly true. Justice is the instrument of love. In our sacramental communities we must share that love which transcends justice.

INTERVIEWER: You once said that the genius of Catholicism is that it has built a fortress that guards the believer against skepticism.

DR. NIEBUHR: I'm glad you mentioned that because it fits in well with what we were talking about earlier concerning the ecumenical movement. We are living in the post-Christian era—I don't like the phrase but a lot of people use it. Anyway we are living in a time when everyone, even Catholics, have a great deal of skepticism. The old metaphors and symbols of their religion don't quite seem to make sense to them. Take, for example, the funeral service, whether it be Catholic or Protestant, where they use the symbol of the resurrection of the body for the immortality of the soul. At President Kennedy's funeral, everyone was impressed that the Catholic Church used the symbols of the ressurection of the body. Now I don't think that anybody really believes in the resurrection of the body. But Christians do believe in eternal life and that man is both mortal and immortal. Mortal in the sense that he is a creature of nature and immortal in the sense that he is a transcendent spirit. This is one of the places where ecumenical contacts help a great deal. We Protestants who are touched by all kinds of heresies, which you regard as dangerous, might convince you that they are a creative source. On the other hand, when Catholics say that "we have a fortress to guard the truth of faith against the acids of modernity," they might teach us something. I notice that that very modern man, Somerset Maugham, said he saw no future for Christianity except in the Catholic Church.

INTERVIEWER: Do you seriously think that many Christians do not believe in the resurrection of the body?

DR. NIEBUHR: Of course. How can they? Our dear friend Father Martin D'Arcy visited us one evening and the conversation centered around the skepticism that one finds in the Protestant church. At one point, Father D'Arcy said: "Any Catholic priest will tell you that Catholics are frequently touched by all sorts of heresies. Sometimes we inquire into them when they are serious enough, but sometimes we don't bother with them." The whole thrust of the Johannine symbolism on eternal life points to what I call the incongruity of human life—that man is both mortal and immortal. Christianity, as seen in both the Old Testament and New Testament, uses the symbol of the resurrection of the body, because for Hebraic thought as opposed to Greek thought there is an assumption that the human personality is one. Thus, you can't have an eternal life without a resurrection of the body. Yet we can't have empirical knowledge about this resurrection, and so it remains a symbol of a reality we can never quite define or grasp. The Church does define it and so we accept it.

When I gave my Gifford Lectures nearly a half a century ago in Edinburgh, I developed a (marvelous for me) friendship with Norman Kemp Smith, a philosopher who was a specialist in Hume and Kant. In one of my lectures I said that Christianity, influenced by Hebrew thought with some Greek accretions especially in John, had projected the idea of the resurrection of the body that was more rational than the notion of immortality. Afterwards, Norman Kemp Smith taught me a wonderful lesson. He observed that I should not have said that the resurrection was more rational than immortality. I should have said that we don't have empirical experience either of the discarnate soul or of the resurrected body. Both are irrational, and both are symbols of a future that is beyond our experience.

INTERVIEWER: You have spent most of your adult life working in the field of theological education. How would you define theology?

DR. NIEBUHR: In this area, I am influenced by Martin Buber, who said that there is no such thing as theology if we define it as a science of God. No one can know God. St. Augustine says that "if thou would comprehend Him, He were not God." Theology is rather a rational explication of man's faith. I would prefer not to use the word science in this context, although I had a professor at Yale Divinity School that claimed theology was an empirical science. This professor meant a lot to me, but I found his courses boring. He was of the school of nineteenth-century empirical theology, and he never was able to convince me that theology was empirical. According to all empirical sciences, the truth emerges when you have controlled experiments. But theology is not like that. Rather, it is historical and must take into account the development of doctrine and the relativities of the historical perspective.

INTERVIEWER: Paul Tillich claimed that your theology was based on an inadequate epistemology. Was he justified in his criticism?

DR. NIEBUHR: It's a legitimate objection, of course. Paul Tillich was a greater philosopher and theologian than I. Even though we were good friends, we were in constant debate over the value of religious symbols. But I believe that his epistemology was also inadequate because it was Neoplatonic. He insisted that people wouldn't believe in appropriate symbols unless they felt them within themselves. Well, what kind of epistemology is that? Tillich produced a Neoplatonic version of Christian theology. But please remember that I am not saying that too arbitrarily. Paul Tillich was a grand spirit who did much to relate biblical truth to Neoplatonic mysticism—the God above all gods, the morality beyond all morality. In one of his books, *Beyond Morality,* he cited the parable of talents. Tillich felt that a horrible injustice was described in this parable. But Our Lord does not say that this parable gave us a norm of justice. Yet for Tillich it meant that all life is like that; the rich get richer, and the poor get poorer. There is no answer to this great conundrum of life, and we can say, Tillich observed, that if we all gather together on the divine ground of our existence, then all things will be set aright. Now this embodies what I regard as a basic heresy. The heresy is that the temporal existence is evil because it is temporal. Much of our debate over symbolism and epistemology can be traced to our different emphasis on the fact that the genius of Christianity was rooted in its Hebraic conception of life. For me, the temporal world is not evil because it is temporal, and individuals are not evil because they are individuals. Mysticism inclines to swallow up individuality, history, and particular situations into a great undifferentiated eternity.

INTERVIEWER: Some have said that in your social picture of redemption you do not adequately emphasize the role of the church.

DR. NIEBUHR: Many of my friends, especially Anglicans, have made that objection, and I think that it may be valid. Even though I am realistic in terms of collective political realities, perhaps I have not sufficiently stressed the role of the church. As a Catholic, you might say that I have no adequate appreciation of the church. Perhaps at issue here is another difference between the Catholic and Protestant church. I won't say I'm right, but I feel that the Protestant church tends to be the American coventicle of middle-class white Christians. I know that the Catholic Church isn't, although it is not without its own problems. Perhaps my critics and former students are right when they say that I don't pay enough attention to the church as an institution. But I have been influenced by the historical realities of the church as I know it—both Protestant and Catholic. For instance, in my days in Detroit, my appreciation for the Catholic Church was postponed because of the Catholic Archbishop. His chief reaction to the Treaty of Versailles was that it had liberated all inferior nations, like the Poles, but had left Ireland in bondage. I have also been influenced in this respect not by sectarian Protestantism, but simply by the critical attitude of some of my secular, political-scientist friends. They viewed religious communities only as they became involved in corruption.

I would like to say, and this is probably one of my recantations, that religion needs an institutional church. I know that a universal church is better than national churches. Organized religion does present problems, but it is necessary.

INTERVIEWER: Over the years you have written an extraordinary amount. Do you have any special method or system?

DR. NIEBUHR: No. My wife would say simply that I am compulsive in my work. I was endowed with a generous supply of energy, and I like to write. I don't regret having written so many articles, because I'm essentially a journalist, not a scholar. I do regret that I wrote so many books. My late brother Richard, who taught at Yale, wrote fewer books and better books than I did.

INTERVIEWER: I notice that you have Altizer's book on your desk. What do you think of the "death of God" theologians?

DR. NIEBUHR: I put it very simply: I think they are stupid. Stupid because they don't realize that all religious convictions and affirmations are symbolic. These young men—I say young because I am an old man—would have been less blithe if they had limited themselves to announcing the dying of the images of God. What do they mean when they say God is dead? The current radical theologians seem to have no interest in the structures of meaning. They do not define a system of coherence. We can only guess at their premises. What becomes of the mystery of creativity that is reflected in the church's belief in God the Father, the Maker of heaven and earth? We must revere the mystery and the majesty of the human story that transcends all human knowledge. These men have not sufficiently digested all the problems of the Christological controversies of the early Christian ages, nor have they understood the existentialism of the nineteenth century. Nietszche said that God was dead, and so did Kierkegaard. But Kierkegaard meant that because of the incongruity of the existing individual, one had to make a leap of faith. This was a leap of faith into the Christ symbol—the ultimate reconciliation that was to come between God's justice and God's mercy.

INTERVIEWER: Will these theologians harm the Protestant belief in God?

DR. NIEBUHR: I don't think they are important enough to be destructive. They are all for doing away with the schemes of meaning that men find useful to explain human nature and the various complexities of history. But they put nothing in their place. They say that it is necessary to clear the ground for new conceptions. What does that mean? Someone is going to rush in with some new symbol. The Communists have already given us a new symbol that has proved inadequate. Rather than merely clear the ground of all irrelevant myths and conceptions, they should work toward a new and relevant conception of God and His mysteries. Of course an absolutely new conception is not possible. We Christians are related to all kinds of non-Christians, and we must be interested in relating the traditions of our faith to modern circumstances. We live in a free society where cooperation is essential. We have an obligation to save each other from our characteristic vices by cooperating with each other. So the "death of God" theologians must try to contribute something positive. Only humble men who recognize the mystery and majesty of life are able to face the beauty and terror of life without exulting over its beauty or becoming crushed by its terror.

❖❖

REINHOLD NIEBUHR was born in Wright City, Missouri, on June 21st, 1892. His boyhood was spent in St. Charles, Missouri, and Lincoln Illinois. He attended Elmhurst College in Elmhurst, Illinois, and Eden Theological Seminary in St. Louis, Missouri. He received his M.A. from the Yale Divinity School in 1915. That same year he was ordained into the ministry of the Evangelical Synod of North America. From 1915 until 1928, he was pastor of a city parish in Detroit. In 1928, he joined the faculty of Union Theological Seminary, and two years later he became Professor of Applied Christianity. He is married and has two grown children. He retired from teaching in 1960 and is now Professor Emeritus at Union and a Research Associate at Columbia University's Institute for War and Peace Studies. He is Contributing Editor of *Christianity and Crisis.*

Dr. Niebuhr's bibliography is extensive. He has written hundreds of articles, and among his major books are: *Moral Man and Immoral Society; The Nature and Destiny of Man; The Children of Light and the Children of Darkness; Faith and History; Man's Nature and His Communities; The Structure of Nations and Empires; World Crisis and American Responsibility;* and *Pious and Secular America.*

Abraham J. Heschel

Rabbi Abraham J. Heschel, with his thick, unruly, gray-white hair and bushy beard, looks like an Old Testament prophet. Solidly built, with an almost military straightness, he gives the impression on a lecture platform and in his photographs of being much taller than he actually is. His manner is paternal, and rarely does he raise his well-modulated bass voice. In aphoristic prose, illustrated by colorful stories, often about Jewish rabbis, he discusses theology in a refreshing way. He uses a common-sense approach and numerous biblical images. Shunning any form of dialectics or closely reasoned argumentation, he speaks simply but persuasively. He does not orate, but engages his listeners in a personal encounter. As someone remarked after one of his lectures: "Hearing Rabbi Heschel is a deeply moving experience."

I meet Rabbi Heschel, as he suggested, in front of the Center for Continuing Education at the University of Notre Dame, where he has just attended a lecture by Fr. Bernard Häring. He is wearing a light gray suit, white shirt, and blue tie. On the way to his room, we talk about the lecture. When we arrive at his room, both of us take chairs next to the window. As it is warm and humid following an unexpected afternoon shower, he opens the windows. On the table next to him is a copy of the documents of Vatican II, and several papers and books are on his bed. He lights up a cigar, and we continue our discussion of Father Häring. In the background, the roar of a low-flying plane can be heard.

INTERVIEWER: What was your impression of Father Häring's talk on holiness in the Church and religious life?

RABBI HESCHEL: Worship is the primary form of religious living. He who doesn't know how to worship doesn't know how to believe and what it means to be alive. In that sense, I would say that worship precedes faith. Father Häring's entire emphasis on the life of worship and prayer is one that I consider valid and indispensable.

INTERVIEWER: Was there anything in his address that you would question?

RABBI HESCHEL: Yes, I have one basic question. In his interpretation of worship and the role of the Holy Spirit, he was exceedingly Christ-centered. This raises some serious theological problems. Is it really necessary for a Christian to believe that the Creator of heaven and earth has resigned His power to Jesus and that God Himself, Omnipotent Father, is unable to reach men directly? What of the psalmist? Would you be willing to say that the psalmist didn't know how to pray? And what of those who do not accept the claim of the Church? Are the Jews and Mohammedans unable to pray or address themselves to God? Father Häring, by saying that the act of worship is an act in Christ, indicated that there is only *one* acceptable form of prayer. As a Jew, I must reject that, and I also consider it dangerous to Christians.

INTERVIEWER: Don't you think that Father Häring would agree that one can pray directly to God? He would probably point to the Divine Office, the official prayer of the Church, which draws heavily from the Old Testament.

RABBI HESCHEL: It is true that the "Hebrew Bible"—a term that should replace the condescending term "Old Testament"—stresses the relationship of immediacy between man and God. But I feel that within the new thinking that is taking place in the Church, there is need of a further clarification on this question. I know that the Church stresses the centrality of Jesus in the process of salvation. I do not think, however, it has had to stress the centrality of Jesus in the process of inspiration and worship.

INTERVIEWER: Is the question "salvation through the Synagogue" important in contemporary Judaism?

RABBI HESCHEL: No. That's not our problem. One of the greatest sources of mutual understanding is that Christians and Jews have different problems. In Christianity, the problem of salvation is paramount. In Judaism, other issues are central. I can best illustrate this by a little story. One of my ancestors was Rabbi Levi Yicchak, a Hasidic rabbi, one of the great saints in Jewish history. He once said: "I know very well that I am unworthy of eternal life, because I am a sinner and have always failed to do the will of God. What will happen to me when I come before the heavenly court? The decree will certainly be that I enter hell, and that will be the will of God. What greater joy is there than to do the will of God? I will utter a benediction and run to hell in order to suffer because such is the will of God.'" We believe in an after-life. We believe that every one of us individually will be called upon to give account of the life we lived. We are *not* saved by the synagogue; our destiny will be determined by what we do or fail to do. The commandment, the *"mitsvah,"* to serve God, is a term more central than the term salvation. Shall I give you another example?

INTERVIEWER: Yes, please do.

RABBI HESCHEL: This is a story of another of my ancestors. His name was Rabbi Dov Baer, the "Great Preacher" of Mezhiritch. He was the successor to Baal Shem, the founder of Hasidism. He was a poor man who made his living teaching little children. But it happened that there were exceedingly few children in the community, and the income he received was not sufficient. On the eve of the Passover, his wife told him that they had no money to buy the matzo, wine, and candles for the feast. He assured his wife that God would take care of them, and he went to the Synagogue to pray. When he returned, he saw candles in the window, and as he went inside, he saw the table set for the feast. He also found a stranger in the house whom he greeted briefly. Then, the family celebrated the ancient rite. Afterwards, his wife told him that this man had come to their house and asked if he could celebrate the Passover with them. He had with him all the necessary supplies. The rabbi was overcome with gratitude and asked the man what he could do for him to repay his kindness. The man said: "Rabbi, I am a happy man, successful, and well-to-do, but my wife never gave me a child. I have uttered many prayers, but God never answered my petition. Would you pray for me?" The rabbi said: "A year from now (using the scriptural way of talking), your wife will be a mother." Suddenly, the rabbi heard a voice from heaven saying: "Since you have made the promise, you shall not share in the life to come." There was a decree in heaven that this man should not be a father and the rabbi should have been aware of this. Since he was a man of spiritual powers, he must have known this. But still he defied it. When the rabbi heard that he would never enter heaven, he was overwhelmed with great joy and started to dance in ectasy. People asked him why he was so happy, and he said to them: "All my life I have had one great fear: that I serve God only to have a share in the life to come. I was never sure if my service was really genuine and pure. Now I know. Now I can serve God out of love, and I will receive no reward. How happy and wonderful will be my life knowing that I am really doing the will of God."

INTERVIEWER: What is the Jewish conception of the after-life?

RABBI HESCHEL: We have no information about it. The only thing we know is what is given to us in the Talmud in the name of one of the sages of the third century. We are told that the world to come is a sphere, a realm where the good people sit with crowns on their heads receiving joy of *visio Dei*—the joy of inhaling the glory of God's presence. That's all we know. We don't know what the *visio Dei* means, or the significance of the "crowns." So we must allegorize, and we say that a crown is made up of the good and sacred moments in our life here on earth and the good deeds that we do in this life.

INTERVIEWER: What happens to the evil man who rejects God?

RABBI HESCHEL: From the Torah, we know only so much about the will of God. The after-life remains a mystery. But we can say that Jewish tradition certainly teaches that there is a way of survival for the wicked that we call Sheol.

Death is not seen as mere ruin and disaster. It is felt to be a loss of further possibilities to experience and to enhance the glory and goodness of God here and now. It is not a liquidation, but a summation, the end of a prelude to a symphony of which we only have a vague inkling of hope. The prelude is infinitely rich in possibilities of either enhancing or frustrating God's patient, ongoing efforts to redeem the world.

Death is the end of what we can do in being partners to redemption. The life that follows must be earned while we are here. It does not come out of nothing; it is an ingathering, the harvest of eternal moments achieved while on earth.

Unless we cultivate sensitivity to the glory while here, unless we learn how to experience a foretaste of heaven while on earth, what can there be in store for us in the life to come? The seed of life eternal is planted within us here and now. But a seed is wasted when placed on iron, into souls that die while the body is still alive.

INTERVIEWER: You mentioned that your ancestors were rabbis.

RABBI HESCHEL: Yes, I can trace my family back to the late fifteenth century. They were all rabbis. For seven generations, all my ancestors have been Hasidic rabbis.

INTERVIEWER: You once wrote that "the dignity of human existence is in the power of reciprocity." When I first read that, I immediately thought of Martin Buber. Was I correct?

RABBI HESCHEL: I will tell you how I understand that statement. Reciprocity has two meanings: in relation to man and in relation to God. I am not sure that Buber used reciprocity in this second sense. In fact, I doubt it. I have found great inspiration in *Psalm* 116:12: "What can I render to the Lord for all His bounties toward me?" This is the basic notion of reciprocity. One of the prerequisites for faith is gratitude. It is the essential attitude that makes a person human. It is out of gratitude that we learn how to praise, how to pray. In the Jewish liturgy, praise is the outstanding form of prayer. We must learn how to praise in order to know how to implore. First we sing, then we believe. Praise precedes faith. If we look at the psalms, we see that above all the psalmist is overwhelmed by sensing the Creator in His creation. He is grateful for every perception— for the moment of being alive.

INTERVIEWER: Have you been greatly influenced by Martin Buber?

RABBI HESCHEL: I would not say so. I consider the important insights in Buber to be derived from Hasidic tradition, and these I knew before I met him. I served as his successor in Frankfurt am Main when the Gestapo would not allow him to teach any more. He asked me to take over his work. I knew him intimately for many years.

INTERVIEWER: What are the significant contributions Buber has made to Judaism and to the philosophy of religion?

RABBI HESCHEL: Permit me to enumerate a few major contributions. First of all, he discovered Hasidism for the West, for the non-Jewish world. And through this he also brought Hasidism to many Jews who were alienated from it and didn't know what it was. Secondly, he wrote widely on Zionism. Thirdly, he was very successful in interpreting Hasidism in modern philosophical terms. Fourthly, he translated the Hebrew Bible into German in a creative way. He was, above all, a profound thinker, a major surprise in the intellectual climate of the twentieth century.

INTERVIEWER: How did Buber feel about organized religion?

RABBI HESCHEL: Let me explain. Jewish thinking and living can only be adequately understood in terms of a dialectic pattern, containing opposite or contrasted properties. As in a magnet, the ends of which have opposite magnetic qualities, these terms are opposite to one another and exemplify a polarity that lies at the very heart of Judaism, the polarity of ideas and events, of *mitsvah* and sin, of *kavanah* and deed, of regularity and spontaneity, of uniformity and individuality, of *halacha* and *agada,* of law and inwardness, of love and fear, of understanding and obedience, of joy and discipline, of the good and the evil drive, of time and eternity, of this world and the world to come, of revelation and response, of insight and information, of empathy and self-expression, of creed and faith, of the word and that which is beyond words, of man's quest for God and God in search of man. Even God's relation to the world is characterized by the polarity of justice and mercy, providence and concealment, the promise of reward and the demand to serve Him for His sake. Taken abstractedly, all these terms seem to be mutually exclusive, yet in actual living they involve each other; the separation of the two is fatal to both. There is no *halacha* without *agada,* and no *agada* without *halacha*. We must neither disparage the body, nor sacrifice the spirit. The body is the discipline, the pattern, the law; the spirit is inner devotion, spontaneity, freedom. The body without the spirit is a corpse; the spirit without the body is a ghost. Thus, a *mitsvah* is both a discipline and an inspiration, an act of obedience and an experience of joy, a yoke and a prerogative. Our task is to learn how to maintain a harmony between the demands of *halacha* and the spirit of *agada*.

The weakness of Buber's conception is in his stressing one aspect to the exclusion of the other.

INTERVIEWER: Did he hold that revelation was a kind of vague exchange?

RABBI HESCHEL: No, not an exchange. Rather, he believed it is a vague encounter. That is untenable. A Jew cannot live by such a conception of revelation. Buber does not do justice to the claims of the prophets. So I have to choose between him and the Bible itself. The Bible says that God spoke to men—a challenging, embarrassing, and overwhelming claim. I have trouble with many of the things He said, but I have to accept them. If I don't accept the claim that God spoke to the prophets, then I detach myself from the biblical roots. Buber was a person of depth and greatness, but on many points he was not able to reach the Jewish people. One of the weaknesses in Buber, who was an exceedingly learned man, was that he was not at home in rabbinic literature. That covers many years. A lot has happened between the Bible and Hasidism that Buber did not pay attention to.

INTERVIEWER: Would you go as far as to say that he had a greater influence on the non-Jewish world than on the Jewish world?

RABBI HESCHEL: Many people say so.

INTERVIEWER: Do you agree?

RABBI HESCHEL: It is hard to know exactly how to measure influence. I must know my limitations. There are certain things I know and other things I do not.

INTERVIEWER: What can Christianity learn from Judaism?

RABBI HESCHEL: To be a witness to the God of Abraham, of Sinai, openness to God's stake in the ongoing history of the Jewish people.

There are many things that Judaism teaches: the importance of the simple common deeds, sanctification of time, and a sense of wonder and radical amazement. But all these things flow from the primary witness to the God of Abraham. The idea of witness, that is, sensitivity to God's presence, is, above all, the primary, existential aspect of Judaism. Other things, such as the mysterious immediacy in relation to God, radical monotheism, and the concept of man, are aspects of witness.

INTERVIEWER: Would you please explain the Judaic concept of man.

RABBI HESCHEL: We start with the certainty that God is involved in human life. This means that the primary task of man is to realize that God has a stake in his life. We also believe that the Jewish people are not the same since Sinai. They are called upon to carry out the commandments of the Torah, the Law. Man is by his very being a man in travail with God's dreams and designs. In the Bible, we read about the creation of all *other things:* "And then God said. And so it was." But when God came to create man, He first had a vision of man. He said: "Let us make man in our vision." In other words, the vision of man preceded the creation of man. We may say that God has a vision or expectation of man. It is our task to recover it. That's why man is a messenger for God—*the* messenger. God is in our midst. Our most important problem is the problem of responsiveness, obedience to the Law, openness, listening to Moses, Amos, Rabbi Akiba; our privilege is being a part of the Jewish community, past and present.

INTERVIEWER: I think that a Christian would agree with all you have said.

RABBI HESCHEL: If he agrees with all that, then he is a Jew.

INTERVIEWER: Perhaps this is what Pope Pius XII meant when he said "spiritually, we are semites."

RABBI HESCHEL: But Christians leave out the possibility and the greatness of Mosaic Law. A Christian theologian would say that the Law is an imposition. We feel the blessing and the love of the Law; we sense God's will. A Jew is committed to the idea that he is able to be attached to God directly. We have the certainty of being able to live a life that is compatible with His presence. In other words, the will of God is within the scope of human understanding. The Torah has not been abolished. We have the gift of the Word. What is the Bible? The presence of God is found in many ways, but above all God is found in the words of the Bible. We believe that we are living in the ancient covenant of Sinai. This is not a matter of feeling or even a matter of faith. It's a reality. God is waiting for the sinner. Up to the last day, God is waiting for his return. Man has to respond. The question of original sin is not of primary importance for the Jew. The problem is not how shall I be saved. The problem is how shall I serve God at this very moment. My challenge is how can I be honest and helpful toward my neighbor in the presence of the Father.

INTERVIEWER: Surely the Hebrew Bible is an essential element of the total Christian view.

RABBI HESCHEL: But what did you do to the Hebrew Bible? You made it an "old" book of Law that very few people read. I have encountered many wonderful priests, whose spirituality I greatly admire who haven't read the Hebrew Bible. Recently, a very fine, inspired priest, a man advanced in years, told me: "I am now reading for the first time the Hebrew Bible. What a great work it is." The fact is that Catholics read only the psalms from the Hebrew Bible. They read papal encyclicals, Christian authors, and, of course, the New Testament. But they forget the Hebrew Bible.

INTERVIEWER: What else does a Jew expect from Christianity?

RABBI HESCHEL: We are a small group always in danger. History has shown that our situation has always been precarious—on the brink of disaster. For almost two thousand years, the Church has tried to understand itself as an antithesis to Judaism. I am not speaking about the results of such hostility. I am speaking about the scandal of rejecting the genuine roots of Christian belief. Jesus was a Jew. His disciples were Jews. Jesus prepared for the Sabbath, sanctified the Seventh Day, read the traditional prayers, and recited and interpreted the Bible.

To answer your question, I would say that the most that Christianity can do is to be faithful to its ultimate roots. Christians must abandon the idea that the Jews must be converted. This is one of the greatest scandals in history. It reminds me of a spiritual Oedipus complex. "Honor your father and your mother." Your mother and father were both Jews. The first thing you could do for us is to be genuine in your Christian faith and to be a witness to the God of Abraham. I recognize in Christianity the presence of holiness. I see it; I sense it; I feel it. You are not an embarrassment to us, and we shouldn't be an embarrassment to you. We can help each other on many levels. The Jews have a good memory of what the Bible means. The Christians have had great experience in proclaiming the message of the God of Abraham to the Gentiles and have been able to preserve many ancient insights and loyalties in their spirituality. A Christian should realize that a world that does not have Israel will be a world without the God of Israel. A Jew, in his own way, should acknowledge the role of Christianity in God's plan for the redemption of all men.

INTERVIEWER: What is the goal of Christian-Jewish cooperation?

RABBI HESCHEL: The purpose of such interreligious cooperation is not mutual refutation. It is to help one another share insight and learning. We must also search for the sources of devotion and for the power of love and care for man. More than ever before we need each other's help, and we need the courage to believe that the word of the Lord endures forever. We must keep ourselves sensitive to God around us and listen to His word in the Bible. Religion is a means, not an end. Over all stands the Creator and Lord of history. He who transcends all.

INTERVIEWER: Recently, a New York minister suggested that Christians join Jews in observing Saturday instead of Sunday as the Sabbath. What do you think of this?

RABBI HESCHEL: It should not be done just for ecumenical reasons. One should not serve God for the sake of the ecumenical movement, but for His own sake. There is much involved here. What is the nature of Christian faith? If it is a biblical faith, then you take the Ten Commandments seriously. So why did the Christians change the Holy Day? I cannot understand it. Historically, it was not necessarily done for spiritual reasons. My task is not to tell the Christian what to do. My task is to help him, not to debate with him.

INTERVIEWER: Your life has been dedicated to theology, the study of the Word of God. What are the main characteristics of Jewish theology?

RABBI HESCHEL: Jewish theology must never be detached from the human situation. The standard of Jewish theology is the degree to which it may affect the life of the Jew, his thoughts as well as his concrete action. A person goes astray if his theory far outstrips his actions. It was a major principle in early Hasidism: Beware, lest your wisdom transcends your fulfillment or concrete service. With every new insight that comes to you, seek to carry out a new act of serving Him. . . . As to the term itself, *theology* is not quite accurate to a Jewish thinker. I once said in my book, *Man is Not Alone,* that the Bible is not man's book about God, but rather God's book about man. In this sense, the real concern is to discover what God requires of man—what is God's expectation for man. Anthropology is central to theology. I often use the term philosophy of religion, but then I have to define it.

INTERVIEWER: What do you mean by philosophy of religion?

RABBI HESCHEL: The term "religion" in the phrase philosophy of religion may be used either as an object or as a subject. In the first sense, philosophy of religion is a critique of religion; religion as a theme or object of examination. In this sense, we employ, e.g., the term "philosophy of science." In the second sense, philosophy has a meaning comparable to the meaning of a phrase such as the philosophy of Kant or the philosophy of Plato.

Now Judaism is a source of ideas, basic insights, perspectives, and teachings. The task of philosophy of Judaism is twofold: radical self-understanding in terms of its own spirit as well as critical reassessment of Judaism from the point of view of both our total knowledge and our immediate situation.

INTERVIEWER: With this distinction in mind, how would you relate it to the contemporary theological quest?

RABBI HESCHEL: We are challenged from two directions, by the insecurity of faith and by the earnestness of our commitment to the Bible. It is necessary to look at the Bible from the perspective of our situation and to look at our situation from the point of the Bible.

Modern theology must seek to recover the uniqueness of biblical thinking, of categories with which to face ultimate problems. The perspective from which we look at reality determines our way of formulating our problems. We have long been accustomed to search in the Bible for answers to nonbiblical problems. The result is confusion. The Bible is the *ancilla theologiae*. What I plead for is a search for the intellectual relevance of the Bible.

INTERVIEWER: Do you have any observations about the direction this search should take?

RABBI HESCHEL: Let us take, for example, the problem of being, which is the central metaphysical problem today. For the biblical mind, being is not the primary question. The Bible is concerned with creation, God's care for creatures. To be or not to be is *not* the question. We have being. The problem is living. The whole conception of the person and of man has been distorted because we have overemphasized ontology. Biblical theology approaches man in a different way. The right question is not "How do I know God?" but "Am I known by God?" This is the basic issue. We have pagan questions, and we seek biblical answers. To understand the Bible, we must know that the Bible has answers to ultimate questions. But first of all, we must know what are the ultimate questions.

INTERVIEWER: Do you think that the insensitivity to God is a major problem today?

RABBI HESCHEL: Yes, it is. But to deal with sensitivity to God is already an advanced problem. We cannot begin with God until we have first dealt adequately with certain pretheological presuppositions. The way I relate myself to this chair will determine the way I relate myself to God. We must analyze some basic pretheological directions or attitudes, such as the sense of wonder, reverence, and gratitude. These prerequisites are not cultivated in our society. Thus, the problem today is not sensitivity to God. We are not even sensitive to God's creation. Unless we know how to be sensitive to God's glory and know something of His presence in the world, we will never know anything about His essence.

INTERVIEWER: You spoke of the insecurity of faith. How should theology face this challenge?

RABBI HESCHEL: First by saying *mea culpa*. Religion has been reduced to institution, symbol, theology. It does not affect the *pretheological* situation, the presymbolic depth of existence. To redirect the trend, we must lay bare what is involved in religious existence: we must recover the situations that both precede and correspond to the theological formulations; we must recall the questions that religious doctrines are trying to answer, *the antecedents of religious commitment,* the presuppositions of faith. A major task of philosophy of religion is, as said before, to rediscover the questions to which religion is an answer. The inquiry must proceed both by delving into the consciousness of man and by delving into the teachings and the attitudes of the religious tradition.

The urgent problem is not only the truth of religion, but man's capacity to sense the truth of religion and the authenticity of religious concern. Religious truth does not shine in a vacuum. It is certainly not comprehensible when the antecedents of religious insight and commitment are wasted away; when the mind is dazzled by ideologies that either obscure or misrepresent man's ultimate questions; when life is lived in a way that tends to abuse and to squander the gold mines, the challenging resources of human existence. The primary issue of theology is *pretheological;* it is the total situation of man and his attitudes toward life and the world. I discussed this in my book, *The Insecurity of Freedom*.

INTERVIEWER: Your recent writings reflect your concern with man's deepening alienation from God and the world's drift toward destruction.

RABBI HESCHEL: I am really a person who is in anguish. I cannot forget what I have seen and have been through. Auschwitz and Hiroshima never leave my mind. Nothing can be the same after that. After all, we are convinced that we must take history seriously and that in history signs of the future are given to us. I see signs of a deterioration that has already begun. The war in Vietnam is a sign that we don't know how to live or how to respond. God is trying us very seriously. I wonder if we will pass the test? I am not a pessimist, because I believe that God loves us. But I also believe that we should not rely on God alone; *we* have to respond. It is so important that all of us, regardless of our religious affiliation, remember that we all stand under the hand of God and must *act* with this in mind. As important as it is to discuss theological subtleties, it is much more important to know how to save men from being liquidated.

INTERVIEWER: Have you any suggestions how the churches may work to save man from destruction?

RABBI HESCHEL: Responsible religious people should discover the real moral problems. The churches should be more concerned with how to save the humanity of man, God's image within man. The prophetic dimension is indispensable. Looking at the past, we may think that the prophet was the most superfluous man that ever lived. The Law was given, the message was there. With the temple and the priests, why was there need for prophets? Apparently, it was within the Divine Plan that besides the Law there be also some men who with prophetic vision could remind others of God's message.

INTERVIEWER: What advice would you give those religious people who tend to become discouraged when they see so much evil in the world?

RABBI HESCHEL: For man to be frustrated is a cardinal sin. Man is not alone in his concern for justice; God is with him. Therefore, we must continue to fight to the last breath. As a criticism, I must say that religious people are often too concerned with trifles and lose sight of greater issues. How can a religious community tolerate violence? This is one of the things I do not understand. I do believe that church members can do much to overcome evil if they unite. Why don't all those affiliated with churches—and synagogues— gather together some afternoon and fill the streets with one voice of protest against the killing of innocent civilians. The protest of these many millions of believers would have a great effect, and President Johnson could not ignore it. They should not cease to utter their disgust that America permits civilians to be killed. This is one practical way to carry out the will of God.

INTERVIEWER: I once read that for the Jews a basic difficulty with Christianity is that the "God of Christians is humble, and we Jews cannot accept such humility." Do you agree with this?

RABBI HESCHEL: No. There is a passage in the Talmud that says just the opposite: "Wherever you find God's grandeur, you find His humility." The divine pathos is a basic category in our understanding of God. I have written about this in my books, *The Prophets* and *Theology of Ancient Judaism, Vol. I.* The issues between Jews and Christians are quite different. We reject the Incarnation; we insist on God's transcendence, and we make absolute the difference between God and man. We don't acknowledge the messiahship of Jesus, because we expected and continue to expect that the Messiah will bring about a radical change in concrete history. We cannot accept the Christian claim that Jesus abolished the Law. To us the Law continues to be valid.

INTERVIEWER: What of Buber's observation that the Church is oriented toward the individual, while Judaism is concerned with the community?

RABBI HESCHEL: This is an oversimplification that is partly true and partly not true. One of the characteristics of Judaism is the complete identity of the people, or community, and the faith. For example, it is impossible for us to write a history of a Jewish church as a church. We only have a community. Christianity is a universal religion; there are many communities in Christianity, but there is no strict identity between community and faith. In other words, in Judaism there is a greater emphasis upon *qahal,* the holy community, in a total way than in Christianity. This can be illustrated by the saying of a rabbi in the first century: "I am willing to be a sacrifice for my people." This can be understood in the sense that "I am ready to give myself up completely, as long as the community remains intact."

INTERVIEWER: The Catholic Church certainly looks upon herself as the *ecclesia,* the sacred, worshiping community. The communitarian aspect is as strong in Christianity as in Judaism.

RABBI HESCHEL: I wish it were, but it isn't.

INTERVIEWER: Do you mean theologically or historically?

RABBI HESCHEL: I am not competent to judge theologically, but historically, Christianity has not stressed the idea of community. Let me give you an example. In my childhood, I could not understand how German and French soldiers, both claiming Christianity as their religion, could kill each other. You call this a community? Maybe you can give me a theological answer for this, but for me it is inconceivable that such a thing should happen in a community. It is fratricide. You are not one people if you kill each other. This is your challenge, and I pray that you can meet it. So far you have not.

INTERVIEWER: Do you have any observations concerning the role of the Jews in the present ecumenical dialogue?

RABBI HESCHEL: We are now at the beginning of a new period in the history of religious cooperation between Christians and Jews. The fact that last year I was appointed the Harry Emerson Fosdick Visiting Professor at Union Theological Seminary is a sign of the change. I have had hundreds of conversations and meetings with Christians, and if I discovered that we have many disagreements, I also discovered that there is much upon which we can agree. It is true that our dogmas and ways of worship are different. But we both worship the God of Israel. We are both committed to the Hebrew Bible as the word of God, to some of the commandments as the will of God, to the sense of contrition, and to the conviction that without the holy, the good will be defeated. Our prayer is for the Christians to continue to serve and to worship God.

However, I have one complaint. Give up the idea of the mission to the Jews, the idea of converting the Jews. It is arrogant to play God. Once the Christians give up this, much of the tension will be relieved. Christianity, as an expression of providence, is no problem for us. It is true that you have a number of ideas that I wish you would modify, and in fact you are modifying many of them.

INTERVIEWER: Some Jews are suspicious of the ecumenical movement and fear that if all Christians unite, then the Jews will again be persecuted.

RABBI HESCHEL: You can't blame the Jews for such fear. I have been stoned and beaten up many times in Warsaw by young boys who had just come out of church. What do you expect the Jews to feel? Do you think I can forget the long history of my people and the horrible things that have happened to us in the last thirty years? The Jew is afflicted with anxiety. The psalmist frequently reminds us that there is no security in this world. But I believe that God will purify the heart and will give wisdom and grace to His sons. I take consolation in the words of Rabbi Johanan Ha-Sandelar, a disciple of Rabbi Akiba, who said: "Every community which is established for the sake of heaven will in the end endure; but one which is not for the sake of heaven will not endure in the end."

❖❖

ABRAHAM JOSHUA HESCHEL was born in 1907 in Warsaw, Poland. He received his Ph.D. from the University of Berlin in 1933 and a year later graduated from Hochschule für die Wissenschaft des Judentums. He taught Judaistic studies at Berlin, Frankfurt, and Warsaw and was the founder of the Institute of Jewish Learning in London in 1940. That same year Rabbi Heschel came to the United States and served as a Professor of Rabbinics and Philosophy at Hebrew Union College in Cincinnati, Ohio. In 1945 he joined the faculty of the Jewish Theological Seminary of America in New York City as Professor of Jewish Ethics and Mysticism. He has also taught at Stanford, the University of Minnesota, and Union Theological Seminary. He is married and has one daughter.

Rabbi Heschel's books include: *Man's Quest for God; The Earth is the Lord's; The Prophets; The Sabbath; The Quest for Certainty; Man is Not Alone; God in Search of Man; Who is Man?;* and *The Insecurity of Freedom.*

Piet Fransen

It is about five o'clock on a cold December evening. Father Fransen's room at Georgetown University, on the eighth floor of one of the new dormitories, gives him a grand view of Washington. The lights are just going on throughout the city. He is at his desk working on a lecture that he is to give the next day. As I prepare the tape recorder, he lights up a black cigarillo and, in a heavy Flemish accent, tells me amusing stories of his recent trip to India and the effect of "jet lag" on traveling theologians of the twentieth century. He is a medium-built man, strong-featured, with lank, graying hair and large eyes. His ruddy, outdoor complexion gives him a decidedly European look. His English is also colorful, and he solves any communication problem quickly by a French or Latin explanation, complete with gestures. Our relaxed and genial conversation is frequently interrupted by his hearty laughter.

INTERVIEWER: In your writings, Father Fransen, you refer frequently to the idea of *diakonia,* of service. Why do you consider this so important in theology today?

FATHER FRANSEN: For one reason, the whole concept of *diakonia* was often lost sight of during the past centuries. The idea, of course, comes from the New Testament, and I was first struck by its importance when I was teaching the course *De Ordine.* In Europe and in many Catholic countries, there is a decided anticlericalism that rests on a medieval conception of the priesthood. In the Middle Ages, the bishop especially, but also the priest, was at times a kind of lord, a prince, a temporal power. For instance, Innocent IV argued that the First Council of Lyons was truly an ecumenical council since there were in attendance *"principes tam saeculares quam clericales."* Contrasting this idea was the Gospel teaching on the nature of the priesthood, I was impressed with Christ's words about the mission of the apostles—and in fact any mission in the Church—that it is a service. Even authority is a *diakonia*. As priests and Christians, our whole life is a participation in the mission of Christ, and Christ always presented His mission as a mission of service.

We have too easily, albeit implicitly and unconsciously, blended together, by a very confused theology, the direct appeal of God's divine authority to one's conscience and the indirect, human exercise of authority "in the name of God." We *overemphasized* the prestige of the human ministry of authority in the name of God, and in so doing, we were inevitably led to *underemphasize* the majesty of God's divine will itself. Both, the superior and the subject, are under the majesty of God's divine call, and both, according to their own mission and status in the Church and in the world, must seek the will of God. Indeed, both have to pray! Both have to free themselves from every kind of self-will, not just the subject, but the superior also. Therefore, the exercise of religious authority and obedience is impossible without a real *spiritual dialogue,* that is, a human and open dialogue with one another, *while* both are listening, and therefor "dialoguing" in prayer with the Holy Spirit speaking in their hearts. This obligation never confuses the different forms of mission in the Church of either the superior, who has without a doubt the "service" to command, or of the subject, who has the duty to obey. But neither commands nor obedience to them can release us from the fundamental obligation to find the will of God.

INTERVIEWER: Karl Barth claims that the work of a theologian can be characterized as a *"ministerium Verbi Divini."* Would you agree with this?

FATHER FRANSEN: Yes, of course. It is the doctrine of the New Testament. Barth is a Calvinist, but I suppose in general that all Protestants would accept the Scriptures as the sole basis of their ministry. They would thus lay a very strong emphasis on the ministry of the Word—the presenting of the Word of God as it is found in the Bible. As a Catholic, I readily agree with this; we have to preach the message of Christ. In all our liturgical functions, it must occupy a central place. But as a Catholic, I must say that our ministry is larger than this. Besides presenting the Word of God in scripture, we have also the ministry of the sacraments and the ministry of religious authority. One of the main differences between Catholics and Protestants is that in the Catholic Church there is a real authority *in the name of God*. Protestants feel very uneasy about that, but in a true sense of sincere ecumenism, we must teach that the Church gets its *mission* of authority from Christ. We must teach this because it is the doctrine of Christ. We have no other choice. I think if our doctrine and practice of ecclesiastical authority were more inspired by the example of Christ, most of the Protestant objections would disappear. As a matter of fact, they were caused by the abuses of authority in the sixteenth century. Did they feel so uneasy with the authority of John XXIII?

INTERVIEWER: You once wrote that we do not possess authority, but authority possesses us. What do you mean by that?

FATHER FRANSEN: That statement is true because our authority is really juridically and existentially a service, a *diakonia*. The Pope, bishops, religious superiors, and all priests must have this attitude. When a priest, for example, gives spiritual guidance, when he hears confession, or when he teaches religion, he must always remember that he is helping, serving others to find God. He must listen to the voice of the Spirit in the Church and must spare no effort in finding what is truly the will of God. On the other hand, if a man *possesses* his own authority, he has to listen to no one; he has only to say "this is my decision, follow it." This should not be the way priests work. It is sad, but too frequently priests equate what they say and feel with the work of the Holy Spirit; they are too dogmatic and self-willed. We must be open, docile, and make an honest, prayerful effort to determine what is the will of God. This is the spirit of our "ministry." This attitude does not necessarily mean weakness, but real courage and fortitude.

INTERVIEWER: This would apply to the hierarchy also when . . .

FATHER FRANSEN: Certainly and why not? Even to the Pope. All in authority have to listen to the Holy Spirit. No one is exempt. Everyone in the Church is bound to pray and to study, and above all to listen. All Christians must develop the existential attitude of openness.

INTERVIEWER: Do you feel that the emphasis on service affects the missionary apostolate of the Church?

FATHER FRANSEN: Most decidedly. When I was in Bombay last year for the Eucharistic Congress, I tried to present my ideas on this subject. Our approach to the problem of converting non-Christians has changed greatly in the last decade. From our own experience and from our study of non-Christian religions, we can better understand how a man can possibly be saved outside Christianity. This is a very serious problem for missionaries, and they sometimes feel that much recent theological speculation is working against them. Believe me I am not imagining this. I remember in Bombay one old missionary who was furious and shouted at me: "Father, you are taking away all the motives that justify our work."

INTERVIEWER: Do you think he was right?

FATHER FRANSEN: Well, in a certain sense what he said is understandable. The missionaries find their work becoming increasingly difficult. I know what they mean. They left their country where they were taught a too narrow-minded doctrine of the Church and of its mission in this world. It was not their fault, nor even that of their professors. God continues to teach us *through history*. In a colonial climate, the conception of the mission of the Church underwent some paternalistic influences. I taught for almost a year in the Belgian Congo just before it became independent. The white man was king; he was considered something special with unique powers. When we would go into the villages, we were received as a kind of supernatural beings. But that is all gone now. So the poor missionaries who are now working in more difficult circumstances say: "Those bad, mad theologians at home are destroying the arguments we use to convert the natives."

INTERVIEWER: How do you answer them?

FATHER FRANSEN: I try to explain that we have a *diakonia* of witnessing, first of all, to our own faithful. But we also have a kind of indirect *diakonia* to others. In India, for example, we meet people who do not accept our religion. It is morally impossible for the most part for them to have any rapport with Christianity, because it is a Western religion related to the old colonial powers. The first thing we have to do, then, is to bring them to the God they do believe in; to purify their faith and to show them the basic moral and religious values that we share. There is no other way of reaching them. At most, we can prepare them for conversion, but the final conversion is up to the providence of God in history. God has His own time, and He can wait till "the fullness of time" is there.

INTERVIEWER: Does this answer satisfy the missionaries?

FATHER FRANSEN: Not always, but it makes good sense to me. Personally, I have always wanted to go to India, and even now I would like to go. I entered the Society of Jesus to become a missionary. I would still welcome the opportunity of working there as a theologian. However, we must not forget that for middle-aged missionaries, it is not easy to adjust to a new situation. It is especially difficult for them since they don't have the time to read or study because of the hard work they are engaged in. I don't think that many of them have the time or the psychological capacity to readjust. It might take a whole generation.

This new situation came about by a deep evolution of human relations in the last decades. First of all, the nations outside the Western world have obtained freedom, and therefore political independence. This goes even further than political independence, and it opens up the possibility of a real development of their capacities according to their own cultural, social, and human traditions and heritage. Secondly, the new nations still suffer from the tragic relics of their struggle for freedom. They are very suspicious of any form of paternalism or tutelage from the white man. On the human level, we must meet them on equal terms, as members of the same human family. Even some politicians of the West have to take the mask of friendship and to "simulate" a spirit of fraternal service when they go in search of power.

The Church, a Western-shaped religious society, at least in its human, social, and cultural expression, suffers from this deep suspicion, more so now than a few years ago. There is no question that the Church should not "simulate" friendship or brotherhood; it has to practice it in full sincerity. This is what I mean by saying God teaches us through history. In the fundamental evolution of our human relations in this world, the Church discovers a new dimension that was already present in the acts and the words of Christ. This was sometimes suspected by the Church Fathers in their confrontation with the Roman Empire which they loved as their own cultural home, but it was mostly forgotten in the closed world of the Middle Ages. Yet, the fact is that the Church has a mission in human history, that Christ and not she is the center of this history. She has to serve the divine plans of God in and through human history. God leads all nations to His glory, and the Church is the Servant of the Lord, ministering to all peoples this witness of love and truth.

This does not mean that the Church should not preach the Gospel. It is her first mission. But she has to do this as Christ did, with the divine patience of Christ and of His Father who waited until the times were ripe. The Church cannot decide when a nation is ripe for the divine harvest, only God can. In the meantime, she is the instrument of God through which this harvest is being prepared. "One sows and another reaps," said Christ.

INTERVIEWER: Isn't it necessary to emphasize in our preaching that everyone, by reason of his baptism and confirmation, is a missionary?

FATHER FRANSEN: Yes, in the sense that all of us must be witnesses to Christ. St. John says: "As the Father sends me, I also send you." So all members of the Church, not only the ordained, are sent to witness to the truth of God. Every man, even the Catholic, participates in paganism; there is a pagan in all of us; all of us are sinners. Thus, realizing this, we must try to bring back men to the truth and reality of God. We must have a dynamic attitude. If we really love Christ how could we act otherwise?

INTERVIEWER: Do you think that all of the active congregations of sisters should engage in catechetical work as part of this dynamic Christ-bringing effort?

FATHER FRANSEN: This is, of course, a very important work, and sisters do it quite well. Some advocate that sisters who are working in hospitals should be free to do other apostolic work, such as teaching catechism. I don't agree with this. I know of several cases, men, women, and priests, who were brought back to their faith by the devotion, love, and patience of the sisters in the hospital. Their life is a witness, a genuine apostolate. To take them out of hospitals to teach catechism is unrealistic, since their life is already a profound and effective form of the apostolate. Their work is already hard enough!

INTERVIEWER: Is the success of the missionary apostolate sometimes hindered by the insistence that the Church has a unique possession of truth?

FATHER FRANSEN: It all depends on what we mean by this. We must say that all truth is entrusted to the Church by Christ, but we cannot say that the Church is in *actual* possession of the truth. In other words, by "I possess" I mean "I have something in my own power." It is against this notion that the Protestants take issue. Decadent scholastic theology was sometimes guilty of fostering a static concept of possession of the divine truth.

But God is richer, fuller, and deeper than anything we can say about Him. We are never in full possession of the truth about God; we are always working gradually toward the fullness of truth. Likewise, at the Second Vatican Council, the bishops in their discussions, their prayers, and study did not arrive at the complete truth. They did not "possess" in the sense that there was no room for further development.

INTERVIEWER: You would not, however, rule out scientific, speculative theology?

FATHER FRANSEN: No, but neither would I say that Catholic theology is deductive. It is wrong to think that the laws of our minds are absolutely the same as the mind of God. I do not accept a deductive theology in the strict sense of the word.

A classic example for me of the deficiencies of this method was our own theological tradition at our faculty of Louvain after the First World War. There some professors used the deductive method, and I must admit that at that time some students liked it. Father

Charles, for example, in the course on the Trinity started with the revealed principles: *Sunt in Deo processiones* and went on to deduce all the known truths about this mystery. For me this is a kind of sacrilege. The *"Konklusionstheologie"* that started in the fourteenth century and developed in the seventeenth century indicates a serious lack of appreciation of God's immensity. We are always pointing toward the truth, but we never grasp it in its totality. Whenever the Church is "defining" a dogma, it is delineating the right frame, the correct perspective, outside of which heresy is to be found. We are told: Think in this direction, and not in that other, because this is not the way to encounter God's reality, which is His truth.

INTERVIEWER: Do you have any special method of teaching theology?

FATHER FRANSEN: First of all, I try to get the facts: revelation, biblical theology, conciliar theology, the *Magisterium,* and the liturgical-dogmatic tradition. This first part of the course is the longest. Once I have all the facts assembled, I try to work out (not in a deductive way, however) a certain view in which all the facts fit into an integrated synthesis. At the end of the course, I always give one thesis that proposes a rich theological synthesis. I accept speculative theology. My synthesis includes those elements that are certain and that come from revelation and others from human philosophy or experience. The latter have some probability, but they belong to the field of human speculation. One has always to keep in mind the different dogmatic values of the various elements of such a synthesis.

INTERVIEWER: Your method seems to be similar to the method used in the positive sciences.

FATHER FRANSEN: I like to compare theology to positive science that establishes the facts, makes experiments, and tries to form certain laws. These laws lead to new experiments and to new laws. Now of course we can't exactly do this in theology. But the idea that I have retained from the positive sciences is that to begin with you must have all the facts, and then you can make a synthesis. We must not forget that our faith is about facts and not about abstract truths. God revealed Himself entering our history *through Christ.*

INTERVIEWER: How does your method differ from deductive theology? Both start with the same facts, don't they?

FATHER FRANSEN: Deductive theology starts with the fundamental truths of faith, but it is not particularly interested in them as historical facts. As Catholics, we believe in the Creed and the dogmas of the Church, but scholastic theology is not interested in the historical background, what we now call the history of salvation. This is precisely my objection against the kind of theology of the last century. You read Billot and others, and you see that they quote frequently from scripture, the Fathers, conciliar statements, etc. But they do not treat these facts in a proper historical perspective. Most of the manuals are not interested in the genuine historical study of the Fathers and make no effort to determine the full context of patristic thought. I think this historical study of the facts has been sadly neglected. St. Thomas was much more historical than the manualists. He was always open to biblical and patristic information. What is still worse is that we don't sufficiently interpret the definitions of the Councils nor the doctrinal decisions of the *Magisterium* in their proper historical context. We treat them as if the fact that those words and that language were used and assumed by and in an infallible statement of the Church caused those sentences to be taken from their real historical background, frame and roots, and changed into certain kinds of Platonic ideas.

The second task of the theologian is to interpret the real meaning of the facts of our faith. This interpretation has of course to be based on the facts themselves. Those facts possess a true divine solidity, but at the same time, they were never revealed independently from human language. Christ did not only act, He spoke. In this lies the fundamental role of Scripture for any sound theology. There we do possess, or better, we do receive the true witness of the early Church and of the first privileged witnesses of Christ's actions and words. The Church, too, does not only live as a religious community in the Spirit, but the Church teaches, witnessing to the work of the Spirit in its liturgy and religious life. For the same reason, there are no sacraments without the words of the sacrament, that is, the liturgical prayers and the testimony of the Church in the homily.

Therefore it is very important that the sacraments should be dispensed in the language of the people. The Word of God is always inseparable from His activity with us.

INTERVIEWER: What importance do you give to the "analogy of faith" in theology?

FATHER FRANSEN: Analogy of faith is another way of finding the true divine meaning of the facts of faith, by comparing the facts and truths with one another. For instance, to understand the mystery of grace, that is of God's love attracting our hearts through conversion, faith and love, one has to compare this mystery with the mystery of Incarnation, in which all grace finds its foundation, and with the mystery of heaven, in which the final reality of grace is being manifested. One also has to compare this mystery with the mystery of our Redemption through which grace was obtained and with the mystery of the Church in which grace comes to life.

Finally, a theologian has to express the result of his prolonged study in a synthesis that has to be formulated in words and ideas of our time. He has a prophetic witness to perform for *his* time and not for the thirteenth century. This work he has to accomplish in the community of the Church. He must work with the Church's authority, the theological witness of his brother-theologians, and the testimony of the faithful. The Spirit of God was given to the whole Church as a living community and never to one person in particular. Whenever a theologian separates himself from this communion of faith, his theological insight suffers. He becomes the more human and poor the more he is separated from the faith-life of the Church. The more a theologian lives in communion with the Church, with the Church of the Apostles, of the Fathers, of the Middle Ages, and of modern times, the richer and the deeper his theology grows toward the very depths of the divine fullness and truth. But any theologian remains a man with limited capacities, and he has finally to remember that there comes a time when the best theology he can offer is the adoration of his silence and prayer.

INTERVIEWER: How did you come to write your well-known article: "Three Ways of Dogmatic Thought"?

FATHER FRANSEN: Several years ago, I was asked to speak at a symposium—Father Rahner was there, by the way—and to present my ideas on how to construct a viable theological synthesis. After a careful study of the history of theology, I discovered that there are three distinct approaches. You can clearly see this in the theology of grace. In early scholasticism we have a method of *psychological* description. Symbolic language and psychological images are used to penetrate the mysteries of the faith. Sin, for example, is described as a sickness, a weakness of the soul, and a hardening of the heart. In the great age of scholasticism, we have *essential* analysis. The study of the truths of faith is based on a philosophical method that was introduced in the twelfth century and was perfected by St. Thomas. Essential analysis is not concerned with the Christian's psychologial experience, nor is it dynamically concerned with the existential problem of any individual Christian. It seeks to know what is the divine intelligibility of revealed truth and to discover the unity and mutual relations among these truths. Finally, there is an *existential* analysis that is more adapted to our modern ways of thought and is greatly concerned with the problem of our personal responsibility. Phenomenology, personalism, and the mystical theology of someone like the Blessed John Ruysbroeck are all existential. These three "ways" each have their advantages and disadvantages.

INTERVIEWER: You mentioned that Karl Rahner was present when you delivered your paper. Did he agree with you?

FATHER FRANSEN: After the symposium, Rahner told me that eventually I would have to make a choice; I would have to decide on one of three ways according to the situation and time in which I live. I realize now that he was correct, and I follow the existential approach. I discovered this especially when I taught the courses on *De Trinitate* and *De Gratia*. The scholastic art of these treatises has little relevance in our times. It has historical value, but you can't spend much time on it as a major part of your teaching.

INTERVIEWER: How would you apply an existential analysis to the highly speculative treatise on grace?

FATHER FRANSEN: You have to read the fully revised edition of my book. . . . (You see I'm a salesman too.) But seriously, my whole treatment of grace is a reaction against the abstract and formal presentation of the past. I am shocked when I hear many priests say that they never preach sermons on grace because it is too difficult, too complicated, too dangerous. It is a terrible thing when priests are not able to preach about the most beautiful, most profound, and most consoling truth of our faith. With all this in mind, I wrote an article in *Lumen Vitae* [12 (1957), 203–232] on the psychology of grace. Then I wrote a small book of about a hundred pages, *Divine Grace and Man* [Desclée, 1962]. This has grown into a four hundred page book that I wrote in Dutch, but it is being translated into English and will be published by Desclée. In the meantime, half of the new translation is already published as a Mentor-Omega pocket book by the New American Library, 1965.

The central idea in all my writings on grace is always the same. It is the idea of St. John and St. Augustine that is the mystery of the love of God. My main theme is from St. Augustine: *"Quia amasti me, fecisti me amabilem."* It is the idea of God coming to us and calling us to live according to the image of Christ guided by the Holy Spirit. The whole approach is existential. Participating in the obedience and the love of Christ for His Father through the power of the Spirit, we become servants with the Servant and sons with the Son.

INTERVIEWER: Do you devote any time in your course to the Molina-Bañez controversy?

FATHER FRANSEN: None. I have a small but very good three page summary made by a professor of our faculty at the beginning of the century. I give this to my best students and have them read it. They should know that at one time in the Church this issue was discussed, and why.

INTERVIEWER: Is there any particular existentialist philosopher who has influenced you?

FATHER FRANSEN: I would hesitate to say so. I think, more than anything else, it is the spirit of the times that has exercised the greatest influence. I live in an interesting climate, a climate of thinking at Louvain which is very stimulating. Also my students influence me. I am always in dialogue with my students in order to understand them. My training was Neo-Thomistic, but after the war I realized that my students did not understand this. It was like a foreign language to them. This forced me to find a way to make the courses meaningful for them. So my students really brought me to an existential approach. I regret that I never had the opportunity to study formally with any existentialist as Rahner did with Heidegger.

INTERVIEWER: Would you like to spend some time in a formal study of existentialism?

FATHER FRANSEN: Of course I would like to have a thorough training in existentialist thought, but I simply do not have the time. The modern theologian is a busy man. It was quite different in the past. The professors in my time led a very simple life. They taught a few courses, studied quietly in their rooms, occasionally writing a learned paper or review. At times, they would attend a few meetings with fellow theologians and perhaps give a retreat to priests. They had a very scholarly, quiet, well-ordered existence. But now a theologian's life is exhausting! Everyone wants you to talk to them. I remember once speaking on contemporary theology for nearly three hours in a tiny Belgian village to a group of some three hundred men. Every night of the week I could go out and talk to people on theological problems. Theologians are in great demand. Theology is nowadays definitely in! Thanks be to God!

INTERVIEWER: In Belgium, do seminary students still study the philosophy of St. Thomas?

FATHER FRANSEN: They do, but as a part in their total training. The whole question of seminary reform is being widely discussed in Europe these days, as it is in this country. I am especially interested in this problem, because I am prefect of studies for our scholasticate, and the rector has asked me to prepare with other professors a plan of a seminary course. One of the first questions we asked ourselves was: Is it necessary to have philosophy before theology? It seems so ridiculous to accept students for the priesthood and keep them for many years, especially in the Jesuits, before they get any adult instruction about their religion. In the Jesuits, with our novitiate, college courses, and three years of teaching in the colleges, it is ten years before you were seriously taught something about your faith. This has to be changed. We started this year to teach a serious course of religion in our novitiate, with exams and discussions. The main topics are the New Testament and the doctrine of grace. They will only be allowed to do the spiritual exercises of St. Ignatius at the end of their first year.

INTERVIEWER: Have you any suggestions as to how a seminary course would be organized if philosophy were taught after theology?

FATHER FRANSEN: We are still discussing this. Actually, I have met only a very few people who want to place philosophy after theology. Some still prefer to keep philosophy and theology apart; others want to teach both at the same time, regrouping philosophical, biblical, moral, canonical, and dogmatic treatises that show some mutual connection and are related with one another. So one could teach the nature of God, the fundamental liturgical attitudes, the religious obligations of worship in the Church, the evolution of the concept of God in the Old Testament, and the revealed doctrine of the Trinity in the same year, and in another year a Christian approach to anthropology, eventually confronted with a Marxist anthropology, general ethics, the fundamental laws of the Church, St. Paul's concept of human existence, and the doctrine of our supernatural vocation in grace. This is what the Dutch seem to look for.

Others, as I said, still prefer to hold philosophy and theology apart for two reasons. First, there is no doubt about the urgent pastoral necessity of a solid philosophical training in our secularized and pluralistic society. Most people will not ask our future priests about the Bible or about the meaning of a conciliar definition, but fundamentally about the immortality of man, his freedom and the meaning of his existence in this world, about peace and war, about social justice and international solidarity. Secondly, every serious philosophical effort is severe, sometimes tedious, and asks for a certain time of patient maturation before one gets the benefit from it. If philosophy were being taught together with theology, there might be some danger of escapism, of evasion into easier matters. I was much impressed by this argument before, but now I am not so sure whether a good solution could not be found that avoids this danger.

INTERVIEWER: Perhaps the younger students at the beginning of their clerical training are not ready for serious philosophical study.

FATHER FRANSEN: Most decidedly. That there is little use in answering questions that are not there is a sound pedagogical principle. Therefore, there is a tendency to reduce the initial philosophical training to two years and to postpone the confrontation with the more fundamental philosophical questions of our days until after theology, or at least at the end of theology as a kind of modern and pastoral preparation to meet the world outside. At that age and with the prospect of entering the ministry very soon, the students would be better prepared, we think, to tackle these important questions.

This system was accepted as one of the many possibilities by the General Congregation of the Jesuits in Rome last year, and seems, as I am told, to have the preference of the Pontifical Congregation of Seminaries and Universities. This congregation feels disinclined, as it seems, to bestow any licentiate in philosophy until after a period of four full years of philosophical studies. This implies that one normally should not graduate in philosophy before his theology.

INTERVIEWER: Would you say that theology today must be pastorally oriented?

FATHER FRANSEN: We should first answer one fundamental question: What is meant by a *pastoral* training of the clergy? This word "pastoral" has almost as many meanings as there are persons who use it. Many students, a few professors, and some bishops seem to think that our clergy needs only a practical training for the parochial ministry. On the other hand, everybody is talking of a coming of age of man. We strive for the emancipation of the laity. We want an adult Christianity. After a few years, the clergy will straggle far behind the elite among the laity. We need urgently an *adult* clergy too, and there is no short cut for this.

INTERVIEWER: Has your own seminary adopted a new plan that restructures the complete seminary course?

FATHER FRANSEN: No. We have a plan, but we have not yet experimented with it. We are, furthermore, hindered by local problems, as whether we should keep our students in our scholasticate or send them to our public faculty in Antwerp, where they would mix with lay students, and get at the same time degrees acknowledged by the state. On our faculty of philosophy, we have a variety of approaches: We have one man who teaches philosophy according to the traditional approach; another is in the phenomenological tradition of Max Scheler; still another teaches the Neo-Thomism of Maréchal. Our students get training in modern philosophy and in scholastic philosophy. However, in Belgium, Holland, Germany (not everywhere), and France you would not find many students who will accept the old, strict type of scholastic theology.

INTERVIEWER: You have written much on episcopal conferences. Do you think they will exercise a great influence in the government of the Church?

FATHER FRANSEN: I would hope so. But it will probably take a century before this is achieved. There is a process of maturation necessary. Do not forget that there is a whole generation of priests, bishops, and theologians who were trained in juridical ecclesiology. They find it difficult to understand the value of collegiality. The Church is a living communion of pope, bishops, priests, and laymen; and collegiality is nothing else than a particular aspect of the Mystical Body. It includes the idea of authority. The reality of collegiality is intimately connected with the idea of the communion of all men within the Church, which is the Mystical Body.

INTERVIEWER: Do you foresee any problems in the practical operation of episcopal conferences?

FATHER FRANSEN: For one thing, the bishops have to realize that completel unanimity is impossible. Most of the bishops in the world were educated in the juridical approach that saw each bishop as a kind of atom and autonomous. But if they have a *collegium,* then they must work together. The only feasible way to arrive at a decision, is to vote and perhaps require a two-thirds majority for important questions.

INTERVIEWER: Traditionally, we have taught that revelation was closed with the Apostles. How do you interpret that?

FATHER FRANSEN: It means that revelation was closed with the coming of Christ. The revelation we are talking about is Christ—the real revelation of God in Christ through His Spirit. I don't think you can give a formal date when revelation terminated. You can't say definitely before or after St. John's death. The genuine revelation was in Christ and His Spirit in the primitive Church. Afterward the Church had only to keep this message safe, to apply it, to witness to this message before the world.

INTERVIEWER: Can you say that revelation reached its fullness in Christ?

FATHER FRANSEN: Yes, but you must also take into account Pentecost. I mean not only the day of Pentecost, but also the pentecost of the pagans—for example, when the Holy Spirit came to Cornelius. There was a special activity of the Holy Spirit in the primitive Church by which the Church gradually discovered herself. Peter discovered the universality of the Church's mission. There is no distinction between pagan and Jew; they are equal before God, and all receive the same Spirit from Him.

INTERVIEWER: Between Christ's Ascension and the end of the Apostolic Age, would you say that there were revelations in the strict sense?

FATHER FRANSEN: I would not like to talk about relevations in the plural, which seems to imply that Christ has communicated a series of particular truths, independent from one another. Christ was the revelation of the Father. The Spirit guided the primitive Church in understanding the mystery of Christ. Revelation is a whole—the full impact of the works and the acts of Christ on the background of the Old Testament. That is the "idea" Newman was speaking of in his fundamental work "On the Development of Christian Doctrine."

INTERVIEWER: For a final question, Father Fransen, do you find anything in the attitude of Christians today that causes you some concern?

FATHER FRANSEN: I am quite worried about something that I see in every quarter of the Church: fear. The Pope, bishops, and religious superiors are fearful of what is happening to the Church. Personally, I oppose such lack of courage, because I think that it is extremely dangerous for the unity and strength of the Church. We must be courageous; we must have confidence in the Lord and the guidance of the Holy Spirit. This is the real spirit of Christianity. We should not be whispering about many things and saying: "Keep silent about this. The people are not prepared for it." In the meantime, the people have to live in the world. I think it is unjust to be so lacking in courage. The simple people have no time to read learned articles or go to conferences. They have to be taught. Unless we do this, they are left without any defense.

INTERVIEWER: In other words, you are saying that we should not encourage the Catholic ghetto mentality?

FATHER FRANSEN: That is just what I mean. I read in the London *Times* some time ago that the Russians have given up trying to interfere with the foreign radio stations that are heard in Russia: Voice of America, BBC, and Radio Vatican. They tried jamming these stations, but finally gave up. So even Communist Russia realizes that you can't suppress the normal interchange of opinion. Yet, in 1966, there are still some who say that the People of God should not be informed. This is cowardice, because we have our own people defenseless in the turmoil of modern ideas, movements, and influences.

INTERVIEWER: You will admit, however, that we can move too quickly in accepting new approaches.

FATHER FRANSEN: You have to be patient. It is an undeniable fact of human existence that we cannot change in one day. All of us need time to adjust to changes. This whole interview is based on the fundamental idea of growth and evolution. We have to prepare the people gradually to accept, for example, the changes in the liturgy, the ways of approaching the sacraments, etc. I am all for this. But what I am against is the idea, which is generated by fear, that insists that we keep the people ignorant. This is nothing else than cowardliness, and it is basically anti-Christian. Whenever I give a priests' retreat, I always give at least one conference on courage. Our bishops and priests need the courage to face facts. They must realize that we are living in the twentieth century. It is impossible to have ghettos in this age. Fifty years ago, in Belgium, there were quiet, little villages that were in no way influenced by the activities of the world. Nowadays these same people have radio and TV, and you see *Time* and *Life* in their homes. My preoccupation is that we priests will lack the courage to face up to the modern problems. We cannot go on living in the past.

❖❖❖❖❖❖❖❖❖❖❖❖❖❖❖❖❖❖❖❖❖❖❖❖❖❖❖❖❖❖❖❖❖❖❖❖❖❖❖

PIET FRANSEN was born in Tournai, Belgium, December 10th, 1913. He entered the Society of Jesus in 1930 and received his philosophical and theological training at Jesuit colleges in Belgium. In 1943, he was ordained to the priesthood. From 1945 to 1947, he did graduate work in theology at Gregorian University in Rome. Since 1947, he has been professor of dogmatic theology at the Jesuit Theologate in Louvain-Heverlee. As a visiting professor, he has taught at the Canisianum in Maastricht, Netherlands; Heythrop College, England; Grand Séminaire de Mayidi near Kinshasa (formerly Léopoldville) in the Congo; and the University of Innsbruck. At present, he is Prefect of Studies and Dean of the Theological Faculty at Heverlee.

Father Fransen is Editor of *Bijdragen,* a Belgian-Dutch research journal for philosophy and theology. He has written numerous articles and is the author of *Divine Grace and Man.*

Jaroslav Pelikan

The buildings of the Yale Divinity School on Prospect Street, New Haven, Connecticut, bring one back to colonial times. The windows are freshly trimmed with white paint. The green shutters blend with the brick walls covered with ivy. The chapel, with its stately white columns, dominates the campus. It overlooks a terraced quadrangle, flanked on both sides by a covered walk. On this spring day in Easter week, little activity can be seen. Someone is busily typing in one of the rooms, and from one of the second-floor windows, a Mozart concerto can be heard. Two divinity students in Bermudas and sweat shirts play a subdued game of "frisbies" on the lawn. It is a sleepy Saturday afternoon.

Jaroslav Pelikan, casually dressed in a brown tweed sport coat, is going over some papers. "How are all my friends in Washington?," he asks as I meet him at the door of his office. At forty-three, he is an intense, energetic person who speaks quickly con brio and frequently emphasizes a point by pounding on the table. He is an outgoing and spontaneous speaker who delights in talking theology. The time passes quickly, and long after the tape has finished, we continue our discussion.

INTERVIEWER: How would you define your primary vocation as a theologian?

DR. PELIKAN: My primary ministry is at my desk and through my work as a scholar. I'm not really an activist, which makes me rather out of style at the moment. I'd rather know than do; I'd rather try to serve the cause by means of scholarship.

INTERVIEWER: Do you think that there is a critical need for scholarship today?

DR. PELIKAN: A great many of our current problems demand scholarship at a high level. We have to ask ourselves what kinds of scholarly work the total life of the Church and its ministry to the world will require. We must find out what are the areas of scholarly inquiry that call for joint Roman Catholic-Protestant study. Both areas that we share, where we have a common interest, and the areas where we diverge must be studied. I would like to see what would happen, for example, if study in the field of Reformation history were carried on jointly.

I will give you an illustration of what I mean. A few years ago in Europe I heard a distinguished European Reformation scholar—he happened to be a Lutheran—talking about the difference between Luther and the tradition. He said that for tradition the virgin birth of Our Lord was a demonstration of His power and majesty since Christ transcended the laws of nature. For Luther, he said, the virgin birth was an act of condescension, since Luther says that "Christ humbled Himself to be born of a virgin." I said to him: "Do you realize that's a quotation from the *Te Deum,* which Luther had sung every day when he was a monk and which tradition had been affirming for centuries!" He didn't see the quotation marks because they were not in the edition that he used. If Reformation studies were being carried on an ecumenical level, this would never happen.

INTERVIEWER: Do you know of any joint projects?

DR. PELIKAN: There are some. In Europe, the institute headed by Professor Lortz at Mainz has done a great deal. At Paderborn, in the Möhler Institute, there is also valuable work being done. The recent appointment of my friend Professor Oberman at Tübingen should be exciting. There should be joint efforts in the patristic area since, after all, many of the things for which the Reformation stood were asserted and defended by the Fathers. The priesthood of believers, for instance, has—to put it quite kindly—been a neglected point within Roman Catholic dogmatic theology, but it is a very prominent feature of early Christian doctrine. It needs to be pointed out that here is something that has been overlooked in post-Tridentine Roman-Catholic theology.

INTERVIEWER: What of biblical studies?

DR. PELIKAN: Ecumenical efforts have been most successful in biblical studies. The Anchor Bible shows us what is possible. But there are other fields where work must be done. Frankly, I have been disappointed—perhaps shocked should be the word—at how little attention has been paid by Roman Catholics to the development of the various forms of vernacular liturgy in the Protestant denominations. Protestant liturgical scholars since the sixteenth century have been involved constantly in the vernacular problem. Some of the silly things that have appeared in the recent Roman Catholic translations could have been avoided if Protestant scholars had been consulted. Take the translation of the Nicene Creed. After all, Anglicans and Lutherans confess the Nicene Creed every Sunday at their services, and they know the problems of a congregation trying to recite this meaningfully. They know some of the pitfalls of translation. For example, *"per quem omnia facta sunt"* is wrongly translated "by whom (suggesting, the Father) all things were made." It should be *"through* whom all things were made," that is, by the Son. Things like that could have been avoided if, as soon as the vernacular liturgy was proposed, an ecumenical conference of liturgical and historical scholars had been brought together.

The assumption, of course, was that translation is a very simple thing. All you have to do is to translate what you see; again, it's a question of finding the quotation marks. So many things in the liturgy are actually quotations from the Scripture and the Fathers that have worked their way into liturgical tradition gradually. To detect these, a sensitive scholarship is called for, the work of scholars who are at the same time literary persons, who know what the genius of English is and where the strength and the weakness of English lie. A one-to-one translation is impossible. What you get is the "You Who" type of thing that appears in the *Gloria*. The present translation is really quite conservative. The substitution of *You* for *Thou* is a step forward, but while you're about it, the whole grammatical structure of the various forms should have been examined.

INTERVIEWER: Wasn't that done by the translators of *The New English Bible?*

DR. PELIKAN: That's right. First of all, a committee of scholars translated from Greek into English. Then a group of literary men took the English translation, ignored the Greek, and tried to make good English out of it. Then it went back again to the Greek scholars to see whether this had done violence to the original. As a result, the recognition that parts of speech perform different functions in different languages helped to shape the final translation. For instance, in *Romans* 11:36, which is also the closing verse of the Epistle for Trinity Sunday, we read in the old translation: "From Him and through Him and to Him are all things: to Him be glory forever. Amen." Now the prepositions *from, through,* and *to* are very powerful parts of speech in Greek. Greek has a great deal of punch in its prepositions. But in English the prepositions are weak-kneed. In *The New English Bible,* this phrase from St. Paul is translated: *"Source, Guide,* and *Goal* of all that is—to Him be glory forever! Amen." Monosyllabic, Anglo-Saxon nouns. Now the words mean something. That's creative translating, instead of following a school-boyish method. Where millions of people don't have the original, the whole purpose of rendition into the vernacular is to make the text meaningful. Someone has said that liturgical Latin is a universal language, so that no matter where the layman goes, he understands as little as he does at home. It's a pity that the Roman-Catholic translation, if it was going to be done at all, was not done with more flair.

INTERVIEWER: Can you suggest any other areas where joint Catholic and Protestant efforts would be useful?

DR. PELIKAN: It seems to me that one additional one is certainly the whole relation of the Church to the world. We have to find out the levels of the Church's relation to the world: collaboration with men of good will, collaboration with theists, collaboration with Jews, and collaboration with those who have been baptized. The distinction among these relations and their implication for the Church's relation to the world is something that remains to be worked out. There's a tendency now in the flurry of ecumenical affection to bring all of these relations into one. This is fuzzy theologically. Baptism is still fundamental, and presumably what divides Christians from all other men is something like their baptism. While we stress what unites Christians to all men, we also have to stress what unites Christians to Christians.

INTERVIEWER: Have Protestant theologians contributed much to this problem?

DR. PELIKAN: I would say so. However, in Protestant theology baptism is not always the crucial problem. In much of Protestant thought baptism does not have an ontological, sacramental structure, but has much more of a sign-character. Tillich speaks of a "latent church," and I think that if you pressed many of the avant-garde Protestant theologians, that would be their primary emphasis.

INTERVIEWER: Does the "latent church" mean that all men are joined together by the very fact that they are created by God and made to His image?

DR. PELIKAN: That is certainly part of it. I sometimes used to say to my late, lamented friend, Paul Tillich, that he ought to call this "latent church" the Society of St. Nicodemus. Some Protestant theologians believe that there are many who have recognized the ultimate issues of life and death and who therefore have, so to speak, the Christian intuition, but who have been alienated by the form of the Church—its institutional life and its language. They find it easier and better to serve the Christian cause—that is to say, the cause of God—outside the structures of ecclesiastical Christianity. They are, as I would say, followers of Nicodemus.

INTERVIEWER: Is Karl Rahner very popular in Protestant theological circles?

DR. PELIKAN: Rahner is becoming increasingly well-known. But very few American Protestants, even among the clergy, read anything but English. Until a couple of years ago, Rahner was simply not known to most. Now that almost every month seems to bring another translation of a book of Rahner or another book about him, he is catching on, and I'm sure that this will be increasingly true, as I can tell in my own graduate students. Unfortunately, Rahner's great historical works are not being translated. For example, his studies on Cyprian's doctrine of penance and his work on Duns Scotus remain untranslated. Thus, the great lack of historical perspective, which is already a problem in American Protestant theology and Roman Catholic theology, is only accentuated when the fruits of historical scholarship are presented in English, but the scholarship itself is not.

INTERVIEWER: This would be true of other authors besides Rahner.

DR. PELIKAN: Certainly. Take Rudolph Bultmann, for example. His theological proposals were translated many years ago, but his great commentary on the Gospel of St. John, which is probably the most incisive exposition of John done in modern times—I would never preach on a text from St. John without consulting it—has never been translated into English. After Bultmann has done the steady, slow work of carefully going through the Gospel of St. John, he is entitled to ask the question: "Is this mythological in structure?" I happen to think that his answer is disastrous, but he has earned the right to ask the question by the work he has done. Today, theologians want to get to the question without bothering with all the preliminary and necessary details. They don't want to do their homework.

INTERVIEWER: Do you think that this antischolarly tendency is widespread among theological students?

DR. PELIKAN: Most decidedly. Some of my very best students are existentially aware of the crisis around them and are committed to doing something about it. Sometimes I think that they're committed to doing *anything,* just doing! As a result, there is a certain impatience with what seems to be the luxury of historical study. This is especially true of students entering the ministry. These students are often quite impatient, and in this they reflect what is probably both a national and an ecclesiastical posture.

INTERVIEWER: How can we go about solving this problem?

DR. PELIKAN: We have to develop styles of scholarship that are truly American. I am happy that scholars such as Rahner, Grillmeier, and de Lubac are being translated into English. But America is a culture come of age, and I think that American scholarship in secular disciplines is asserting itself as something more than simply the importation of continental material.

INTERVIEWER: In other words, American theological scholarship is too derivative?

DR. PELIKAN: Right. I once quipped that within American Roman Catholicism the books are written by émigrés and converts. Father Walter Ong has said that an American Catholic intellectual is one who is devoted to the dream that he can take what some Frenchman had said and translate it for the man in the street. Protestant theology also has been too dependent on European scholarship. We have to develop our own styles of scholarship that speak to the American way of doing things and that will be heard by our European brethren.

INTERVIEWER: Can you mention any concrete examples?

DR. PELIKAN: There are several possibilities, but two approaches seem appropriate to theological-historical scholarship. First, there is American literary criticism, which has become a style of scholarship unto itself. It is no longer dependent either on German philological criticism or on the British style of literary analysis. The American "new critics" are a breed apart. If this makes the kind of sense it does out of Milton or Browning, I would like to see it applied to St. Paul or Clement of Alexandria.

Secondly, there are the social sciences, which are, after all, largely an American discovery as a scholarly field. Sociology in Germany as late as the period after the Second World War was still being taught by professors of philosophy. If we applied the methods of social science to Church History, we might have some interesting results, especially if you believe that the Church is not just the clergy and that the history of the Church is not just the history of the clergy. Why should books on Church History be divided according to popes? If the Church is the people of God, then you ought to be able to say something about the life of the people. How do you find out what people believed and what the religious life of the people was in the ninth century? There *are* ways of beginning to find out, ways that have been developed largely under the leadership of the social scientists.

INTERVIEWER: Perhaps you might explain how the method of the social scientists might be used in a specific area.

DR. PELIKAN: Canonical legislation would be a possibility—not with a view towards finding out what found its way into Canon Law, but with a view towards finding out what was going on in the parishes. You would try to discover what evils and practices were condemned because the law simply went through the *form* of condemning them and what things were *in fact* part of the common life of the people. I would like to know more about the history of divination or the history of marriage. Everyone these days is writing a book on the sacrament of marriage, but I would like to know what percentage of the marriages in ninth-century Europe were performed before a priest. I suspect that there were very few. Now what happens to the definition of marriage and of its sacramental character? It seems to me that the strict definition is the proper one here, namely, that the priest is the *witness*.

INTERVIEWER: Has this type of investigation been done at all?

DR. PELIKAN: There have been approaches to it and largely, I must say, under secular auspices—in history departments where there is interest in social and economic history. Right now economic history is a very exciting field of historical study. This is not without implications for the study of the history of the Church.

INTERVIEWER: You seem optimistic about the future contributions of American theological efforts.

DR. PELIKAN: I am optimistic that American theology *can* contribute something; I am not optimistic that it *will*. That's an important distinction. I don't know whether it will, because I don't know whether it will be permitted to. We are in a position where the manpower problem is a serious one in the schools of the Church, both Protestant and Roman Catholic, at the higher levels. It is increasingly difficult to get, and especially to hold, capable people in these positions. So the historical and theological scholarship in the schools of the Church is not a very promising thing. The seminaries on both sides are not staffed as well quantitatively or qualitatively as they ought to be. Many of the seminary professors are so busy that they themselves are not engaged in research and are simply passing on what they received in class.

INTERVIEWER: A more basic issue is the renewal of seminary education.

DR. PELIKAN: This is the hidden problem in what came out of Vatican II. If something really significant can be done about the seminaries in the next thirty-five years, then Vatican II will have hands and feet. Otherwise, it will just be a nice thing for some future Church historian to study. There is much work to be done with the whole problem of priestly vocation. The priestly vocation is still projected on assumptions concerning the life of the parish and the family that are no longer valid. It is still assumed that a boy makes a decision to become a priest earlier than in fact he does. A great many boys, some of the best ones, who would consider a priestly vocation in later years during college or shortly after it, face the necessity of doing penance for having gone to a school such as Yale for their college years, instead of having gone to a minor seminary, which is academically *no better* than Yale, at least.

INTERVIEWER: The seminaries will only be as good as the men operating them. Do you have any observations about seminary professors?

DR. PELIKAN: Some of us who are responsible for graduate students have to ask ourselves what we can do in the next twenty years in the training of seminary professors. Are the American bishops prepared to take some chances in order to get some quality people into the seminaries so that the implications of the Council can be carried out, and so that the ecumenical movement can get beyond the era of good feeling to a really meaningful encounter? The requirement that a seminary professor must have an ecclesiastical higher degree needs to be scrutinized. That seems to me to be a guarantee neither of orthodoxy nor of scholarship. It is simply a guarantee of conformity—and conformity and orthodoxy are not the same thing.

INTERVIEWER: The proliferation of seminaries is a related problem.

DR. PELIKAN: There are too many seminaries that are too weak. Also the multiplication of colleges is drawing off further men—

something that the Church can't afford. Too many men and too much money are being put into academically marginal operations. The Church should have fewer and better places to prepare young men for the priesthood.

INTERVIEWER: Many seminaries are situated in isolated areas. Do you think that they should be moved closer to a university?

DR. PELIKAN: By all means. It is essential that we weigh carefully the question of the relation of seminaries to a broader academic context. I think that a seminary belongs in a university, or at least in a college, since each of the major fields of theological study has its non-theological counterpart. Minor seminaries should be related in a more creative way to colleges and to major seminaries.

INTERVIEWER: Are Protestant seminaries facing similar problems?

DR. PELIKAN: We have far too many Protestant seminaries and far too many weak ones. We are not exercising the kind of stewardship in manpower and resources that we should. The institutional autonomy of a school can be preserved, yet collaboration could be achieved in many fields.

The formation of priests and ministers has been shaped more than it needs to be by a certain kind of defensiveness, a negativism and asceticism that is seen more as a refuge than a fulfillment. Protestantism needs to learn again. Ascetical theology is an important part of Christian theology from the New Testament on. But it has to be seen primarily as a form of fulfillment of creation—as a way of being set aside for a purpose and therefore as a constructive force and not as a sniggling, petty thing. Emotional development, mental health, and similar issues need to be related to seminary formation.

INTERVIEWER: Some problems might be solved if more attention were paid to the selection of seminary students. What kind of candidate should we be looking for?

DR. PELIKAN: Here I think the characters of the various denominations must be considered. My late friend Father Weigel used to say that if you ask a Jew about his rabbi, he will say that he is learned; the Protestant will say that his minister is eloquent; the Roman Catholic will say that his priest is kind. I always thought this was very telling. The object of the training of a rabbi is to make him a scholar in the Law for all his life. The object of Protestant training has frequently been to make the student a good preacher, and of Catholic training to make him a kind priest, a good confessor, and a man for the people. This has changed in the life of each community and is changing more and more.

INTERVIEWER: What changes have you observed?

DR. PELIKAN: One of the most important, recent phenomena is the emphasis on pastoral counseling in the Protestant churches. Protestants expect their pastor to be a *pastor* and *counselor* and to take an interest in their personal needs. If he regards himself in a primarily rhetorical role today, he is missing the opportunity to be a true minister. The sociology of the Roman Catholic parish has shifted. Father Fichter's *Priest and People* is a hair-raising book. But is does suggest that you cannot prepare men for seminaries or even admit them on the basis of some stereotype of what they are going to be. If one of the implications of Vatican II is a new stress on preaching, then we are in for trouble. I fear that what I have heard during many a Mass—a moralistic ten-minute homily on the Gospel for the day, ending with a financial appeal or a warning against the sins of the flesh—will be typical. I'd just as soon they wouldn't preach!

INTERVIEWER: Has there been a decrease in candidates to the Protestant ministry?

DR. PELIKAN: There seems to have been a significant decline. Yet the overall population and the Church population are increasing. I am even more worried about the quality within the quantity of vocations. I've sometimes said to people facetiously that if we could drop the bottom twenty-five percent in quality, we might be better off. What has happened, of course, sociologically, is that the service of the Church is no longer the only or the best way for a young man from a less than privileged background to move up. If he's bright, concerned, or alert, he can go into dozens of fields. The ministry is not even the only way for somebody who wants to serve humanity. We've been saying this, and maybe we've oversold it. There has been much talk, in the public press and elsewhere, about the new concern for the secular. I believe that theologically, as well as tactically, the counterpart to the commitment to the secular is a commitment to a sacramental Church that can be relevant in a secular way. That means the whole sacramental life of the Church, including "the eighth sacrament," which is the proclamation of the Word of God and which is as sacramental as any of them. The sacramentality of the proclaimed Word has to be re-examined. Here an important key is the seminaries. It is not the only one, but one of the essential ones.

INTERVIEWER: In the last few years, have you detected a tension between university theology and pastoral or apostolic theology?

DR. PELIKAN: Decidedly so. This is a long-standing problem on the European continent, where the theological faculties of the university became the equivalent of other university faculties engaged in research and were sometimes indifferent or even hostile to the needs of the Church. In the Lutheran Church in Germany, for example, the situation got so bad that in the nineteenth century the Church established its own seminaries. A man would graduate from the theological faculty of the university and *then* go to the Church's seminary. This is still true in much of the Evangelical Church in Germany. When university theologians, scholars who are primarily engaged in research and teaching, have a sense of the Church and of their responsibility to it, things work out well. However, in the case of Protestant scholars, there is not the same kind of ecclesiastical structure as in the Roman Catholic Church. It's largely an individual matter. You can do as much or as little as you want. When the professors have this commitment, university theology can be most fruitful in relation to the life of the Church. In itself, the tension is wholesome, but we have to find ways of institutionalizing it by keeping the lines of communication short.

INTERVIEWER: What do you think of the two-track system in theology schools? One course would be academic and directed to the training of scholars, and the other course would be seminaristic to train men for the ministry.

DR. PELIKAN: I think that there should be more than two. But, above all, there should be interaction between them. I am not sure if I like the distinction between academic and seminaristic. Any good university ought to have a department of political science as well as a school of law, a department of anatomy as a branch of the biological sciences as well as a medical school. If the university is interested in training practicing lawyers and healing doctors, it must also be interested in training political scientists and theoreticians and in training research scholars in anatomy and physiology. I believe that both the professional schools and the research departments benefit from being part of a single institution. Where it is possible, students should be permitted to move from one to the other, in either direction, as they develop. This would help to shape the character of their vocation.

There are analogies between that and what we ought to be doing in theological studies. The danger is that the research program might go off by itself and maintain an Averroistic doctrine of double truth in relation to the Church. This would allow seminaries to draw away from the academic and develop their own kind of obscurantism. They would say: "All this research is all right for the scholars, but what good is it for us who are out in the parishes? Our people don't really care who wrote the Epistle to the Hebrews."

INTERVIEWER: How do you answer this objection?

DR. PELIKAN: It's true that many a layman is not interested in the academic disputes about the authorship of Hebrews. But the clergy must realize that the implications here can be very serious and will help them to teach people of simple faith. The division of theology into hermetically sealed compartments is a danger and must be avoided.

INTERVIEWER: Do you find that the "death of God" movement has had any effect on your students?

DR. PELIKAN: I'm not sure it's a movement. It may well be the greatest theological nonevent in the last fifty years, created by the newspapers and television. But some of the men who have been identified with it have been important, particularly on the collegiate level, to young men who are now theological students. These young men, as juniors and seniors in college, were *engagé* by one or another of the protagonists of the idea that all traditional forms have lost their meaning. Such students, who had a deep human concern and moral commitment, came to the seminary more committed to certain human values than to the explicitly Christian cause. They were more interested in the figure of Jesus than in the institutional Church. Some of our best students have been influenced by these ideas, and yet they are now in a program that is presumably supposed to train them for the ministry. While I think that in many ways this approach is a form of bankruptcy, the questions it is asking are important—too important to be trivialized, either by its friends or by its enemies.

INTERVIEWER: Has the improved Luther image helped ecumenical understanding?

DR. PELIKAN: Yes and no. Yes, where Protestantism still takes the Reformation seriously enough for this to be a factor.

INTERVIEWER: Would that be in the United States?

DR. PELIKAN: Certainly it is not as true in the United States as it is on the continent. Luther is a national-cultural-religious hero in Europe, and the new recognition of his person and character has been significant. In this country, Protestants have begun to discover Luther and Calvin in a way that they hadn't before, even apart from the ecumenical dimension.

INTERVIEWER: Do you have any concerns about the ecumenical movement?

DR. PELIKAN: I will be honest with you. I have deep anxieties about what is going on. Fifty years ago, the average Protestant congregation in the United States believed something very much like the Apostles' Creed—and it had no contact with Roman Catholicism! It had an evangelical piety, which you can see in prayers and hymns. If you have ever heard free prayer in a Baptist or Methodist church, you sense its authenticity, not of just a religious experience, but of Christian commitment and, in its own way, of dogmatic substance. Salvation through the Blood of Christ is an overriding theme of traditional evangelical Protestant piety. I think that it had a great deal to contribute to the total Christian cause including the Roman Catholic cause. If Roman Catholicism had heard this fifty or seventy-five years ago, many mistakes would have been avoided and a positive gain would have been achieved. For various historical reasons, Protestantism and Catholicism were on separate tracks, but only now have they discovered each other, when it may be too late.

Interviewer: You mean, then, that the loss of dogmatic substance within both Churches has serious ramifications for ecumenism?

Dr. Pelikan: That is just what I mean. After 1854, 1870, and 1950, along with changes within the structure of Protestant piety and preaching, the ecumenical encounter, while welcome, also becomes quite poignant. For that matter, to be candid, there is a greater loss of dogmatic substance also within Roman Catholic piety at all levels than anyone can measure. In other words, when we were both fairly rich (but not as rich as we thought we were), we should have come together to strengthen the name of Christ. Now we are poor (and poorer than we know we are), and now we *are* coming together. Things have changed in all sorts of interesting and sometimes distressing ways. What's the point of reviewing Reformation arguments about prayers for the dead, if you believe that prayer is a form of auto-suggestion? Why debate the Assumption of the Blessed Virgin, if you deny the virgin birth, the Ascension of Christ, or the Resurrection?

Interviewer: You seem to imply that there will be some difficult days ahead of us.

Dr. Pelikan: I am not a pessimist, and I dedicated a good part of my life to ecumenism long before it became fashionable. But I think that we are in for some very rough times here as these questions get sorted out. I hope we are in for honest times also. The fundamental problem is doctrinal; the question of doctrine must come to the center, where it belongs. We can't lose sight of this when we come together to talk about moral issues, social action, and similar questions. There are some words that are going to have to come back— words like orthodoxy, dogma, and heresy. There *is* such a thing as a *heretic!* There are separated brethren, but there are also heretics. The word "heretic" has been used too freely in the past and thrown around carelessly. Maybe it was good that it was given a rest, but we still have to ask these questions.

Interviewer: Who is prepared in American Christianity to discuss doctrine?

DR. PELIKAN: I honestly don't know. The products of Roman Catholic seminaries? The products of Protestant seminaries? I don't know who is qualified, but I'm afraid that if dogma is not discussed, the ecumenical movement will turn into a palsy-walsy thing. On both sides doctrine has in one way or another been ignored, either by a certain kind of catechesis, which isn't really a consideration of Christian doctrine but the recitation of formulas, or by a kind of Jesus-piety, which is shared by pietistic Catholics and Protestants.

INTERVIEWER: Perhaps a way to recover the concern for dogma would be to relate it to the Church's worship.

DR. PELIKAN: Dogma is what the Church prays. It is an effort to give an account of the fundamental presuppositions of the Church's worship and service. You can't tinker with worship and suppose that by that kind of tinkering the dogmatic foundation will be repaired. Many, unfortunately, are unable to recognize or to cope with the problem, and so they dismiss it. The dichotomy you mentioned earlier between university and seminary theology includes an anti-dogmatic as well as an antiintellectual tendency. The Church becomes a place where you are marshaled for action or inoculated for eternity. The sacramental ministry of the Church is seen by the activists on both sides as the place where you get new picket signs for next week's rally and by the pietistic quietists on both sides as the place where you get your dose of help from the seven sacraments or through evangelistic ditties.

INTERVIEWER: What do you think of Father John Courtney Murray's observation that there is only *one* problem in theology today—the problem of development?

DR. PELIKAN: I certainly agree with Father Murray on this and have maintained this for more than a decade. Last year, at Yale, Father Walter Burghardt and I gave the St. Thomas More lectures, taking for our subject "Doctrinal Development and Catholic Unity." We limited ourselves to three patristic doctrines: original sin, *Filioque,* and Mary, and developed them from the Greek and the Latin side. We asked ourselves some basic questions. How is it that doctrine develops at different rates and in apparently different directions within different parts of the one Church? What does this imply about the nature of doctrinal development and, even more, about the definition of Catholic unity? Is a dogmatic definition a step forward, or is it an admission of failure?

INTERVIEWER: Do you have any suggestions how theologians should approach the problem of development?

DR. PELIKAN: I believe that those of us who are fundamentally traditional in our dogmatic concern and vocabulary should be working on this problem. The "systematic" theologian of the Protestants and the "dogmatic" theologian of the Roman Catholics should start becoming "constructive." They had better realize that you cannot start either with the dogma of the Church or with the hackneyed apologetic that used to pass for fundamental theology. You have to follow the example of the great apologists of the Church and start with your own historical situation. When the historical situation included dogma, liturgy, canon law, and the dominance of the institutional Church in the culture, it was possible to start with all that. But that isn't the case any more. Now the question should be—and this is where Rahner has been very helpful—what is there in the life of our churches in relation to the world that has dogmatic import? I think there is much that has.

INTERVIEWER: Perhaps a good place to start would be the devotion that much of the secular world along with the religious world has for the figure of Christ.

DR. PELIKAN: I agree. There is a residual loyalty to the person of Christ among those who find the forms of the institutional Church repugnant. To say, as we have said hundreds of times, "You cannot accept Christ without His Body," may be correct, but it is a certain kind of institutional defensiveness that is axiomatic and altogether irrelevant. It indicates an unwillingness to recognize where the power of the Spirit of God is at work in the world.

The recent movie, *The Gospel of St. Matthew,* was interesting in that the Church press was divided in its opinion. The basic division was over the question whether a Communist can portray the life of Christ meaningfully. Is there more to Christ than any man has ever imagined? In Rome, a few years ago, a Marxist told me that the letters S.C.V. on the Vatican license plates did not stand for

"Santa Città Vaticana," but for *"Si Christus videret!"* Even he could not shake off his loyalty to the figure of Jesus Christ. This is what is meant by saying: "the fullness of the Godhead dwells in Him bodily." There follows the recognition within Him of aspects of this fullness that we have not seen as clearly as we should. This is something that does have dogmatic import.

INTERVIEWER: This concern for the reality of Christ was of prime importance for St. Athanasius about whose theology you wrote a book some years ago.

DR. PELIKAN: That's correct. Athanasius was not afraid to take a Gnostic word, *homoousios,* which had been spattered by all kinds of controversy, and press it into the Church's service. He took Platonic and Philonic metaphors of light and darkness and made them an instrument of orthodoxy. We ought to be a little less timid and ask ourselves about this loyalty to Christ that is so great and really quite touching in the world. But we often act as though we owned Christ. The Church may be His Body, but He is still the *Lord* of the Church and not just the *head* of the Church. His Lordship over the Church transcends the Church. I have the feeling that we must begin to speak the truth about where we are doctrinally. We must be much more concerned about doctrine, about true doctrine, right doctrine, and orthodoxy.

INTERVIEWER: This should drastically affect the preaching in the churches.

DR. PELIKAN: Yes, the preaching will change on both sides. I hope that it will become more biblical. Another interesting thing has happened in this area. Amid great skepticism about basic dogmatic truths, there is a seriousness about the Bible. You see it on college campuses; the students will read the Bible. They may not believe very much of it, but they know that this is where they have to be engaged.

INTERVIEWER: But they become involved only if they understand the real meaning of faith.

DR. PELIKAN: We have to present a realistic notion of faith. It might help if by implicit faith we meant that one comes with his doubts and hesitations to stand in the association of those who, in their doubts and hesitations, have a commitment and confession. That is to believe what the Church believes. I want to be part of this community, even though at a given moment, if you asked me what I, in my little selfhood, believe, I could put it all on a 3" by 5" index card. But "I believe in one God, the Father Almighty, the maker of heaven and earth, and of all things visible and invisible," because I believe myself to be a part of the community that confesses all of this. Catholics and Protestants have to realize that the cultural matrix of the Church has changed and many things that the Church presupposed can no longer be presupposed.

INTERVIEWER: This might help explain, as you suggested in *The Shape of Death,* why so many today deny the immortality of the soul and the resurrection of the body.

DR. PELIKAN: There is no doubt that a change has taken place. From the days of the Greek Fathers in the second century to the nineteenth century, we can say (though it is impossible to prove it) that most intellectuals in the matrix of the Church believed in the immortality of the soul. The Church confessed the resurrection of the body on the basis of this general belief and spoke about the seriousness of death and sin in grim terms. Today, I'm sure that most "nonchurched" intellectuals, or at least those born in this century, do not believe in personal immortality. Previously, the Church echoed the secular belief in immortality. The kind of optimism you found in theologians, both Catholic and Protestant, sounded like that of the world around them. Now the kind of skepticism about immortality you hear from some theologians echoes the spirit of the world around them.

INTERVIEWER: Your book, *The Riddle of Roman Catholicism,* which appeared in 1959, was most successful. Could you tell us something about it?

DR. PELIKAN: In relation to the Vatican Council and the Kennedy campaign, it probably came out at the right time. I lightened up its scholarship as much as I could, and perhaps more than I should have. I tried to take account of my audience more than I usually do. Therefore, it is more popular and more "Protestant" than I would have made it if I had been writing it for myself alone. But I think it helped; it had a positive effect on a considerable number of readers.

INTERVIEWER: If you were to rewrite it now, what changes would you make?

DR. PELIKAN: There would have to be a complete revision. I have been urged to do this. It would require now a saturation in conciliar materials. When I wrote the book in 1958, not very many people were interested in these matters. I felt, as an historian of the Reformation and the early Church, that it was time to open these questions. After all, Friedrich Heiler's book, to which Karl Adam wrote an answer, was never translated into English. In a sense, I wanted to get something ecumenical started. If I, as a scholar concerned with history, were to do the book over, I would take the first two chapters and examine historically the formation of Catholic Christianity. In what sense is the Apostolic Church catholic, and in what sense is it not? Also, there is the question of Roman Primacy. Both of these questions are too easily answered in current study, perhaps also in my *Riddle,* and they need to be reconsidered.

INTERVIEWER: What was the Catholic reaction to the book?

DR. PELIKAN: Some of it was sick, but basically the reaction was generous. The funniest reaction came from Rome. It happened this way. The publishers bound up a special copy and sent it to Pope John. They asked me to send a Latin letter along with it. I got a note back from a priest friend in Vatican City who had transmitted my letter. He said that one of the Cardinals had read it and said: "From the fluency of his Latin, it is obvious that he is not an American Catholic." This confirmed me in my deepening conviction—to which I referred in response to your first question—that although such books are necessary, my own primary vocation is to be a scholar and historian, a spokesman for the tradition in an ecumenical age.

❖❖

JAROSLAV PELIKAN was born on December 17th, 1923, in Akron, Ohio. He received his seminary training at Concordia Seminary, Saint Louis, Missouri, and was granted his Ph.D. from the University of Chicago in 1946. That same year he was ordained into the ministry of the Lutheran Church. He has taught at Valparaiso University, Concordia Seminary, and the University of Chicago. Since 1962, he has been at Yale University and is the Titus Street Professor of Ecclesiastical History. He is a member of the Commission on Faith and Order of the World Council of Churches. He is on the editorial board of the *Catholic Theological Encyclopedia* planned by Corpus Instrumentorum, Inc., and on the National Board of Trustees of the National Conference of Christians and Jews. Since 1955, he has been Departmental Editor for Religion of the *Encyclopaedia Britannica* and editor of *Makers of Modern Theology*. He is married and has two sons.

Dr. Pelikan's writings include: *From Luther to Kierkegaard; Fools for Christ; The Riddle of Roman Catholicism; Luther the Expositor; The Shape of Death; Obedient Rebels;* and *The Christian Intellectual*. He is editor and translator of sixteen volumes of the American edition of *Luther's Works*.

John Meyendorff

*D*umbarton Oaks Research Library is located in the exclusive
Georgetown residential area of Washington. This lovely home with
magnificent gardens was formerly the residence of the Bliss family.
On the property there is also an excellent museum of pre-Columbian
art designed by Philip Johnson. The porter at the door of the faculty
entrance takes my name and then rings for Father Meyendorff. In
a few minutes, I hear the "click, click" of leather heels, and Father
Meyendorff, with a neat black beard, flashing eyes, and a friendly
smile, comes through the door. He greets me warmly and then
leads me down book-lined corridors and up a narrow stairway to
his small study. Outside, it is a cold, gray day, but his study is cozy
—perhaps a bit overheated. He sits behind the desk, and I take a
chair to his left. His English is good and the French flavor of his
speech is in no way a hindrance to communication. We speak softly,
so as not to disturb the other scholars who are working on their
research projects in adjoining rooms.

INTERVIEWER: You were born in France and received all your
education there. Is there a large Orthodox colony there?

FATHER MEYENDORFF: I am from Paris, and I have lived most of
my life there. My parents left Russia after the Revolution. Between
the two World Wars, Paris was the center of Russian immigration
and became the intellectual center for Russian scholars, artists, and
theologians. They started several fine schools, among which is the
Orthodox Theological Institute of St. Sergius where I studied. The
Institute has produced quite a number of theologians who are now

dispersed all over the world. I suppose that there were about 200,000 Russian immigrants in Paris between the two wars. This is not an extremely large number, but it was composed largely of the intellectual elite of Russia. Now, of course, this number is decreasing. In addition to this Russian background, I followed the normal course of French secondary and university training.

INTERVIEWER: In your theological training were you influenced by French Catholic theologians?

FATHER MEYENDORFF: During my student days, I was in constant contact with Catholic theology. The relationships between Catholics and Orthodox in France were quite genial throughout the last thirty or forty years. The ecumenical movement that we are witnessing today was something that was going on in Europe in a less official way for a long time. This was especially true in the field of theological research. We always felt that the Orthodox and the Catholics were able to dialogue and to work together in the study of Patristics and the Liturgy. In Europe, this was the normal state of affairs.

INTERVIEWER: When you came to this country, were you surprised at the lack of cooperation between Christians?

FATHER MEYENDORFF: In a way, yes. Perhaps I was spoiled by my European experience. There is no question that the ecumenical movement began much later in this country than in Europe. However, because of Vatican II there are many encouraging signs. The atmosphere has changed drastically, and there is a much freer exchange between all Christians now in the United States. The relationship between the Orthodox and the Catholics has also made some progress. The Roman Catholic Church in this country had always been a solid block of Christians. It discouraged dialogue with others. On the other hand, the Orthodox came here as immigrant groups and generally without much intellectual or theological leadership. Frequently, they were fearful of Rome because they came from those areas in eastern Europe where Rome and Orthodoxy had clashed bitterly. There was a lot of mutual distrust that made exchange almost impossible. We should be grateful that things are changing for the better.

INTERVIEWER: Do you have any reservations about the present direction of the ecumenical movement?

FATHER MEYENDORFF: I do not want to sound pessimistic. But a movement that begins with such great vitality and energy often has later to rethink its aims in a more sober light. The Second Vatican Council gave ecumenism the "big push." The movement started quickly, and almost everywhere was encouraged. It all happened so suddenly that many were not prepared. I do not think that all the Orthodox or the Catholics in America are sufficiently prepared to understand that the ecumenical dialogue implies more than just embracing everyone you see. We cannot forget the necessity of deeper dialogue that means listening to what others are saying. The very heart of ecumenism centers on the problem of *truth,* and that means that study, prayer, and understanding are all needed to see things in their proper light. The Protestants have the merit of having initiated the present ecumenical dialogue. They have an openness to dialogue with other Christians because they have no strong ecclesiological commitment. Roman Catholics and Orthodox are much closer in that they both have a well-defined ecclesiology.

INTERVIEWER: Do you foresee the Orthodox playing a greater role in ecumenism in the years to come?

FATHER MEYENDORFF: I hesitate to be a prophet about this. But I am convinced that the Orthodox Church must play a central role in uniting all Christians. The Orthodox Church has participated in the World Council of Churches from the very beginning. We have made the necessary statements concerning our position, and we have never felt that we were in any way relativizing our faith or our ecclesiology. The World Council of Churches is essentially a meeting place with organized dialogue. It has done a tremendous job.

On the other hand, the Vatican Council has given all Christians great hope. The Orthodox have felt the change in the climate of dialogue and negotiation. The very fact that Orthodoxy became a part of the Western ecumenical scene has mellowed some of the fanatical anti-Latin animosity that was a product of the Middle Ages. Psychologically, the grounds for reunion are improving. However, a condition for future progress is to avoid going off on side-tracks like "intercommunion" and emphasis on the Uniate Churches. The very existence of the Uniates is a major problem in the eyes of many Orthodox. Positively, we should avoid all polemic or apologetic arguments that would base their argument not on doctrine, but on history. The Roman Catholic manuals of theology in the past had a rather low opinion of the Orthodox Church and claimed that after the schism, the Orthodox Church, split by nationalism, lost its vigor and doctrinal purity. Orthodox books would also center their polemics on historical issues like the Inquisition. Thanks to the Vatican Council and the renewed interest in ecumenism such arguments are becoming rare.

INTERVIEWER: Are Orthodox efforts toward reunion hampered by the fact that most of their churches are in Communist countries?

FATHER MEYENDORFF: Almost ninety percent of the Orthodox faithful live in Communist countries where the political situation does not favor free discussion of theological issues. In spite of these difficulties and lacking any effective central power, the Orthodox of Communist countries still are generally interested in feeling and manifesting Christian solidarity in confronting militant atheism. This is seen in some of the theological periodicals. Exchanges of professors and students has been helpful in this area.

INTERVIEWER: Is the problem of doctrinal development widely discussed by Orthodox theologians?

FATHER MEYENDORFF: Yes, it is. There is very little difference between the Roman and Orthodox view on this question. We say that development is never a new revelation. Rather it is a deeper understanding of the implications of the death and resurrection of Christ—the essential content of the Christian Gospel applied to our times.

INTERVIEWER: How is development of doctrine assured if Orthodoxy refuses to recognize as legitimate any ecumenical council after the eighth century?

FATHER MEYENDORFF: It is true that the ecumenical council is the greatest witness to truth and a manifestation of the presence of the Holy Spirit in the Church. However, the notion of the ecumenical council is not devoid of historical ambiguities. An ecumenical council of the fifth and sixth centuries is a quite different thing from an ecumenical council in the twentieth century. For one thing, in the early centuries, the emperor normally called the council. Later on, there were no councils in the East because the Byzantine emperors, who saw themselves as world emperors, felt that unless the West was represented, there could be no genuine "ecumenical" council. The Council of Florence technically was "ecumenical" because politically it included the whole world. Nevertheless, it was rejected by the Orthodox Church. But there have been other councils in the Orthodox Church that have made important doctrinal pronouncements and are universally accepted, without claiming formal "ecumenicity." St. Gregory Palamas, for example, was a leading figure in the fourteenth century and was involved in a theological debate on the grace and knowledge of God and the relationship between nature, God, and the world. A series of local councils (1341, 1347, 1351, 1368) made doctrinal definitions on this point and the Orthodox Church accepted them. There are many other instances when the Orthodox Church exercised its full teaching power, but hesitated in calling its councils "ecumenical" for political reasons. The local Council of Jerusalem (1675), for example, dealt with Reformation confessions of faith. Its statements too were universally accepted. For us, the highest doctrinal authority is the *concensus* of Church, which may or may *not* be expressed through a formal "ecumenical" council.

INTERVIEWER: Is the *"filioque"* issue still a burning question in Orthodoxy?

FATHER MEYENDORFF: It is a critical question for two reasons. First of all, there are some Orthodox theologians, Vladimir Lossky to name one, who center all the differences between the East and the West on the *"filioque"* problem. I am not convinced by all their arguments, but I do agree that the ecclesiological implications that the *"filioque"* issue brings up are important. The original Creed did not have the *"filioque"* in it. It read simply: "I believe . . . in the Holy Spirit, the Lord, the Giver of Life, *Who proceeds from the Father."* The West added *"filioque"* so now the Creed in the West reads: *". . . Who proceeds from the Father and the Son."* In fact it was not until the start of the eleventh century that Rome started using the *"filioque"* addition, even though it was approved by the local Council of Toledo in 589. Now the ecumenical councils forbade any changes in the Creed, while this addition was made without any approval from an ecumenical council. It was a unilateral interpolation—the East was not consulted at all. So you see the ecclesiological significance of this. Secondly, there is a theological doubt about the value of the *"filioque"* addition. It implies an Augustinian view of the Trinity that is quite different from that of the Cappadocian Fathers. My own opinion is that the Augustinian view of the Trinity could have been considered as the individual speculation of one Father of the Church and thus coexist with the usual patristic view. But the commitment of the Roman Church—especially at the Council of Lyons (1274)—to this one-sided theory, created between East and West a doctrinal issue of first magnitude.

INTERVIEWER: Let us consider a practical ecumenical problem here in the United States. How do the Orthodox feel about Eastern Catholics—those in communion with the Holy See?

FATHER MEYENDORFF: That is a very delicate and difficult question, which we have touched already. Traditionally, and there is perhaps no need to limit this to the United States, the majority of the Orthodox today look at the Eastern Catholic Church as a kind of war machine directed against Orthodoxy. They look at them with the greatest distrust and disfavor. In the past, and perhaps even now, there were some good reasons for such distrust. Personally, I feel that we should move from this emotional ground that is so dangerous and try to understand just what the problem is. Using a more theological and objective approach, I would make two observations. First of all, we Orthodox have to understand that the Roman Church claims to be and understands itself as being *the* Catholic Church—the universal Church of Jesus Christ. The Roman Catholic Church claims it has the right to appeal to the needs of all cultures and all mentalities—in a word to be truly catholic. We cannot blame the Roman Church for adopting this attitude that is part of its doctrinal self-consciousness. It is a fact that the Romans believe this way, and we Orthodox have to get used to that. It is simply naïve to get offended by it. Secondly, we hope that interest for the Christian East will lead our Roman brethren to a rethinking of their theology. If the Roman Catholics of Eastern rite would understand their existence primarily in terms of representing the Eastern Christian *theology* in the Roman fold, they would perform a useful ecumenical task. In practice, however, their role has generally been the opposite: to serve as instruments of the East's latinization. Finally, the danger of "Uniatism" is that it often convinces the Roman Catholic Church that the differences between Orthodoxy and Rome are not doctrinal, but only ritual. This is wrong factually and creates the myth that reunion can be achieved "cheaply."

INTERVIEWER: Surely the Liturgy should provide a natural meeting ground for Orthodox and Roman Catholics.

FATHER MEYERDORFF: Yes, but no responsible Orthodox thinks for a moment that the main problem between Rome and Orthodoxy is a ritual one. That these Eastern rites exist in the Roman Church symbolizes the deep tension that exists between Rome and Orthodoxy. By using them, Rome reminds us of the sort of unity that she pretends to offer. She presents this unity to us in a ready-made form. Ecumenically, this results in tension, not in a solution. There is nothing ecumenical about Catholics having Eastern rites. There is only a self-affirmation by the Roman Church that she is the Catholic Church. We challenge that affirmation because we are Orthodox; we have the same self-conscious belief about our Church. The Orthodox Church claims to be the true Church of Christ, the one and only Catholic Church. This is the heart of the problem, and there is no point in talking our way around it. The problem of interrelation between doctrine and rite is a complicated one, full of intricate presuppositions and cultural and historical ramifications. Not every theology fits every rite. That the Roman Church maintains Eastern rites in its own fold does not mean at all that its theology becomes acceptable to us.

INTERVIEWER: Doesn't the Orthodox Church in the United States find it difficult to maintain its Eastern traditions?

FATHER MEYENDORFF: Here, in America, we are faced with the challenge to create a Western Orthodox Church. I don't think that

Eastern culture as such has much of a future in America. The whole frame of reference here is Western. The basic tradition of the Church, however, can flourish in the East and West. I am not sure what road the Orthodox Church will take. By using Eastern rites we do in fact Westernize them. The expression becomes naturally different, not necessarily the theology. I remember a few years ago I was in the Middle East and concelebrated the Liturgy with the Metropolitan of Beirut. It was the same Church, the same faith, but somehow it was a different religion. The form was so different. I am myself Western trained, and although my theology is Orthodox (I hope!) and my historical roots are in Byzantium, I deeply feel that the Eastern Liturgy celebrated in the East has a character somewhat different from what an average American understands. The Orthodox Church must have its own *aggiornamento*; otherwise, you have the Church becoming a fossilized museum. In fact, the Byzantine Liturgy, in its essential nucleus and meaning, is not necessarily "Eastern" and can become meaningful to Americans if properly celebrated.

INTERVIEWER: The vernacular has become an important instrument for liturgical renewal in the Roman Church. How does the Orthodox Church feel about the vernacular?

FATHER MEYENDORFF: The Orthodox Church is traditionally committed to use the vernacular in its Liturgy. The Byzantine Liturgy was translated in various languages during the years of missionary expansion in the ninth and tenth centuries. However, now we have the same problem that the Roman Catholics had in the United States in the last century. You were forced to have German, Italian, and French parishes. Now you have, as we do, young people who want the Liturgy in English because they don't understand the language of their parents. They feel that they cannot fully participate in the worship of the Church in a foreign language. However, for us, the problem has never been a matter of principle, but rather of pastoral exigency. Today, most Orthodox churches in this country use English quite extensively. Some parishes use English completely and others combine English and the older languages. The Greek Archdiocese is an exception. It does not allow English for the official worship of the Church, but only for sermons and Scripture readings.

INTERVIEWER: In your book, *The Orthodox Church*, you wrote: "The Orthodox Church, therefore, takes part in the ecumenical debate as the guardian of the true faith, the faith of the Apostles and Fathers of the early Church. It maintains that all Christians must return to the one true faith, the faith of the first ecumenical councils, as the condition for true reunion." Would you qualify that statement at all in the light of Vatican II?

FATHER MEYENDORFF: Both Orthodox and Catholics share one thing in common. We both are committed to the belief that Christ founded one Church, not several. It is theologically improper to speak about "churches" in the plural. The one Church is an historical reality. But there is also the fact of a major schism that divided the Roman Catholics from the Orthodox Catholics. However, neither of us would say that this schism implies *total* separation from what the one Church essentially is, for, indeed, wherever there are elements of the Christian faith, there are also elements of the one Church, elements of unity in Christ, However, total unity can exist only in the total unity of faith, a joint and total commitment to a single body, fully visible. From the Orthodox point of view this unity of faith and of commitment is *the* sign of union. We don't talk about canonical uniformity or obedience to a particular see as a condition of unity. The expression of unity for us is the unity in faith, not a jurisdictional submission to any particular center. The relationship between the *Church* and *truth* is crucial. It is truth that makes the Church one.

INTERVIEWER: Orthodox theology has always stressed the sacramental presence of Christ in the local church. What do you think of Congar's observation that "the East has poorly succeeded in realizing the ecclesiology of the Universal Church"?

FATHER MEYENDORFF: It all depends on what he means by the ecclesiology of the Universal Church. This has to be specified. Orthodox ecclesiology maintains that the notion of the Body of Christ as used by St. Paul is to be applied to the sacramental reality of the local church and not to a geographic universality. The fullness, not a part of Christ, is present in the Eucharist. Of course, this total presence of Christ in the local church is also to be manifested through a universal unity of faith and action of all the local churches, forming the Universal Church. It is obvious that, at times, the Orthodox Church has historically failed to manifest this unity sufficiently.

INTERVIEWER: Does the Orthodox Church feel the need for some central organization which would strengthen the unity of the various local churches?

FATHER MEYENDORFF: The Church in the third and fourth centuries was not centrally organized, yet there was a very deep sense of unity that was not based on a unity of discipline. The Orthodox Church of today presents a unity of witness that is similar to that. Of course, it is not as spectatular as the unified, juridical, and legalized structure of Rome. However, the Orthodox Church is not against organization in principle. In fact, there are many in the Church today who feel that we are badly in need of more organization. This is being expressed in many Orthodox publications. However, the theologians who advocate some kind of central organ of administration understand it as something that would operate according to ecclesiastical law (not divine law). This organ would only act in accord with the Church and in harmony with its consent.

INTERVIEWER: Would you please explain how this consent of the Church is determined?

FATHER MEYENDORFF: It cannot be defined exclusively in judirical terms. Of course, the term *consensus ecclesiae* is mentioned in Vatican I. The Council said that infallible statements of the pope are of themselves irreformable and "not because of the agreement of the Church"—*non ex consensu ecclesiae*. As it is well known, this passage constitutes one of the greatest obstacles for us. However, we could perhaps understand that doctrinal statements do not have to be *formally* voted upon by the Church—the Church is not a democracy. But the absence of a *consensus ecclesiae* should not exclude at least a *sensus ecclesiae,* with which every authority has to reckon. There is a moral agreement on essential truths that all Christians must express. This is what Orthodox theologians mean when they refer to "reception" of a doctrine by the Church. After a council, or an individual bishop, or a local church, makes a doctrinal statement there is a period during which the Church reflects on it. There is a time for the Church to commit herself to one position or another. There are numerous examples of this in the history of the Church. The Council of Nicea, for example, occured in 325, but for almost a century, it remained a controversial issue until the Church finally approved it.

INTERVIEWER: This brings up the question as to who possesses the authority to teach in the Church. Does it reside in the Church as a whole or in some specific members of the Church?

FATHER MEYENDORFF: The teaching authority resides in each bishop in his diocese, and the bishops gathered together as a college. This authority is divinely given; it is a grace bestowed by God on the episcopate in accordance with their function in the Church. However, like every other grace it can be betrayed by individual members. In other words, no one is infallible in using His grace. It can happen that a bishop betrays his episcopate by teaching a doctrine that will be ultimately rejected by the Church. The teaching of the Church is done under the guidance of the Holy Spirit, and the infallibility resides in the Church as a whole.

INTERVIEWER: Are there any occasions when you can say that the Church is speaking in an infallible, irreformable way?

FATHER MEYENDORFF: This is the most crucial point of debate between ourselves and Western Christianity. *The* Western concern is over a definable, clear criterion of truth. It is almost a kind of original sin for Western Christianity, both Roman Catholicism and Protestantism. The Protestant notion of *sola Scriptura* is a response to the claim of papal infallibility. Now in modern Protestantism where biblical criticism has shown that the Bible is a *human* document also you find much confusion. As an Orthodox I must say that the highest possible witness to truth you can have is a ecumenical council of the universal episcopate gathered together in the name of Christ. But even here there is no *absolute* guarantee or formal "security"; no one must accept it with *blind* obedience. There has to be a personal commitment; I must believe in my heart that the bishops gathered together are the Church for me. This does not always happen. Take St. Maximus the Confessor. He was told that all the Patriarchs and the Bishop of Rome himself had signed a Monothelite confession of faith. He told them that they were wrong and that they had been disloyal to their faith. Or you have the Monophysite churches of the East rejecting the Council of Chalcedon on the basis that it was simply not true. . . .

INTERVIEWER: Why have any teaching authority in the Church if the individual Christian can reject this authority even when it is present in its highest form—in the ecumenical council?

FATHER MEYENDORFF: The individual Christian will be a sectarian if he rejects an ecumenical council on the basis of his own private opinion. If he is to reject it, he must do so in the name of the whole Church, in the name of the continuing teaching of the past. We Orthodox do not believe in private interpretation of Scripture. On the contrary, one of the most valuable contributions to nineteenth-century Orthodox ecclesiology is the notion of *sobornost*—the idea that the knowledge of God is always collective and not individual; one must always share in the mind of the Church. The opposition of one person against all the bishops is an extreme case and requires extreme daring, but it ultimately simply preserves human freedom and responsibility in principle.

You asked why the *Magisterium* of the Church is needed. The normal, human existence of the Church requires that there be someone in the Church who teaches. The bishops receive the grace to teach, and this has kept the Church growing through the centuries. Here the image of the Church as a body may help us. In the normal functioning of the Body of Christ, the bishop teaches the faithful, and the latter obey him in all docility and loyalty. But there are certain times when normal functions of the Body are temporarily troubled, when some members, even some leaders, lose or twist the true message of Christ. These cases will occur, I suppose, till the end of time, without threatening the existence of the Body as such, based on God's commitment to Israel and to this New Covenant with humanity through Christ. It is this *divine* commitment that makes the Church to be the Church, not any formal criteria.

INTERVIEWER: Do you think that the Roman Catholic doctrine of the Teaching Authority of the Church as the guardian and teacher of truth is correct?

FATHER MEYENDORFF: Historically, this doctrine has emphasized the juridical aspects of the Church's teaching power. Some of the results were not always good. Because of the presence of a permanent, infallible, and direct Teaching Authority, the individual Catholic feels less responsible for what he says. He knows that if he is wrong, eventually he will be told. In the meantime, he is more or less free to say what he wants. The Orthodox in the absence of the same kind of permanent and absolute authority has to be fully responsible for what he says, and this leads very often to a kind of blind conservatism that characterizes much of Orthodox thinking. The Old Believers in Russia are a good example of this.

INTERVIEWER: How did the Orthodox react to the decree of Pope Paul VI and Patriarch Athenagoras I withdrawing the mutual excommunication pronounced against each other by Rome and Byzantium in 1054?

FATHER MEYENDORFF: Both Pope Paul and Patriarch Athenagoras have a very good feel for the symbolic. This lifting of the excommunication was an excellent example of it. However, the meaning of their gesture must correspond to the events of 1054 themselves. In fact, the incident of 1054 is not that significant, and it is made up of a combination of misunderstandings and confusions. It is good to get rid of these. It would have been much better and more significant, however, if the Roman Church had made, for example, a formal rehabilitation of Photius. The schism with Photius took place in 867. In 879–880 there was a Council at Constantinople, and both the East and the West agreed on union. They discussed the topics that divide us today. Pope John VIII (872–882) sent legates to that Council that restored Photius and with the Eastern Church condemned the famous addition of the *"filioque"* to the Creed. Till he died, Photius was grateful to the Pope for restoring unity in the Church and frequently referred to John VIII as an example to those who wished to deny the moral authority of the Roman popes at Byzantium. The decisions of this Council must be thought of as the very model of the way the Orthodox Church views Christian unity.

Now this Council was recognized as an ecumenical council in the West until the Gregorian reform in the eleventh century. If this Council could now be jointly accepted as ecumenical, we would make a significant step forward to unity.

Interviewer: The Second Vatican Council has allowed Catholics under certain conditions to receive the Eucharist from non-Catholic ministers whose Church possesses valid orders. Do you see this as an ecumenical advantage?

Father Meyendorff: The Orthodox reaction to this was not favorable. The Orthodox bishops in the United States made a statement in 1964 (published in *St. Vladimir's Quarterly,* 9, 1965, No. 1), about intercommunion that was decidedly negative. The problem behind intercommunion is a basic one and cannot be lightly passed over. The Eucharist is a sign of unity achieved; it's a sign of the one Church of Christ. When you take Communion in the Church, you acknowledge that this Church is your Mother. You also acknowledge that the bishop is your teacher and that you believe in his doctrine. To allow Communion to nonmembers is to imply that there is a separation between doctrine and the sacraments. The "validity" of the sacraments is thus separated from the tradition of the Church. This is bad theology and bad ecumenism. Taking Communion is not simply a magical act—it's a full commitment to the life of "the Church" in its entirety. It is only on the blessed day when we will understand the same Church to be "the Church," that we will be able to take Communion together. Therefore, we consider the statement of Vatican II on this matter as unfortunate.

Interviewer: Isn't it true that intercommunion has been practiced between Latins and Orthodox for several centuries?

Father Meyendorff: Yes, intercommunion was practiced in some of the Greek islands until the eighteenth century. It was found also in some remote areas of Europe where Roman Catholics were without their priests for years. Sometimes it happened because of necessity, ignorance, or misinformation.

However, these are exceptions and not in themselves positive ecumenical signs. My point is that we must situate sacramental validity, especially that of the Eucharist, in the total framework of unity of belief. Earlier we spoke about the local Church and the fullness present within it. This applies here too. When fullness of faith is present, one local Church recognizes and accepts another local Church. Schism occurs when this mutual recognition *in the same fullness* is not possible. It does not mean that the two Churches have nothing in common, but it does mean that they do not share *all* in common. It means that they have differences on what God wants them to be. The Orthodox feel that the Eucharist is the ultimate expression of our unity in Christ. It would be impossible to establish intercommunion before accepting together a common commitment to the same one Church.

❖❖

JOHN MEYENDORFF was born in Neuilly-sur-Seine, France, on February 17th, 1926. He completed his secondary school education in Paris and graduated from the University of Paris (Sorbonne) and the Orthodox Theological Institute of Paris. Father Meyendorff, a Russian Orthodox priest, came to the United States in 1959; his special field of research is Byzantine spirituality and ecclesiology. He is Professor of Church History and Patristics at St. Vladimir's Orthodox Theological Seminary, Crestwood, New York; Harvard University Lecturer in Byzantine theology at the Dumbarton Oaks Research Library and Collection; and Adjunct Professor in the Department of Religion, Columbia University. He has done research work in the field of Byzantine studies under the auspices of the Centre National de la Recherche Scientifique. He is a member of the Commission on Faith and Order of the World Council of Churches.

His publications include, besides many articles, the following books: *A Study on Gregory Palamas; The Orthodox Church;* and *Orthodoxy and Catholicity.*

Francis J. Connell

It is the afternoon of December 8th, and the temperature is an un-seasonable seventy-two degrees in Washington. As I park my car before the Redemptorist College, I see Father Connell slowly walking back and forth on the front porch, engrossed in his breviary. He is wearing his black religious habit with its soft, white collar. His oversized rosary is attached to a cloth belt. We enter a starkly furnished parlor that has a crucifix on the wall and a few volumes of the writings of St. Alphonsus on a corner table. The fresh smell of floor wax and furniture polish permeates the room. Father Connell is a small man with curly white hair, bright eyes, and a ready smile. He looks almost frail. He speaks hurriedly with the trace of a Boston accent, makes his point, and eagerly awaits the next question.

INTERVIEWER: For many years you taught dogmatic theology. What prompted you to start teaching moral theology?

FATHER CONNELL: In all, I have taught theology for forty years: twenty-two years in dogma and eighteen in moral. I taught dogmatic theology at the Redemptorist Seminary in Esopus, New York, until 1940. That year, Bishop Corrigan, Rector of The Catholic University of America, invited me to come to the University to teach dogma. I accepted with the permission of my superiors. However, in the summer of 1940, Bishop Corrigan asked me if I would teach moral theology instead, since his moral theologian, Monsignor O'Brien, had been called back by his bishop to be rector of the seminary in Cincinnati. I accepted.

INTERVIEWER: Wasn't it difficult for you to make the change?

FATHER CONNELL: In the beginning, it was somewhat difficult, but it did not take me very long to get used to it. I was impressed by this thought: One who knows dogmatic theology well is really best qualified to teach moral theology. After all, theology is *one* science. I feel that too often theology is split up unnecessarily. Although I am not actively engaged in teaching now, I feel that as Dean of Religious Communities I am still in the work of education. I consider it a great privilege to have been occupied in the work of Catholic education for forty-eight years.

INTERVIEWER: What theologians influenced you the most?

FATHER CONNELL: I had the advantage of having had Father Garrigou-Lagrange when I was a student at the Angelicum in Rome. He surely was an outstanding theologian and, of course, a convinced Thomist. I was fortunate to have taught theology for six years before I began to do graduate work. I had read all the authors of the day, but I think that I most admired the Dutch theologian, Father Van Noort. His work on dogmatic is magnificent. It is now being translated and updated by the Sulpician Fathers Castelot and Murphy. When I began to teach moral theology, I used mainly Merkelbach, O.P., and Regatillo-Zalba, S.J. Of course, I also used St. Alphonsus.

INTERVIEWER: How did these authors affect your theological method?

FATHER CONNELL: First of all, I have always tried to be *clear* and *simple* in my presentation. I think that characterizes Father Van Noort and the others I mentioned. I regret to say that some of the theologians today do not possess this quality. I always distrust one who is vague. My idea has been this: If a man *really knows* something properly, he can express it clearly, no matter how sublime and abstract the subject may be.

INTERVIEWER: From your own experience, what role would you say the moral theologian plays in the Christian community?

FATHER CONNELL: The moral theologian must give guidance to people; he must explain to them how they must conduct themselves. Of course, the theologian is not a member of the Church's teaching authority—the *Magisterium*: he is not an *official* teacher of the Church. And yet, as our Holy Father Pope Paul VI has recently mentioned, theologians and Scripture scholars are supposed to guide those who do officially teach in the Church. The *Magisterium* learns from theology.

INTERVIEWER: How does the belief of the faithful enter into the operation of the *Magisterium*? In other words, what is the value of the *sensus fidelium*?

FATHER CONNELL: The *sensus fidelium* is synonymous with the *ecclesia discens*—the learning Church. Recently, there have been some who believe that the *ecclesia docens*—the teaching Church—must follow the *ecclesia discens*. This is wrong. It has always been that the Church gives doctrine and the faithful learn doctrine. To say this does not mean that there should not be any communication between them or that the teaching Church can learn nothing from the faithful. The common belief of Catholics can influence the teaching authority. Today's feast of the Immaculate Conception is a good example of that. In the Middle Ages, as you know, there was a great deal of discussion among theologians as to whether Mary was conceived immaculate or not. On one occasion, a pope said to a group of theologians that if they taught that Mary was conceived in sin, the people would rise up against them. However, this does not change the principle that the Church's obligation is to teach and the faithful's obligation is to learn.

INTERVIEWER: How many people have come to you for advice over the years?

FATHER CONNELL: In all truth and humility, I can say that I have been called upon to give advice on many occasions. Bishops, priests, religious and lay people are continually writing me. In one way or another—either by my teaching, through letters, conferences, and retreats—I have come into contact with about one-quarter of the priests in this country, which would number about fourteen thousand. Many people write me about moral problems. Since I came to Washington twenty-six years ago, I suppose I have sent out on an average of two or three thousand letters a year. That means that I have done my bit in supporting the U.S. Post Office by sending out over fifty thousand letters.

INTERVIEWER: Do you receive many quack letters?

FATHER CONNELL: Some. A quack letter demands no reply. Sometimes, the individual writes anonymously and gives no address. I have received many letters from people who were to my mind extreme one way or another. But I have always tried to answer them kindly, even if it only meant saying: "I can't agree with you. My position is etc." I think that is the proper way to handle such things. I have always tried to answer the most critical letters in a kind way.

INTERVIEWER: I am sure that some of the letters you receive must be amusing.

FATHER CONNELL: They certainly are. One day, I received a letter from a woman who was quite irate about the Russians sending a dog into space. She objected violently to my position that it is all right to use animals in scientific experiments. She told me that dogs make better friends than people and that she was going to light a candle in St. Patrick's Cathedral in New York for a month with the prayer that I would suffer as much as the good dog suffered. She finally suggested that they send up some Catholic brat into space, but not a dog. I couldn't deny that there are some Catholic brats! Perhaps she had some very harrowing experience with them.

INTERVIEWER: Your life has been very productive. Do you have any special techniques that enable you to get so much done?

FATHER CONNELL: I believe that if a person starts out with the idea that he should do as much as he can for the cause of Christ, then he can accomplish a great deal without unnecessary strain. God has been good to me by giving me excellent health. I am still fairly healthy at the age of seventy-eight, and I have always led an active life. I have a very wonderful example of dedicated work in our founder St. Alphonsus, who took a vow never to lose a moment of time. I can say that while I have never taken such a vow (it would be too much for me), I have always tried to use my time wisely. My educational background helped me develop good habits. I am proud that I am a graduate of the Boston Latin School, which is a public school. From the day we entered it, we were told that we had to work if we were to get through. If you didn't work, you did not graduate. The first time I went to a Catholic school was when I went to Boston College, which is run by the Jesuits. I spent two years there before I entered the Redemptorists. I might add here that I was encouraged to apply for membership in the Jesuits. I decided against it, since (as I said) I didn't want to spend my life in a class-room. So I joined a missionary society, the Redemptorists, and I've been in a classroom ever since.

INTERVIEWER: You have published many books and articles. Would you explain how you go about your writing.

FATHER CONNELL: My only ambition has been to write clearly and simply. I believe that even the most profound and abstract doctrines of our faith can be put simply. I don't mean that you can under-stand these mysteries fully, but you can present what we under-stand of them simply. I used to tell the young men who wrote dis-sertations under my direction that they must not spend too long in doing research before they write. Theological students are inclined to read widely and to fill out index cards by the dozen. They hesitate to write a word until they have exhausted the subject. You know that eventually they won't use a quarter of the cards they have made out. My system is this: Select a topic and think about it seriously by asking yourself questions. Write down *all* you know about it. Then study and read more. This will result in your chang-ing and developing the original text. I think that's the better way. Once you have something down on paper, it is easier to work with. I have rewritten some of my articles four or five times before I was satisfied with them.

INTERVIEWER: Do you keep extensive files?

FATHER CONNELL: Yes I do. I pity those who come after me and have to go through my files and examine them to see what is worth-while. Besides keeping carbons of all my letters, I also have files with my notes, conferences, and relevant periodical material. I have tried to keep abreast of theological development by reading books and periodicals. As a moral theologian, I also must know what is hap-pening in the world, and so I read many newspapers and news magazines. I try to read articles on both sides of a question and to give a fair hearing to those who do not agree with me. I have never felt any personal resentment to anybody who disagreed with me. Rather, I admire them. But it is very difficult to keep up with everything that is written today.

INTERVIEWER: What method did you employ in teaching theology?

FATHER CONNELL: I used the same method in all my years of teaching theology. I received it from my Boston Latin School background, and I think it very productive. For the first ten minutes of each class, I would ask questions about the material covered in the previous class. This method was intended to encourage the students to study what had been taught the day before. I sometimes found out by questioning the students that I hadn't explained the matter completely, and it gave me an opportunity to clarify it. I have always encouraged questions from my students. Some questions were often unnecessary, but I would never indicate any sign of impatience. If one student has a question, there is a good chance that several others in the class have the same problem. The principal purpose behind all my teaching is that the material should be sufficiently explained so that everyone understands what I have to present.

INTERVIEWER: Some have called you a *conservative* theologian. Is that an accurate description of your theological position?

FATHER CONNELL: I would like to point out that I have not always been labeled conservative. Twenty-five years ago, I was regarded as a liberal theologian! I regret very much that this dichotomy—liberal or conservative—has to be used at all. To my mind you can and should be *both* liberal and conservative. The theologian must realize that there are developments in theology and that new problems have to be faced and answered. But on the other hand, he must also realize that his solutions must not oppose what the Church has taught for centuries. A theologian has to be *conservative* in regard to the certain teaching of the Church, but *liberal* in the sense that he is willing to accept new ideas that develop but do not deny the Church's traditional doctrine. The distinction between liberal and conservative is largely due to the press at the Vatican Council. I was at the Council for the four sessions and also a member of the American Bishops' Press Panel. The impression was given by many of the reporters that a man had to be either a liberal or a conservative.

There was no account made of the fact that the vast majority of the bishops were and are both. The same applies to theologians.

INTERVIEWER: Do you think that theology has changed radically in the last ten years?

FATHER CONNELL: Some theologians have changed, yes. But I cannot see how theology has changed. I do not see how it could change radically, since it takes its principles from Revelation as taught by the Church. There has surely been a significant progress in theology over the last decade, but this does not mean that there has been a denial of what went before. I encourage any kind of theological research and study as long as it aims at the truth. This is the primary goal of theology. It is a sad fact that today a man is judged not so much by whether he seeks truth, but by whether he is a liberal or a conservative. A man must seek truth in every field of science, and theology is no exception. Truth, truth, always truth!

INTERVIEWER: It has often been said that Catholic theology before the Second Vatican Council was largely irrelevant. Do you agree?

FATHER CONNELL: Certainly not. Before Vatican II, Catholic theologians were, on the whole, moving ahead. I fully admit that they did not consider all the problems that should have been treated. I think that we have to discuss seriously contemporary problems. But I cannot understand how theology can be unfaithful to the heritage of the past.

INTERVIEWER: American theology, both Catholic and Protestant, has depended greatly on European scholarship. What future do you see for a proper American theology?

FATHER CONNELL: I can only speak for Catholic moral theology. I think that we have many fine Catholic moralists in this country. European scholarship has been overrated, at least in the field of moral theology. Fathers Ford and Kelly have contributed much to American theology and in many respects were far ahead of European theology. Because of the peculiar American experience, perhaps our theologians are well suited to discuss the problems of Church-State, racial injustice, war and peace.

INTERVIEWER: In looking back over your years as a theologian, do you think that you would have been more successful if you had been less of an activist?

FATHER CONNELL: I don't think so. No. God has been good to me by keeping me active—giving me many opportunities for work in the field of theology. I attribute all I have done to His great graces. I have failed in many respects. My feeling now, after fifty-three years as a priest, is one of deep gratitude to God for giving me His help. I hope God will give me a few more years to continue my work. I have tried to do His will. I think, in all humility, that I have contributed something to the Church by my work. I know that not all would agree with all my solutions; nevertheless, this much I have heard from many sources: my solutions have been clear, definite, and without ambiguity. While some might not agree with my solutions, they were at least understandable.

INTERVIEWER: Isn't it precisely in this area that you have also been criticized? Some would say that you seem to have an answer to every moral problem.

FATHER CONNELL: I know what you mean, and I have also heard that. But you must remember that my solutions were based on serious study. What might have appeared to be an unprepared answer was really the fruit of many years of study. When people have a moral dilemma, they want an answer—yes or no. I have never left people up in the air. Some answers I have given have been my own opinion, and I could see merit in an opposing view. Other answers I have given without any hesitation, since they were the teaching of the Church. The problem of contraception would be an illustration of this.

INTERVIEWER: You have been engaged in many controversies in your theological career. Your discussion in the early fifties with John Courtney Murray, S.J., on the Church-State problem perhaps attracted the greatest interest. What was your position?

FATHER CONNELL: I said that the *ideal* situation is where the State recognizes the Catholic Church as the one, true Church. Father Murray believed that the Church and State should be separated. I insisted that in the ideal situation they should not be separated, even though in particular conditions they might be.

INTERVIEWER: Does the *Decree on Religious Liberty* of the Second Vatican Council cause you to change your views?

FATHER CONNELL: Not in the least, because it says nothing about this question. In passing, it did mention that in certain places there is a union of Church and State, but it neither condemned nor approved this. The *Decree on Religious Liberty* is an excellent statement, and I am in full agreement with it. Father Murray deserves great credit for the labor he put into it. Remember that religious freedom is by no means freedom of conscience. That phrase was left out of the document completely. Religious liberty is based on the dignity of man and the means that man should not be subjected to any coercion on the part of civil authority in religious matters, either to do what is against his conscience or to refrain from doing what his conscience dictates, unless public order is concerned.

My controversy with Father Murray was on Church-State, and that is not the same as religious liberty. *Ideally,* the Church should be recognized by the State and its rights acknowledged. There should be a union in this sense. In fact, the Church for centuries has claimed certain rights that the State would back by natural law. We have, for example, the matter of marriage impediments. The Church still claims she has a right to make impediments for the marriages of all baptized persons. That is taking over what in the natural order would belong to the State. The State has the right to make impediments only for unbaptized persons. This means that the State is *per se* obliged to recognize the Catholic Church as having this power.

In the *practical* order, I have always held that it is best, even in Catholic states, to have a recognition of all people. Every man should be allowed to do what his conscience dictates. My argument was based on the principle of the greater good. Nowadays, it is based on human dignity.

INTERVIEWER: What advice would you give to young theologians?

FATHER CONNELL: Speaking to young Catholic theologians I would say two things. First of all, seek the truth. Objective, unbiased truth must be the primary goal of the theologian. Don't be led astray by a thing because it is new and don't stick stubbornly to something simply because it is old. The Catholic theologian has to go on the principle that the Church is infallible and can teach with authority. This infallibility is not restricted merely to what is contained in Revelation, but it extends also to truths that are connected with Revelation.

Secondly, I would say that young theologians should seek the truth reverently, since theology is also wisdom. Prayer and theology go hand in hand. I recommend to every Catholic theologian, whether he be lay or clerical, a deep devotion to the Blessed Sacrament. Believing that Christ is truly, really, and substantially present in the Eucharist, we can derive great help from Him. We should also have a devotion to Mary, the Seat of Wisdom. Through her, we may hope to receive true wisdom from her Divine Son.

❖❖

FRANCIS J. CONNELL, born in Boston, Massachusetts on January 31st, 1888, graduated from Boston Latin School in 1905 and attended Boston College for two years. In 1907, he entered the Congregation of the Most Holy Redeemer and was ordained to the priesthood in 1913. He did graduate work in theology at the Pontifical University of the Angelicum. He taught dogmatic theology at the Redemptorist Seminary in Esopus, New York, from 1915 to 1921 and again from 1924 to 1940. He came to The Catholic University of America in 1940, where he taught moral theology until his retirement in 1958. In 1957, he was appointed Dean for Religious Communities at The Catholic University. He had been on the Editorial Board of *The American Ecclesiastical Review* since 1943. He was a *peritus* at the *Second Vatican Council* and a member of the American Bishops' Press Panel. He died in May, 1967.

Father Connell wrote a large number of pamphlets and articles on theological questions. Among his books are: *Morals in Politics and Professions; Outlines of Moral Theology; Father Connell Answers Moral Questions;* and *Spiritual and Pastoral Conferences for Priests.*

George Lindbeck

As I arrive for my appointment with George Lindbeck, I find him standing on the small landing near his office in the Yale Divinity School carefully emptying the contents of his large bag. Books and papers are neatly piled on the stairs. "I've misplaced the key to my office," he explains smiling, but not without a note of annoyance. "I thought it might have dropped into my bag." His search proves fruitless, so we go instead to the pine-paneled faculty meeting room, which is quiet and most suitable.

Dr. Lindbeck, a slightly built man, looks youthful enough to be a Yale graduate student. He does not look forty-three. He is a serious person who speaks slowly and with deliberation. When a question is asked, he pauses some time before answering and even then is cautious in his choice of words. His voice is strong and affirmative. He smokes a large-bowled pipe with which he occasionally gesticulates. The fragrance of Amphora tobacco fills the air.

INTERVIEWER: How did you become interested in Roman Catholic theology?

DR. LINDBECK: My own original specialization is the history of doctrine with particular reference to the Middle Ages, that period from Augustine to the Reformation. The first few years of my teaching were almost entirely confined to that area. I also gave occasional seminars, or parts of courses, on the early Luther, that is, the relation between Luther and late scholasticism. Then, gradually, I found myself working more and more with contemporary Roman-Catholic theological developments. Because of my interest in this and medieval theology, I was asked to attend the Second Vatican Council by the Lutheran World Federation. Since that time, contemporary Roman-Catholic theology occupies about half of my time, and the more historical courses that I taught previously occupy the other half.

INTERVIEWER: What will you be teaching this year?

DR. LINDBECK: I will have one course on "The Medieval Tradition in Philosophy: God and Metaphysics" in the period from Aquinas to the Reformation, followed by a semester on contemporary trends among "Neo-Thomists" (assuming that Rahner and Lonergan can be thus classified). I will also have a seminar on Rahner's theology and a course, which will probably be my continuing major lecture course from now on, on comparative dogmatics or symbolics. I am not sure what the Catholic name for it in English would be, but the Germans call it *Konfessionskunde*. It's a comparative study of the major theological dogmatic traditions in Christendom—Catholic, Protestant, and Orthodox. Perhaps you are familiar with the book by Algermessen, which is the standard Roman Catholic work on the subject.

INTERVIEWER: Protestant Bishop Hans Lilje of Hannover said in 1957: "Each generation of Protestants must re-think the decisions of the sixteenth century. We must be able to say why we today are not Roman Catholics." Do you think that this is still a pressing task for contemporary Protestantism?

DR. LINDBECK: In terms of the view of nature and the development of doctrine that is so important today, I think that it is the obligation of the Church at *all times* constantly to re-think its understanding of revelation in light of the situation in which it now exists—which is always somewhat different from previous situations. But doctrine must also be seen in the light of the heritage of the Church, the tradition in which the Church has understood revelation in the past. Bishop Lilje's recommendation seems to me to be simply saying that Protestants must carry out the task that is a fundamental task within all Christian traditions. We all must re-think the meaning of God's revelation to us in terms of the present situation.

INTERVIEWER: As a Protestant theologian, how do you look on the reforming character of the Protestant Church? In other words, do you feel that the Protestant Church, which began as a reform movement, has become a permanent, independent reality?

DR. LINDBECK: There is a sharp division among Protestants on this question. There are two possible options. Some would think of the Protestant Reformation as *constitutive* of a new type of Christianity. Others would consider the Reformation as being in essence a *corrective* reality within the Church.

INTERVIEWER: Didn't the reformers themselves have primarily a corrective intention?

DR. LINDBECK: That would be more true of Luther than Calvin. Already by the second generation of Protestants, which Calvin represents, you get a kind of hardening of the lines on the question of church order. By and large, Calvin tended to think of the task of the Reformation as that of re-establishing the original order of the Church, which he thought of as having been more or less totally lost in the course of the centuries. In this, there was a sharp contrast with the basic Lutheran view, which saw the matter of order as that of reforming the Catholic order in the Church. There was no opposition to the historical episcopacy for the Lutherans, since they justified their developing an ordering of the Church that was outside the historical order as an emergency measure. It was something that they hoped would be transitory and temporary. On this question, you have to distinguish between the Reformation tradition as represented by Calvin and Luther.

INTERVIEWER: What would be the arguments of those who opt for the Reformation as constitutive?

DR. LINDBECK: For one thing, there is the question of *sola fide* and justification. They appear to hold that this insight into the meaning of the Pauline doctrine is fundamentally different from anything that had existed before—perhaps it didn't even exist in the mind of St. Paul. This would be one point on which the constitutive group would differ from the original reformers who thought of the doctrine of justification as simply a re-establishment of the Pauline doctrine. The development of historical scholarship has shown that one cannot identify the Reformation doctrine of justification and the Pauline doctrine. The Reformation doctrine presupposes the whole development of Augustinian individualistic-predestinarianism and of the penitential practice of the Middle Ages that concentrated on the problem of comforting the anguished conscience. To put it in modern categories, the Reformation doctrine of justification is more existentialist than it is in St. Paul, where it is more eschatological. In St. Paul, there is a greater emphasis on what God is doing in *His* world than on the individual, authentic self-understanding. When the Reformation's more individualistic and existentialized understanding of justification is made central to the Christian faith (that is, constitutive), then it becomes something fundamentally new and can't be incorporated into the historical Catholic tradition.

INTERVIEWER: How would those who hold the corrective view answer this?

DR. LINDBECK: They would agree with the historical analysis regarding the difference between the Reformation understanding of justification and the doctrine of St. Paul. But they would say that one has to view the Reformation insight like all other doctrinal insights as historically conditioned. Thus, the reformers understood the Gospel in terms of concrete problems and circumstances. But must it follow from this that the particular formation of the doctrine of justification at the time of the Reformation is forever an article of faith by which the Church stands and falls? Therefore, those who hold a corrective view of the Reformation ask if it is not possible now—in different circumstances—to see the basic thrust of Trent on justification and the Reformation teaching as complementary rather than opposed. They would agree with Hans Küng's analysis of the relation of Catholic and Protestant views of justification.

INTERVIEWER: Do you personally subscribe to the corrective interpretation?

DR. LINDBECK: Very definitely. I cannot conceive of Protestantism as a separate branch of Christendom. We must consider Protestantism as a reform movement within the Universal Church, and its purpose is to assist in the formation of circumstances that make its separate existence unnecessary. It works toward eventual reunion. I don't use the word "return," even though I can think of an objective sense in which it may be used correctly. But, psychologically, the word has been thoroughly spoiled for us.

I can also agree with Karl Rahner who once said that he could conceive of a Catholic theologian holding a genuinely Reformation position and remaining a good and loyal member of the Church. This person, of course, would understand the Church to have a closer or denser historical relationship to the original revelation than other communities. He would be obligated to remain in the Church unless the Church by her highest teaching authority insisted that he believe something that he felt was directly contrary to the Gospel. As far as I can see, it would be very hard to demonstrate such a contrariety. There would, on this view, be no need for a "Reformation" Roman Catholic to understand either the Marian dogmas or papal infallibility as clearly directly contrary to the Gospel.

INTERVIEWER: Do you have any difficulty with these dogmas?

DR. LINDBECK: My difficulty with them—and I think this would be generally true of those who hold to the corrective view of the Reformation—is that the Catholic Church has dogmatized matters that cannot be dogmatized. There would be no fundamental problem if the Roman Catholic stance had remained that of the Orthodox—to see such teachings as theological opinions in the technical sense. A Protestant might say that these teachings have such a relationship to our earliest testimonies to revelation that, even though they are acceptable theological opinions, they cannot be dogmatized, because they are clearly not required by the *norma normans non normata*.

INTERVIEWER: But the fact is that certain teachings *have* been dogmatized.

DR. LINDBECK: Yes they have. And where do we go from there? You can comment on this from the point of view of what it means for someone who is *within* the Roman Catholic community and what it means for one who is *outside* this community. For the latter, the problem is not so much with a particular dogma, but whether the Church as a teaching body has the right to speak infallibly about these particular truths. However, it is important to go on to analyze these problems more precisely. I think that for non-Catholics—certainly for Orthodox and on a more implicit level for Protestants—to question the right of the Church to dogmatize one is *not* questioning the fact that some of the decisions of the Church are irreversible. I suppose it would be possible to interpret infallibility in such a way as to make it more or less equivalent to irreversibility. Then we must investigate the criteria for determining when dogma is irreversible.

INTERVIEWER: The witness of Scripture would be a primary criterion.

DR. LINDBECK: By all means. The Church in making a dogmatic decision must submit herself to the superior authority of the primary witness to the original revelation—namely, Scripture. So that a decision which is not demanded by Scripture becomes a decision on a lower level than one that is demanded by Scripture. The way in which one distinguishes these two levels of decision is by saying that there are decisions that are dogmas and other decisions that are less than dogmatic and might be called pastoral.

INTERVIEWER: Is there any other criterion that should be used in determining dogma?

DR. LINDBECK: Another criterion that the Protestant would insist on—this time in conformity with the Orthodox—is that a doctrinal decision becomes permanent and irrevocable in terms of its acceptance by the Universal Church. It thus becomes the reflection of the belief of the Church, rather than a purely juridical, definable act of a specific authority.

INTERVIEWER: Does the Protestant principle of *sola scriptura* apply here also?

DR. LINDBECK: The actual operative superiority and significance of Scripture in the life of the Church has to be emphasized. I am talking here about the original deposit of faith that is summed up in the culminating revelation of Jesus Christ. If the Church is to make the fact of the finality of revelation really operative in its life, then it must constantly check, judge, and review everything it does in light of Scripture. One cannot identify formal, dogmatic statements about Scripture and the *Magisterium* with the operative significance of Scripture and the Church.

INTERVIEWER: We must say, therefore, that there should be a dialogue between the Church and Scripture.

DR. LINDBECK: Yes, there is a dialogue between the Church's doctrine and revelation as witnessed by Scripture. The Church is in dialogue with its starting point; it allows itself to be questioned by that starting point. There is a danger in every church that its responses to the original revelation will tend to rival and substitute for the revelation itself. Then you have a kind of illegitimate supplementation pretending to be on the same level as revelation. The significance of *sola scriptura* is as a kind of additional assistance to the Church to keep itself constantly in subjection to the original revelation. However, it doesn't guarantee it.

Protestants, and this is true of those who hold the constitutive interpretation of the Reformation, can absolutize an historically conditioned, optional development so that it comes to have the same rank as the original revelation. Yet conversely, even in the absence of the protective dogma of *sola scriptura* and the substitution for it of an incorrect understanding of the authority of the *Magisterium,* it is still possible, from a Protestant point of view, that a church could effectively subject itself to the authority of the original revelation. I suppose this is what Karl Barth had in mind when he said that Protestants should consider the possibility that the Roman Catholic Church in its present renewal is actually being more faithful to the Word of God than are the Protestant churches.

INTERVIEWER: Do you foresee a thoroughgoing renewal in the Protestant church?

DR. LINDBECK: If the present kinds of development continue, it seems very unlikely that the Protestant church will undergo a renewal and reform of a depth and extensiveness that is taking place within the Roman Catholic Church. The reason for this is obvious. The magisterial and disciplinary authority of the Protestant churches to make effective decisions on a communal level has atrophied. It is extraordinarily difficult for Protestant groups, either as individual groups or as a totality, to make common, effective reformatory decisions. They cannot make decisions like those expressed in *De ecclesia* or *De sacra liturgia* of Vatican II, with all their potentially immense significance for the restructuring of the life of the Church. Such decisions would be much more difficult to make for Protestants because of their magisterial weakness.

INTERVIEWER: Does Tillich mean the same thing when he says that more "catholic substance" has been preserved in Catholicism than in Protestantism?

DR. LINDBECK: What we are talking about here is the *reason* why it has been preserved. Also one would have to ask oneself precisely what is meant by Tillich's phrase. I'm not sure that everyone would agree with everything that Tillich had in mind. Yet I would say that the sacramental presence, the Real Presence of Our Lord in the Eucharist and other sacramental celebrations, has been much more vividly maintained in Catholicism. The sense of sacramental presence has largely vanished from the concrete life of Protestant groups —most of them at least. Clearly, it is easier to *reform* the sense of sacramental presence than it is to *restore* it. That's why liturgical renewal is so much more difficult in Protestantism than in Catholicism.

INTERVIEWER: Has the liturgical renewal made any advances in Protestantism?

DR. LINDBECK: The liturgical renewal in its formal phase has been active and progressive in Protestantism and not only in Anglecanism and Lutheranism, but also in the less historically minded churches. You could say that it has progressed as far as it had in Catholicism before the Second Vatican Council. But how in the world are the Protestant churches ever going to make a common decision about it? The liturgical renewal in the Catholic Church has been immensely and immeasurably accelerated by the decisions of Vatican II. I think that this has helped us, too. On the practical level the Protestant liturgical renewal has run into problems and the Catholic Church has had the same ones. The liturgical movement in this country before Vatican II had relatively little effect on the overwhelming majority of Catholic parishes. This is true even today, I suppose. Both Protestants and Catholics have active groups working diligently for liturgical changes and improvements, but they have very little impact on most parishes.

INTERVIEWER: Were there any special influences during your student days that directed your interest to ecumenical theology?

DR. LINDBECK: I will limit myself to academic considerations, to what might be called the level of intellectual history. In college and the seminary I became very interested in proofs for the existence of God. The skepticism of modern man became a problem for me. Being of a somewhat rationalistic turn of mind, I very much wanted to know whether or not the existence of God could really be demonstrated. In that way, I got interested in the classical proofs of St. Thomas and in the works of his modern interpreters, Gilson and Maritain. It was through this road that I really first began working with Catholics. I went on to do my dissertation on Duns Scotus, and I spent some time as an auditor at the Pontifical Institute of Medieval Studies in Toronto. I also spent close to two years in Paris working largely with Roman Catholics on medieval matters at Ecole Pratique des Hautes Etudes.

INTERVIEWER: What was the immediate result of these associations?

DR. LINDBECK: It made me very much aware of Roman Catholicism. I had what I judge is a typical reaction for both Catholics and Protestants when one discovers that there are vast numbers of this strange group, that one had always looked at with suspicion, who really have many common beliefs. I recognized that the unity between myself and Catholics was the deepest of all unities—belief in the same Lord and Master. Jesus Christ is the center of our lives. I was deeply moved by this, because naturally I had a whole set of stereotypes about Catholics.

INTERVIEWER: Was it at that point when you began to work on the Reformation?

DR. LINDBECK: I had been interested in the Reformation before this, but this led me to a greater interest on the question of what really was involved in the Reformation protest. My own heritage and my intellectual leanings led me to do a lot of work on Luther and others. I started to wonder about the possibilities of *rapprochement* and of overcoming the division that took place at the Reformation.

INTERVIEWER: Was there any one man who influenced you more than others?

DR. LINDBECK: I have a hard time saying that any individual

professor was determinative of this interest. The *way* in which I have approached matters has been very deeply influenced by some of my teachers. But I don't know of any of them who actually shared this interest. Gilson at Toronto and Paul Vignaux in Paris were not particularly interested in the ecumenical problem. So my interest in ecumenism was more a by-product of my studies rather than a direct suggestion by any of my teachers. However, I would say that the person who most influenced me in this regard was somebody who was never a teacher of mine, but with whom I worked in very close association in Europe when I was there in 1957 and again in the summer of 1960 and 1962–64. His name is Professor Skydsgaard of the University of Copenhagen, and he has been deeply interested in ecumenical problems since the 1930's.

INTERVIEWER: What future do you see for the ecumenical movement now that the Council is over?

DR. LINDBECK: It's hard to know where to start on a question like that! There are so many things that one could say. Perhaps the easiest way to put it would be to say that it seems to me that we are moving into a period in which intensive and persistent activity needs to be carried on at many levels. There is work to be done on the level of theological decisions and exchanges; on the level of co-operation in social and ethical issues; and on the level of common worship, *communicatio in sacris*. My own impression is that we are beyond the stage at which the prudential consideration of the threat of indifferentism is a major factor any longer. I don't think that *communicatio in sacris* in the present period is likely to lead to indifferentism. We also need grass roots lay exchanges. The *Living Room Dialogues* are excellent for this. All these things have to be pushed simultaneously and as much as possible. It is futile for one thing to move ahead of the others.

INTERVIEWER: Recently, in an address, you referred to the "decision theory" of doctrinal development. Would you please elaborate on that?

DR. LINDBECK: Any attempt to place the dogmas of the Church in historical context must take seriously modern historiographical work. This leads in the direction of what I call decision theory.

The Protestants talk about it a great deal. Germans use the word *entscheidung,* which means decision, for dogma. A *dogma* is a decision. The idea is that the Church from time to time is confronted with the necessity of choosing between alternatives, and from this decision emerges a dogma.

INTERVIEWER: How would this relate to Newman's theory of organic doctrinal development?

DR. LINDBECK: I can perhaps best answer that question by briefly sketching the two theories. In Newman's theory, I think it would be fair to say that you have a great use of organic analogies. The development of dogma is the result of the fact that truths that were present in germinal form in the beginning gradually unfold. What was implicit becomes explicit. The consciousness of the Church of the original revelation becomes more and more articulate. The growth is cumulative and continuous.

In the decision theory, one thinks of the problem in more historical terms. Doctrine in general and dogma in particular constitute the responses of the Church in historical circumstances relative to the revelation that is witnessed in Scripture. Tradition, too, must be used. The newness of a dogma is determined by the situation from which revelation is viewed. The historical circumstances in which the Church interprets revelation change continually. Instead of continuous, cumulative development, you have the history of dogmatic growth becoming a matter of looking at the same object from different perspectives.

INTERVIEWER: Don't you have to account for the element of cumulativeness?

DR. LINDBECK: Certainly. This cannot be avoided in any theory of development. If the Church is to be responsible in its consideration of what revelation means for us in our particular circumstances, then it must take into account how it has understood the same data in the past. In the decision theory, there is an enlargement of insight and understanding that occurs when you see the same thing from different perspectives. In a cumulative organic development, that which existed in the past provides the foundation of the new development. In contrast to this, I would say that while we have to understand the past, we must understand it in terms of relevant intelligibility. This does not mean that the Church was wrong in her past decisions. It simply means that we must see these decisions as historically conditioned, and their relevance for the present might be minimal.

INTERVIEWER: It might help to clarify matters if you could illustrate what you mean with a concrete example.

DR. LINDBECK: Chalcedon would be a good example. Karl Rahner discusses the Chalcedonian decision that was directed, in part, against the Monophysites, which were a constant peril for the Church. The "two natures" formula becomes understood very differently, Rahner points out, in a situation in which Monophysitism is not a major problem or where one is not aware that it is a major problem. In other words, the formula of true God and true man can easily come to be understood "unconsciously," as he phrases it, in terms of half divine and half human rather than fully divine and fully human. In a situation in which the peril comes from those who deny Christ's divinity, the formula might mean, "unconsciously," that Christ is not fully human. The emphasis might change. In the Monophysite sitution, it was quite clear that the Church was affirming that Jesus Christ was fully man. But in the later period, because of the absence of the Monophysite peril, you have, Rahner suggests, a kind of implicit Monophysitism present in the Church. Then, too, you have the problem of the language used in the Chalcedonian formula. Is the language of the two "natures," based as it was on Greek philosophical thought, altogether adequate or relevant to us in our day? This is what I mean when I say that a particular doctrinal formulation may become less relevant in the course of time when one looks at it in its concrete historical situation. You can say this and also say that the Church decided the only way it could have according to the original circumstances. This should not be condemned as relativism. To be sure, dogmas are historically conditioned and so in a sense are relative: they are relative to a situation. However, they do present one particular, true aspect of the reality being dealt with—whether this is relevant to every age or not.

INTERVIEWER: How can a Catholic theologian use the decision

theory of development to explain the Marian dogmas that he claims are implicitly contained in Scripture?

DR. LINDBECK: I think Roman Catholics have grave difficulties whichever theory is adopted, not only with the Marian dogmas, but also with papal infallibility and primacy as including immediate and universal jurisdiction. If you take the decision theory by itself, I think it would be possible to interpret dogmatic development, as a whole, *through* Trent as depending on a kind of direct, objectively verifiable progress rooted in Scripture. In other words, Roman Catholics could argue that the various dogmas through Trent are *directly necessitated* by the scriptural witness. This is more correct than to say that they are implicitly contained in Scripture. In one sense, the Church cannot deduce any of her dogmatic truths from Scripture. The conceptuality of Nicea, for example, is not found in Scripture. But one can say that when the Church is confronted with a dispute in a matter vital to the faith, it must make a decision. In the case of Nicea and after, when the choice was between *homoousion* and *homoiousion,* the Church had to decide for *homoousion* as the only alternative consonant with Scripture. If the Church had existed in India and not in the Greek world, it presumably would not have come up with the same formula. We just don't know.

However, the papal and the Marian dogmas do not seem to be required by Scripture in any comparable way. Particularly in reference to the latter, the question arises whether the Church, even from the Roman Catholic point of view, was ever in a position where it had to settle the issues one way or another. Could it not have left them open as the Orthodox have done, who by and large have the same Marian beliefs as Roman Catholics, but refuse to make them into dogmas? Further, and more crucially, the papal and the Marian dogmas cannot be represented on objective exegetical grounds as the only ones among the available alternative views that can be harmonized with Scripture. These dogmas go beyond Scripture in such a way that the Protestant fears that, in practice, even if not in theory, they add to the supremely authoritative public revelation that centers in Christ, which was—as the traditional phrase puts it—"closed with the death of the last apostle" (or "apostolic writer") and is testified to by the Bible. In short, from the perspective of Reformation Protestantism, the main difficulty with the most recent phase of Roman Catholic doctrinal development is that it seems to involve something suspiciously like "new revelation" and thereby threatens to undermine the sole lordship of the Incarnate Lord over theology and the Church.

I hasten to add, however, that the present biblical renewal in Roman Catholicism represents a major countervailing tendency, and that, as even so staunch a Protestant as Karl Barth has remarked, Protestant churches may find, if they refuse renewal, that the Roman Catholic Church is in practice, even if not in all of its doctrinal statements, becoming more faithful to the lordship of Christ and the biblical witness than they are.

❖❖

GEORGE A. LINDBECK was born in Loyang, Hanan, China, on March 10th, 1923. He received his secondary education in American preparatory schools in North China, Hongkong, and Korea. He earned his B.A. from Gustavus Adolphus College in 1943, his B.D. from Yale in 1946, and his Ph.D. from Yale in 1955. He has also studied at the Pontifical Institute of Medieval Studies at the University of Toronto and the Ecole pratique des Hautes Etudes at the University of Paris. Since 1949 he has taught at Yale and at present is Associate Professor of Historical Theology. Dr. Lindbeck was "delegated observer" from the Lutheran World Federation to the Second Vatican Council and Research Professor of the Lutheran Foundation for Ecumenical Research in Strasbourg, France. He is married and has one daughter.

In addition to having written numerous articles on medieval theology and contemporary Roman Catholicism, he is editor of *Dialogue on the Way: Protestants Report from Rome on the Second Vatican Council.*

Henri de Lubac

Spry and trim at seventy-two, Henri de Lubac is, as John Courtney Murray once described him to me, "a princely fellow." Despite a bit of shrapnel in his head from World War I that causes him frequent pain, he appears ebullient and energetic at the time of our interview. His short white hair and clean-cut features give him a boyish, almost puckish look. Our conversation is in French, which he speaks very quickly. Marvelous facial expressions and graphic gestures accompany his words. He is at first alarmed to discover that I plan to record our interview. However, after I solemnly promise (as a Benedictine, not as a journalist, he insists) that I will show him a copy of the text before it is published, he acquiesces. My first question is about Teilhard de Chardin.

INTERVIEWER: Did you know Père Teilhard de Chardin personally?

FATHER DE LUBAC: I was much younger then Père Teilhard, much younger indeed. Nevertheless, we were good friends for many years. He was a fine man—very kind and always eager to encourage younger people. He came from an excellent family, and his parents were totally Christian in the best sense of that word. His mother was a very saintly woman who was a vigorous apostle of the Sacred Heart. Père Teilhard frequently paid tribute to her, and he felt that it was to her that, fundamentally, he owed the best of his thought. As you know, I have written two books about Père Teilhard. One is *La pensée religieuse du Père Teilhard de Chardin* and the other is *La Prière du Père Teilhard de Chardin*. I have tried to defend him against unjust accusations, some of which were not only false, but also calumnious. I have also tried to bring out the religious and spiritual aspects of his work.

INTERVIEWER: In your writings, you also mentioned certain reservations about his theories.

FATHER DE LUBAC: In *some* areas, yes. I have never attempted to make a general criticism or analysis of his work, because I do not feel that I am competent. For instance, I have left aside any discussion of the purely scientific aspects of his teachings.

INTERVIEWER: What value does the Teilhardian vision have for modern theology?

FATHER DE LUBAC: First of all, I would say that there are many admirable things in his writings. However, I have the impression, and I may be wrong, that as he got older, Père Teilhard more and more systematized his thought. The result was that his thought became more restricted or narrow. I believe that the finest and most beautiful things he has written date before World War II, although he also wrote some fine things after it. Secondly, I believe that he will have much influence on theology, precisely because he is not a professional theologian. You know that it is not always the theologians who are responsible for progress in theology, just as it is not always the philosophers who push philosophy forward. It is often men who are on the fringe or outside a particular science who, because of their contributions, force those working in the field to transform some of their perspectives. Père Teilhard, for example, because of the vision of the world that he proposed, has raised questions in Christology that the theologians must dig into.

INTERVIEWER: Would you say that Père Teilhard was a good theologian?

FATHER DE LUBAC: Yes. However, there are some of his critics who, either to criticize him or to excuse him, say that he had a poor theological background. This is not exactly true. He had a solid theological course at Ore Place in Hastings, England. Each year, for four years, his professors selected him to take part in the annual theological *"disputatio."* He proved on these occasions that he had a good grasp of the classical sources. Yet, it is true to say that he was not a professional theologian. He had other interests. Between his philosophy and theology, he spent three years teaching physics and natural history in Cairo, and right before the war in 1914, he was sent to Paris to prepare for a career in science. Later on, his approach was more spiritual than theological, if one can distinguish these two.

INTERVIEWER: For Teilhard, then, human experience was integrated within the broader context of Christian commitment.

FATHER DE LUBAC: Yes, his experience was at the same time human and Christian. This explains the great hold he was able to have on people's minds and hearts. They saw in him a unique blending of human and Christian experience. His temperament, which was most attractive; his religious sentiment, developed by his fine family; and his scientific genius—all these elements fitted together perfectly. Yet, he did not confuse these various elements, and he knew how to distinguish between nature and grace as well as how to separate scientific reflection from faith.

INTERVIEWER: Do you think that Teilhard's influence can be seen in the documents of the Second Vatican Council?

FATHER DE LUBAC: I feel that Père Teilhard had no *direct* influence on the Council texts. But he certainly did help (he was by no means the only one) to create an atmosphere, an orientation that affected the Council. It was not surprising that his name was mentioned in the *aula* of St. Peter's both favorably and unfavorably.

INTERVIEWER: Can we say that it is in the *Constitution on the Church in the Modern World,* that Teilhard's influence is most in evidence?

FATHER DE LUBAC: I regard this text as a whole to be excellent. However, I believe that if the *redactores* had on some occasions been more inspired by the thought of Teilhard, they would have made the text more strongly Christian and pastoral. This document speaks about the temporal order, about our love for the world, and how the work of God is carried out by man in time, in the world. The text correctly shows that in the last analysis everything we do in this world must be in terms of our final, eternal destiny. In Teilhard, there is an eschatology that is stronger and more coherent. Admittedly, it would have been difficult to reproduce this in a conciliar text without introducing a personal element that would have been unsuitable in those circumstances. While Teilhard is a man passionately taken up with this world and concerned fully with the work that man must do in this world, he is for all this a man who, like St. Paul, realizes that this world will pass. He showed in his own life that a person must dedicate himself to his work wholeheartedly, but detach himself from everything that is transitory. Everything must pass through death in order to be transfigured. Teilhard's life is a vivid argument against those of less vigorous faith who say that concern for the world means losing oneself hopelessly in the world. The enthusiastic interest with which he viewed man in his earthly setting, far from turning him away from the eternal world, directed all his vigor and optimism to the eternal. He always considered illusory human desires in relationship to Christian hope.

INTERVIEWER: Do Teilhard's references to transcedence and cosmic evolution reflect Eastern thought-patterns?

FATHER DE LUBAC: I don't think that Père Teilhard was directly influenced by Oriental thought. However, it is possible that he was influenced by Vladimir Soloviev. A small book on Soloviev has just come out in Germany from Herder that was written by Father Karl Vladimir Truhlar, a professor of spirituality at the Gregorian University. I have not yet read the book, but I have spoken to the author. He compares Teilhard and Soloviev. When Teilhard was still young, he could have come into contact with the thought of Soloviev by a popular book by Father Michel d'Herbigny. It is quite likely that Teilhard read this book, although I don't believe that he even mentions Soloviev by name in any of his writings.

In a more general way, I would say that there is a certain resemblance, a certain atmosphere that is common to both Teilhard and Oriental Christian thought. This may be explained by the fact that Teilhard during his theology course was a reader of Greek Patristic texts. St. Irenaeus and St. Gregory of Nyssa were his favorites, and he refers to them occasionally in his writings. It is not surprising that he would have much in common with Eastern Christians. More than once have I had Easterners tell me that they felt at ease in the thought of Teilhard; they detect something familiar to them, a certain feeling or "resonance" that appeals to them.

INTERVIEWER: Was there any *rapprochement* between Père Teilhard and the French existentialists?

FATHER DE LUBAC: Mutual repulsion. Here is what happened. Père Teilhard spent the whole of World War II in China. Right after the war, toward the end of 1945, he came back to France. He returned by plane and was forced to leave many of his belongings in Peking. They haven't been recovered yet, but we have some reason to believe that they are not completely lost. When he arrived in Paris, he found himself in the midst of "black" existentialism, that excessively excited atmosphere that followed the Liberation. He strongly opposed it. He gave several lectures that were followed by debates in various Paris *salons*. These meetings often became quite heated. It was from this time that some accused him of being overly naïve and simplistic. For him, existentialism was a destructive thing, and he opposed it with horror. Of course, as sometimes happens, he did not fully understand the people who questioned him so vigorously.

INTERVIEWER: You have written several books on Buddhism. How did you first get interested in that field?

FATHER DE LUBAC: In 1929, only two weeks before classes began, I was named professor of fundamental theology at the theology school at Lyons. At the end of that year, I was called to the office of our dean, Father Podechard, a Sulpician. He said that at most schools in France, even normal schools, courses in the history of religions were being offered. He felt that it was not right that our young priests who were studying for the doctorate in theology should be ignorant of these matters. Since the school at Lyons did not have enough money to establish a special chair for this, the dean asked me if I would teach a course in the history of religion and incorporate it in my course of fundamental theology. I was foolish enough to accept his offer. I was not at all prepared. I had never taken any formal courses in that subject; I hadn't written any books on it, nor did I know the necessary Oriental languages. However, I managed somehow to get a course together. At that time, we had cycle courses, which meant that every year the courses changed. I never worked harder in my life. It was necessary to take broad topics, and one of the subjects I lectured on frequently was Buddhism. Later, in 1950, when I had some leisure time, I was able to work over my courses, and using the Paris libraries, I could check my citations and references. This way I was able to publish three books on Buddhism.

INTERVIEWER: In 1951, you wrote that despite many good popular works on Buddhism, this subject remained, even for cultured people, a *terra incognita*. Is that still true today?

FATHER DE LUBAC: I think so. I will tell you a story that will illustrate what I mean. In my book, *Rencontre du Bouddisme et de l'Occident,* I wrote that people are so badly informed about Buddhism that they confuse it with Hinduism. I sent out a few complimentary copies of the book, and a few weeks later I received a most enthusiastic letter that began: "You have written a wonderful book on Hinduism." This proved to me, first, that the person had never read the book and, secondly, that I was correct in saying that there is great confusion in this area.

INTERVIEWER: Are there any religious insights in Buddhism that would be especially useful for Christians today?

FATHER DE LUBAC: That is a very difficult question to answer in a few words. The expression "useful" is not suitable; it's not found in the vocabulary of Buddhism. Buddhism, as the world's largest religious phenomenon (if we can speak of "religion" here—"religion" is analogical or perhaps even equivocal) has a view of the spiritual world totally different from ours. Above all, it is a mystical spirituality. Buddhists believe that one can arrive at "deliverance" only by passing through some kind of monastic state. Buddhism is essentially mystical, and one cannot approach "deliverance" until one has first rejected exterior, restricting elements in the world. But this does not really touch the heart of the matter. . . .

INTERVIEWER: Bergson has said that Buddhism is an incomplete mysticism because it lacks warmth. Do you agree?

FATHER DE LUBAC: What Bergson says is true, but that does not explain the difference between Buddhist and Christian mysticism. There is much more to be said on this subject, but we don't have the time now. I would suggest you read a book that has just appeared, *La mystique et les mystiques.* It is a group effort published by Desclée de Brouwer and edited by my confrere and former provincial, Père André Ravier. It compares the various religions of the world in terms of their basic spiritual intuitions. There is a chapter on Buddhism and Hinduism and an excellent treatment of Protestant mysticism. It is the best work of its size on the subject, and I hope that it will be translated into English.

INTERVIEWER: Romano Guardini has great respect for Buddha. He feels that Buddha might be considered a precursor of Jesus Christ, and that we must explain the significance of the teachings of this genius of the East. What are your thoughts on this?

FATHER DE LUBAC: I have great respect for Guardini's opinion, because he knows his subject well. I think that we might find something analogous to Buddhism in the Old Testament in the writings of Ecclesiastes, Coheleth. The *vanitas vanitatum*—the nothingness of the things of this world—reminds me of the spirit of Buddhism, which produces emptiness. One cannot desire *nirvana* even with the purest kind of desire, for in so doing you would have in your desire something worldly, and this would be an imperfection. Buddhism is, in a certain sense, the *vanitas vanitatum* pushed to its ultimate limit.

INTERVIEWER: In your book, *The Drama of Atheist Humanism*, you said that the main element in positivist humanism is the annihilation of the human person.

FATHER DE LUBAC: That book was published in 1945, although parts of it were first found in a series of studies that appeared in *Cité nouvelle*, from 1941 to 1943. It is out of date now, because much has happened in the last twenty years; there has been a considerable development in contemporary atheism. However, if I were writing it now I would replace the word "annihilation" with the word "disintegration."

INTERVIEWER: An American philosopher recently called Simone Weil a modern Gnostic because she insists on the great abyss between God and the world and feels that any action on one's own behalf is hopeless. Do you agree with that interpretation?

FATHER DE LUBAC: There is certainly truth in it. One can discover Gnostic tendencies in some of her writings, but other things she says seem to contradict that. She is still popular in France, and in certain cases her influence is good. She loved God and Christ, but she never joined the Church. Even though she rejected Judaism completely, she refused to become a Catholic. In a way, she was an anarchist who feared the social structure of the Church. Throughout her life, she was a great admirer of the Greeks. In that, she was not at all in conformity with the fashion. Platonism today has a "bad press," and it is misunderstood. When people hear the word Platonism, they think of the soul on one side and the body on the other; one must despise the things of the body completely. This is a caricature of true Platonism.

INTERVIEWER: Could you tell us something of your intellectual formation and the men who influenced you?

FATHER DE LUBAC: I entered the Jesuit novitiate in England in 1913. At that time, the Jesuit Province of Lyons had all their houses in England. I was drafted in 1915 and spent almost five years in the army. On my return, I had a great thirst for knowledge, and I read everything I could. I read the Fathers, especially St. Irenaeus. I also read some French translations of Newman, since at that time my English was not up to the difficult style of Newman.

There was one man who influenced not only myself but my whole generation. That was Père de Grandmaison. He was a professor of theology for about ten years and also at one point superior of the Jesuit house of studies in Paris. What an admirable man he was. He was an excellent religious, a man of exceeding good will, and deeply spiritual. He had great intellectual, literary, and artistic gifts. During the war, I think it was around 1915 or 1916, he wrote a long article on Jesus Christ for the *Dictionary of Apologetics* of Father D'Alès. The article was a résumé of his course in fundamental theology. It was excellent, and I read it several times. He wrote many articles, and he once published a series of articles on personal religion in *Études*. These were gathered together in a book after his death and were translated into Italian by the present Pope when he was a Monsignor.

INTERVIEWER: Did you know Father Rousselot?

FATHER DE LUBAC: Pierre Rousselot wrote a famous doctoral dissertation at the Sorbonne in 1908 on the intellectualism of St. Thomas. Gilson in the last few years has cited it on several occasions. Père Rousselot was something of a genius—what a pity that he died so young. He was killed at Eparges, near Verdun, in the spring of 1915. He was only thirty-five. I never knew him, but he was a close friend of Père Teilhard. They spent a year together at Ore Place (1908–9), and they met again in Paris from 1912 to 1914, where Rousselot was professor of dogma in the theological faculty.

INTERVIEWER: What of Teilhard de Chardin? Did he influence you?

FATHER DE LUBAC: It was not until 1922 that I got to know Teilhard. By that time I was already twenty-six years old. I began to correspond with him, and occasionally we would meet. His influence, if you will, was by degrees; it was never an overwhelming kind of influence. I am no Teilhardian. I love Père Teilhard deeply, and I admire many of the things that he has written. But I cannot say that I am a Teilhardian or that he has left his mark on me. Perhaps I was not interested enough in science, I don't know.

INTERVIEWER: How would you describe your theological method?

FATHER DE LUBAC: Quite honestly, I have no special theological method, and my personal contribution to theology, as far as doctrine is concerned, is meager. Directed by circumstances, I have read much, and I have tried to explore, in certain fundamental areas, the totality of Christian thought as it appeared in the course of history in order to show its richness, its organic depth, its unity in diversity, and its creative vigor that is evident even today. Thus, I have worked on the relationship between the Church and the Eucharist, the spiritual understanding of Scripture, and the fundamental problem of the "supernatural" end. The eternal problems of the knowledge of God and of the mystical life have also been the subject of several of my writings, even when these appeared to deal with a more specific subject. I have likewise published the posthumous writings of many of my confreres whose work was most valuable. For example: Yves de Montcheuil, Auguste Valensin, and Pierre Teilhard de Chardin. In all my work, my only ambition has always been and still is to make the great Christian tradition known and loved in order that contemporary thought may derive nourishment from it. I believe more than ever that a deep grasp of this tradition, which is never a burden but a living force, will allow us to accomplish the work of renewal that the recent Council has enjoined.

INTERVIEWER: As one who possesses an enviable "habit" of theology, would you please give a few words of advice to beginning theologians.

FATHER DE LUBAC: Very briefly, I would tell them not to spurn the interior, spiritual life that in many places is minimized. Because of a false idea of community in the Church, some people run the risk of misinterpreting the value of a rich and vibrant spiritual life. This is needed, of course, for all people, but even more for Christians and especially for priests and theologians. There is no substitute for a well-developed, solid spirituality. Theology cannot be separated from the life of faith. Furthermore, critical research in the essential areas of theology must go hand in hand with spiritual enthusiasm and prayer. Otherwise, it quickly becomes dry, sterile, and misleading.

❖❖

HENRI DE LUBAC was born at Cambrai (Nord), France, on February 20th, 1896. He entered the Society of Jesus in 1913 and two years later was drafted into the French army. In the service until 1919, he was wounded in action and received the Croix de Guerre. From 1920 to 1928, he pursued his philosophical and theological studies at the Isle of Jersey, Canterbury, and Hastings in England and at the Jesuit Scholasticate in Lyons. In 1927, he was ordained a priest, and a year later, he received his doctorate in theology. He was named in 1929 Professor of Fundamental Theology and the History of Religions in the faculty of Catholic Theology at Lyons. At present, he is an honorary professor of that faculty and resides in Lyons. At the Second Vatican Council, he was a *peritus* and a member of the Theological Commission. He is a consultor for the Secretariat for Non-Christians and for the Secretariat for Non-Believers. Since 1953, he has been a member of the Institut de France (Académie des sciences morales). He was editor of *Recherches de science religieuse* from 1945 to 1950. He is a member of the Executive Editorial Committee of *Concilium*.

Father de Lubac in 1941 began, with J. Daniélou and C. Mondésert, *Sources Chrétiennes*—edited translations of ancient Christian literature, of which 118 volumes have appeared so far. He has written a great number of articles and nearly thirty books, which include: *Catholicism; Aspects of Buddhism; Surnaturel-études historiques; Paradoxes; The Un-Marxian Socialist; The Drama of Atheistic Humanism; The Splendour of the Church; Augustinisme et théologie moderne;* and *Teilhard de Chardin—The Man and His Meaning.*

Barnabas Ahern

This was perhaps the most difficult of all the interviews to arrange. Father Ahern was enthusiastic about the idea, but we could never settle on a suitable place to meet between his travels to Africa, Europe, and South America. We tried several times, but always without success. I finally managed to arrange a meeting in late August.

He is to arrive from Oregon via New Orleans in mid-morning, and I am to wait for him by the information booth in Grand Central Station, New York City, at high noon. I am there a few minutes before twelve, and clutching my tape recorder, I stand among the frantic, hurrying weekend travelers (more of them than ever because of the month-long airline strike). Commuters, campers, vacationers, and half a dozen priests pass, but no Father Ahern. Finally, just as my hopes begin to dwindle, I am startled by a light tap on the shoulder. I turn around, and there is Father Ahern, who, with a laugh in his voice, greets me with the words: "Good things come to those who wait." He is a tall, thin man, slightly stooped. His narrow face and thin features are quietly ascetic, belying his great energy and drive. He speaks quickly and excitedly in a Midwestern accent.

Our first stop is in the cool Oyster Bar in Grand Central for two bowls of clam stew. We then walk over to St. Agnes Church on 43rd and Lexington Ave. An obliging young curate who had known Father Ahern in Rome brings us to the pastor's comfortable room. Here, amid the sounds of the busy street and the muted rumble of the subways, we speak together of the ancient Scriptures.

INTERVIEWER: Father R. A. F. Mackenzie has defined biblical theology as "the doctrine of God contained in Scripture, analyzed and systematized in biblical categories." Do you think that is an adequate description?

FATHER AHERN: Yes, I think this description is both accurate and adequate. Perhaps, however, it would gain in clarity if the phrase "doctrine of God" were substituted by the fuller phrase, "the teaching about God and God's ways with man."

INTERVIEWER: Do you agree with the traditional placing of biblical theology in the category of what is called positive theology?

FATHER AHERN: Here we find ourselves in an area of semantics. There is undoubtedly a basic reason for distinguishing positive from speculative theology. Positive theology, which includes both biblical and patristic studies, is primarily concerned with the positive affirmations of revealed doctrine contained in Scripture and in the Fathers. Speculative theology, on the other hand, is chiefly concerned with the analysis and presentation of revealed truth in the patterns of thought that are peculiar to various cultures and philosophies. In our own day, however, the line of demarcation between these two areas of theology is growing ever more faint. On the one hand, scholars are becoming more aware that the affirmations contained in Scripture and in the writings of the Fathers were presented in the cultural, religious, and philosophic thought-patterns of the day. On the other hand, scholars working in the field of so-called speculative theology are utilizing more and more the new scholarly insights into the contents of Scripture and patristic sources. As a result of these new approaches in theology, the terms "positive" and "speculative" no longer serve as apt designations of the various areas of theological study. I believe, therefore, that today we should designate the various disciplines of theology with labels that are much more precise, e.g., Isaian theology, Pauline theology, Johannine theology, Platonic theology, Aristotelian theology, Thomistic theology, Scotian theology, etc. In theology, we have reached the age of specialization; general titles are no longer scientifically exact.

INTERVIEWER: How did St. Thomas consider biblical theology?

FATHER AHERN: The term "biblical theology," as referring to a precise kind of theological investigation, is wholly modern. For St. Thomas, all theology was biblical; like the Fathers of Vatican II, the Angelic Doctor regarded Sacred Scripture as "the soul of theology." It is true, he consistently unfolds the contents of revealed truth in the thought-patterns and categories of Aristotelian philosophy. But, as he makes clear in the very first question of the *Summa*, the "sacred doctrine" that he proposes rests wholly on the principles presented by divine revelation. Throughout all his writings, therefore, Thomas worked with the assurance that his theology was a human explication of the truths contained in the Bible. His commentaries on Sacred Scripture show that, though he lacked the modern scientific understanding of many aspects of the sacred text, he did have a penetrating insight into its doctrinal contents. This insight guided and inspired him in all his theological work. Hence, he often quoted Sacred Scripture and sought always to present its doctrine faithfully. As a result, though his writings show the structure of the scholastic method and of Aristotelian categories, the emergent doctrine is often a full and beautiful unfolding of the revealed doctrine contained in Sacred Scripture. I cite as an example St. Thomas' treatment of God in the first part of the *Summa*. True to the dichotomy of his human method, Thomas treats first of God as He is in Himself and then of God as He is in His activity. But when one views his doctrine as a whole, one realizes that in this bifurcate treatment Thomas has truly presented the God of the Scriptures.

INTERVIEWER: In reading Scripture, one gets the impression that the inspired writers are preoccupied with the *activity* of God.

FATHER AHERN: It is true that Scripture presents God as one who acts. In celebrating His attributes, the sacred writers make their affirmations within the context of His saving activity. Thus, for St. John, the being of God may be summed up in the action-phrase, "God is love" (*1 John* 4:16). One could even say that the world of God's being, as the Scripture envisages it, is the world of men whom God created for His glory. This glory itself is the radiance of His saving activity among men. A similar emphasis on functional activity is found in the biblical portrait of Christ. He is hailed as Son of God only at that moment when, through resurrection, He experiences His messianic enthronization and begins to act with the full saving power of His Father (cf. *Acts* 2:36; 13:33; *Romans* 1:4). In Scripture, therefore, the divinity of Jesus as *Kyrios* is intimately associated with His Resurrection precisely because, in the biblical perspective, divinity is always seen in the light of that saving power that belongs uniquely to God.

INTERVIEWER: You would say, then, that the biblical concept of God is not exclusively functional?

FATHER AHERN: Yes. It would be false to conclude that the biblical concept of God and of His Son is limited to the functional and phenomenological level. The living awareness that the sacred writers had of God's unique activity contained eminently a living awareness of God's unique being. In fact, because their thoughts about God and His Christ were so rooted in the "acts" of God, their knowledge of what divinity is in itself was much more real and true than thoughts about God ever could be if they were derived merely from philosophic speculation. Nothing could surpass John's revelation of the intimate life of God in Chapters 14-17 of the fourth Gospel. No affirmations of the unique being of God and of Christ could be more apodictic than Paul's quotations drawn from early Christian hymns (cf *1 Cor.* 8:5–6; *Phil.* 2:5–10; *Col.* 2:15-17). If some wonder at the paucity of such material in biblical writing, especially in comparison with the abundance of material on God's activity, it must be pointed out that the uniqueness of God's being is best witnessed to by the believer's silence about God. When one knows God truly in a living way, through contact with His activity, he feels that he really has very little to say about one whose transcendent being is almost totally above the thoughts of men: "One cannot lessen, nor increase, nor penetrate the wonders of the Lord. When a man ends he is only beginning, and when he stops he is still bewildered" (*Sir.* 18:4–5). If the writers of Scripture thus affirm the transcendence of God's works, how much more were they aware of the transcendence of His being.

INTERVIEWER: Oscar Cullmann has been criticized for concentrating solely on the functional level of Christology. Is this criticism justified?

FATHER AHERN: I think that this criticism is unjust. The critics of

Cullmann have argued wrongly, I believe, that he recognizes no other dimension in Christology except the functional. He is too firm a believer and too erudite a scholar to affirm that New Testament theology views Christ only from a functional perspective. It is true that Cullmann emphasizes the functional aspects of the New Testament portrait of Christ, precisely because this feature dominates the biblical presentation of Christ. As the incarnation of God's saving power, Jesus both as *Christos* and *Kyrios* is presented within the context of the salvific activity that characterizes the biblical portrait of God Himself. Hence, I think it is true to say that the perspectives and emphases that appear in Cullmann's writings are really the perspectives and emphases of the New Testament itself. It is an injustice to Cullmann, a writer on *biblical* theology, to require that his studies conform with the Christological doctrine that emerged from later controversy and doctrinal development. If we identify "theology" with the speculation, analysis, and doctrinal developments introduced by the Eastern and Western Fathers, we should say that Cullmann is dealing with the pretheological doctrines of the New Testament.

INTERVIEWER: What do you mean by pretheological language?

FATHER AHERN: When we use this phrase, we do so to indicate that Sacred Scripture and the writings of the very early Church Fathers antedate the philosophic thought-patterns, clarifications, and analyses introduced by the later Fathers of East and West and rendered classic by the great Councils of the Church. The perfecting of theological formulation that is observable in the progressive development of doctrine from Nicea through Ephesus to Chalcedon resulted in thought-patterns and vocabulary that hardly accord with the Christological affirmations to be found in the New Testament. In the light of the Christology that emerged from the reflection of the Fathers during the great Council debates, some of the New Testament affirmations about Christ sound almost adoptionist, e.g., "Let all the house of Israel know assuredly that God has made him both Lord and Christ, this Jesus whom you crucified" (*Acts* 2:36).

INTERVIEWER: In other words, the functional emphasis of the New Testament is based on its Semitic milieu.

FATHER AHERN: That's right. It must be remembered that Scripture has a theology all its own, drawn from Semitic thought-patterns and emphasizing the activity of God and of His Son as the best insight into their nature. Since the emphasis of later thought is rather on the ontological, its statements will often seem out of harmony with scriptural affirmations. For this reason, therefore, we have to make clear that biblical theology with its perspectives is different from the theology developed by the Fathers who were trying to make revealed truth meaningful to their contemporaries by speaking a vocabulary and using philosophical structures that were familiar to them. So it is that we often speak of biblical doctrine as "pretheological," not to deny its theological character, but to indicate that the theology of the New Testament comes from a different milieu than that which created the theology of the Fathers.

INTERVIEWER: Could you give some examples of this "prethcological" language of the New Testament.

FATHER AHERN: I think the best examples are to be found in the Christological texts to which I have already alluded: *Acts* 2:36; 13:33; *Rom.* 1:4. Both of these texts view the divine and messianic lordship of Christ as a derivative of His Resurrection. Such a concept jars against our post-Chalcedonian emphasis on the ontological and eternal divinity of Christ's nature. But only a moment's thought suffices to show that the affirmations of Scripture have their own validity. Viewing all things from the perspective of salvific activity, the sacred writers like the first Christians recognized that Resurrection introduced Jesus to an entirely new way of life. The Resurrection was for Him a true messianic enthronement. Previously, the Word made flesh had lived upon earth with all the limitations of His humanness: "He had to be made like His brethren in every respect" (*Heb.* 2:17). Bound by the limitations of His life upon earth, the Man-Jesus did not share fully in His Father's lordship; His very mission involved Him in the ministry of the "Servant of Yahweh." Once He had completed His mission, however, He was free to enjoy and to exercise all the saving power that was rightfully His as God's Son. His Resurrection from the dead, therefore, marked for Him the beginning of a new way of life as the Man-

God sharing fully in the lordship of His Father and in the exercise of the Father's power to save men through the activity of the Holy Spirit. Functionally, through the exercise of this saving activity, He shared fully in the lordship of His Father only from the moment of His Resurrection; this is the point of emphasis in the New Testament. Ontologically, through His divine nature, He was always God's Son; this is the point of emphasis in post-Chalcedonian theology.

INTERVIEWER: What are your observations about modern exegesis and the analogy of faith—the relationship between revealed doctrines?

FATHER AHERN: The analogy of faith is undoubtedly an imperative criterion for biblical exegesis. No sound scriptural interpretation can contravene truths that are certainly known to have been revealed by God. Otherwise, we would be faced with the anomaly of an all-truthful God contradicting Himself. But it is needful to emphasize that we are speaking only of truths that are certainly known to have been revealed. Hence, the control of scriptural interpretation by the analogy of faith must be exactly understood.

The history of theology shows that many times the *Magisterium* of the Church has proposed revealed truth in the language and thought-patterns of a contemporary human philosophy. In so doing, the Church focused her attention not on the philosophic character of the definition, but on the truth which God has revealed. The human reasoning that accompanied the deliberations of the Fathers and the cultural or philosophic background of the language that they used do not form part of the Church's magisterial teaching. These elements were looked upon by the Fathers simply as an apt and convenient way of expressing the truth and of making it meaningful to men of their own age. Hence, the truth revealed by God and proposed by the *Magisterium* of the Church does not bring with it a canonization of the human elements that were utilized in its definition. As human elements, the paraphernalia of dogmatic definitions are subject to reconsideration and perfecting.

To give an example: In defining the eucharistic faith of the Church, the Council of Trent made crystal clear that, at Mass, a wondrous change takes place whereby Christ becomes personally and bodily present in His dying and rising that He may be received by us through faith. In the formulation of this revealed truth, the Fathers at Trent were thinking in the Aristotelian categories of substance and accident. These philosophic thought-patterns were apt and meaningful for men of the sixteenth century. But the Tridentine definition does not canonize these human elements of expression. The revelation of the Eucharist as presented in the New Testament knows nothing of these Aristotelian categories; but who would question the validity of its mode of expression? Hence, we must be very careful not to overextend the principle of the analogy of faith. To invoke every human element in a definition of faith as the norm and criterion for scriptural interpretation would be to impose a merely human control over the Church's seeking for the exact meaning of God's word in Scripture.

INTERVIEWER: Do you feel that the analogy of faith restricts the Catholic exegete?

FATHER AHERN: The basic principle that must guide every Catholic exegete is that no true scriptural interpretation can contravene a truth that is certainly known to have been revealed by God. The exegesis of Scripture, as a form of literary interpretation, is not an exact science like mathematics. Though at times texts are so obviously clear in their meaning that all interpreters will be in agreement, there are many other instances where complete certainty is very difficult to reach. At other times, the conclusions of an exegete will carry a very high degree of probability, but will not compel acceptance by other interpreters who prefer equally probable interpretations. In this whole matter of possible and probable interpretations, the Catholic exegete enjoys a wide range of liberty. When, however, a possible or probable interpretation would involve a conclusion contrary to revealed doctrine, the Catholic exegete knows instantly that, although the interpretation may seem probable, it is really false. Thus, an interpretation of the texts pertinent to the eucharistic institution, if it rules out the real presence of Christ, must be rejected by the Catholic exegete as false since it contravenes the certain teaching of Catholic faith. In this way, the analogy of faith is a great help, since it provides at times a sure guideline for the acceptance or rejection of possible interpretations. Actually, however, since the Church has explicitly defined the meaning of so few texts, the analogy of faith functions rather rarely with compelling force.

If we look for a comparable guideline in the ordinary *Magisterium* of the Church, we shall achieve only minimal success. First of all, when one is thoroughly familiar with the writings of the Fathers and Doctors of the Church, he realizes that often their exegesis of Scripture texts presents so many possibilities that it is impossible to speak of the unanimity that is essential for obligatory teaching. Secondly, the use of Scripture texts in papal documents (even in the documents of the solemn *Magisterium*) does not *in itself* constitute an obligatory norm for Catholic interpretation. In the case of a definition by the solemn *Magisterium,* it is clear that the Teaching Authority of the Church includes its use of Scripture within the definitory scope of its pronouncement.

INTERVIEWER: Let us talk about a concrete situation. How would you apply the analogy of faith to the matter that you just mentioned, that is, the interpretation of the words of eucharistic institution as presented by the Synoptics and St. Paul?

FATHER AHERN: It is obvious that the account of the Last Supper is open to several possible interpretations. Catholic exegesis, in accord with the definition of Trent, has always held that the words of the text show clearly that Our Lord became personally and bodily present under the appearance of bread and wine. This interpretation was bolstered by pointing out that Christ did not say "This represents my Body," rather "This is my Body." This argument that is found in Cardinal Wiseman's *Lectures on the Eucharist* has recently been questioned by the non-Catholic scholar, Joachim Jeremias, who proposes a contrary interpretation of what took place at the Last Supper. First of all, Jeremias points out that the Aramaic words that Christ uttered would not have included the copulative; He would have said simply *Den Bisri* ("This, my Body") and *Den Idmi* ("This, my Blood"). He then goes on to show that, even if Christ thought in the actual copulative form ("This is my Body"), such an affirmation would not *in itself* refer to His real, bodily presence. For, as Jeremias shows, very often the Prophets of the Old Testament made similar statements as they performed their prophetic actions that, though fully efficacious, were merely symbolic. Thus, after the symbolic action of cutting off his hair and destroying it, Ezechial cries out, "This is Jerusalem!" (*Ezech.* 5:5). With this mimed action and the accompanying words, the Prophet foretells and efficaciously launches the destruction of Jerusalem.

In the light of the mimed actions of the Prophets, Joachim Jeremias evolves his own interpretation of what took place at the Supper. He identifies the conduct of Jesus with the conduct of the Prophets. As heralds of God's word, which is infallibly efficacious, the Prophets of Israel through their prophetic words and deeds actualized God's powerful will among their people. In the same way, according to Jeremias, Jesus at the Last Supper performed a prophetic action that efficaciously launched and gave meaning to the death that He died on the morrow. Hence, though Jeremias recognizes fully the efficacious power of Christ's action at the Last Supper, his explanation does not involve the personal and bodily presence of Christ under the appearance of bread and wine. The interpretation presented by Jeremias, therfore, runs counter to Catholic faith in the reality of Christ's bodily presence in the Eucharist.

INTERVIEWER: What do responsible Catholic exegetes think of Jeremias' interpretation?

FATHER AHERN: Two outstanding Catholic exegetes, Jacques Dupont and Pierre Benoit, have given considerable attention to the study of Joachim Jeremias. They agree with his criticism of the arguments that Catholic apologetics have previously used to corroborate the traditional understanding of Christ's action at the Last Supper. They recognize also the merit of Jeremias' suggestion that Jesus, like the Prophets before Him, was engaged in the performance of a prophetic action. Yet, with the analogy of faith to guide them, they develop Jeremias' line of argument to the point where Jeremias' insight is brought into accord with Catholic doctrine. They point out that, in performing His prophetic action, Christ used bread and wine, which are not symbols of death or sacrifice, but of nourishment. The use of these symbols and Jesus' command, "All of you eat of this," bring the whole action of Christ within the context of the sacrifice-banquet of the Covenant. For, while the words He uttered point to sacrifice, the very use of bread and wine and the command to eat point to real participation. Hence, just as in the sacrifices of the Old Covenant the participants really shared in the sacrifice by eating the flesh of the sacrificial victim, so in Jesus' prophetic action He invites His disciples to receive the real victim who would be offered in the sacrifice that inaugurates the new Covenant. Obviously, therefore, the victim must have been really present. In this explanation, what is best in the insight of Joachim Jeremias is preserved while, at the same time, Catholic faith in the real presence of Christ in the Eucharist is safeguarded. Not all Catholic exegetes, perhaps, will accept the explanation of Dupont and Benoit. But whatever interpretation they present must take into account and keep intact the truth of Christ's real and bodily presence, which Catholic teaching assures us God has certainly revealed.

INTERVIEWER: You insist on the real presence as one of those cardinal truths that no sound scriptural interpretation can deny. What other scriptural themes would you put in this category?

FATHER AHERN: As I have said before, we must not unduly multiply the instances in which the analogy of faith is compellingly directive in the exegesis of Catholic scholars. Strictly speaking, the definitive action of the solemn *Magisterium* has guaranteed for us the meaning only of the eucharistic institution passages, the Matthean text on Peter's primacy, St. Paul's affirmation on original sin (*Rom.* 5:12), and possibly the Johannine passage on baptism (*John* 3:5). At the same time, however, the essentially constitutive elements of salvation history are also rendered secure by the analogy of faith. For it is the very essence of Catholic faith that it be rooted not in mere doctrines and ideas but in the really historical interventions of God in human destiny. Hence, the creation of God's chosen people through the salvation event of Sinai as well as God's extraordinary intervention through the illumination of the Prophets in the course of Israel's history must be accepted as historical realities. So, too, the constitutive elements of the early *kerygma* preached by the Apostles must be regarded as fully historical. The fact that Jesus is the Incarnate Son of God and that He did preach, work miracles, expel demons, died a redemptive death, and was resuscitated from the dead as the messianic Son of God—these are areas which are not open to question in Catholic exegesis. To rule out all miracles and expulsion of demons from His earthly ministry or to considerably reduce their number, to suggest that Jesus did not really die on the cross or that He was not really raised from the dead—suggestions like these are not only contrary to the moral certainty of history, but are also contrary to the essential tenets of Catholic faith. Hence, because of that faith, the salvific events in man's history and the inspired interpretation of these events as presented in Sacred Scripture represent truths to which the Catholic exegete must assent and to which his exegesis must conform.

INTERVIEWER: Would you restrict the objects of our faith to salvific events?

FATHER AHERN: Everything revealed by God, whether it be the inspired interpretation of an historical event or the inspired teaching of a doctrine flowing from the very nature of salvation, is truly the object of faith. In other words, faith is man's total acceptance of the light of God's revealing word, which renders meaningful to man the divine act of salvific intervention. Hence, both the *word* and *deed* of God are inseparably connected as the object of faith. This truth is well expressed in the recent conciliar *Constitution on Divine Revelation:* "The plan of revelation is realized by deeds and words having an inner unity; the deeds wrought by God in the history of salvation manifest and confirm the teaching and realities signified by words, while the words proclaim the deeds and clarify the mystery contained in them."

In some instances, the word of God revealing inheres immediately in the deed of God to form the object of faith. Thus, the birth of the child Jesus, an historical fact, is also truly an object of faith since God has revealed that this was the birth of His own Son. In other instances, the connection between the revealing word and the deed is recognized only on reflection. Thus, Our Lord's teaching on charity in the parable of the Good Samaritan will strike some as a word that has no immediate connection with a salvific deed. The fact is, however, that the parable serves to unfold and clarify an essential consequence of Christ's incarnation, whereby all men became brothers bound to one another by the exigencies of love. In every instance, therefore, the revealing word is in some way inseparably connected with the salvation deed of God, i.e., the redemptive Incarnation of His Son. Hence, the object of faith embraces both the word and deed of God.

INTERVIEWER: I notice that in your listing of the objects of faith you omitted the Ascension of Our Lord. Do you consider this event an object of faith?

FATHER AHERN: The Ascension of Our Lord, if it is regarded as a merely phenomenological fact apprehensible by the senses, is not *in itself* an object of faith. God's revealing word is essential if an historical event is to be seen not merely as an event, but as a salvific event, an object of faith. The Ascension of Jesus, therefore, as an object of faith, could not be His mere local elevation from the earth. This at most was an external sign of the supernatural event that was realized in the very Resurrection of Jesus. At that moment, the one resuscitated from the dead was not a mere man, like Lazarus, brought back to merely physical life. He was rather the Son of God whose restoration to life as a man involved a full human share in the power of the Father, i.e., an "ascension to God's right hand." This "ascension" is an essential and wholly supernatural element of Christ's rising from the tomb. It renders Christ's resuscitation from the dead the truly supernatural and salvific event that we call "resurrection." This "ascended" character of the risen Christ is strictly an object of faith since it is knowable only through the illumination given by God's revealing word. That word was uttered by St. Peter in *Acts* 2:32–33: "This Jesus God raised up. . . . Being therefore exalted at the right hand of God, and having received from the Father the promise of the Holy Spirit, He has poured out this which you see and hear." The Ascension, therefore, as an object of faith is essentially contained in the mystery of Christ's Resurrection.

INTERVIEWER: Are you saying that no historical event, no Ascension, took place forty days after the Resurrection?

FATHER AHERN: No. All I am saying is that the tree must not obscure the forest. That Our Lord was seen by His Apostles during the forty days following His Resurrection and that a final moment came when He was no longer visible to them form part of the history of salvation. The all-important feature in Luke's description of how He eventually left His Apostles is the manifest symbolism of the biblical account. The peculiar literary character of this account makes clear that Luke's concern is not with the historicity of a phenomenological fact, but with the sign-value of the biblical description. It is significant that Luke alone describes this event—and in a style that is typically midrashic. It is well known that John in his Gospel combines all three events of Resurrection, Ascension, and giving of the Spirit, placing them all on Easter Sunday, to show the fullness of the Resurrection. It is to be noted, too, that the consistent preaching of the Apostles centered in the theme, "He has risen," without any mention of the Ascension except as an element in the theological contents of the Resurrection (cf. *Acts* 2:32–33). Hence, the value of the Lukan description of Jesus' Ascension is not to be found in the reality of a phenomenological fact, rather in its important doctrinal teaching that He who rose from the dead was the Son of God who shared fully the power of His Father. Just as this truth is represented by the figure of speech, "exalted at the right hand of God" (*Acts* 2:33), so too it could be represented by the sign-value of Luke's description of Christ's last departure from His Apostles.

INTERVIEWER: You seem to imply that the Ascension as described by St. Luke is open to several interpretations. Would you indicate these?

FATHER AHERN: I see two possible interpretations. There could have been a phenomenological elevation of Christ from the earth in the way in which Luke describes it. The purpose of such an event in God's plan would be to strengthen the faith of the Apostles with an earthly phenomenon that would symbolize in a human way the strictly supernatural "ascension" that had taken place at the very moment of Christ's Resurrection. On the other hand, in view of the significant points that I previously indicated, it could be that the Lukan description of the Ascension is a purely literary device, popular among biblical writers, that the author introduced in order to teach allegorically the "ascended" character of the risen Christ who, at the very moment of His Resurrection, was enthroned "at God's right hand." This interpretation, developed at length by Père Benoit in an article that appeared in the *Revue Biblique,* is supported by the early liturgies of the Church that always celebrated the mystery of Christ's Ascension as part of the mystery of His Resurrection.

INTERVIEWER: How can the latter interpretation be maintained when Christian tradition and the belief of the faithful for centuries centered in a specific historical event that took place forty days after the Resurrection?

FATHER AHERN: It is unfortunate that we tend to identify customary attitudes of religious thought in the Church with dogmatic tradition. As the *Constitution on Divine Revelation* has made clear, tradition is the word of God as it lives in the faith of the Church. Its formative element and its controlling factor is God's revelation. Without this essential element "tradition" becomes merely a customary way of human thought without any more value than any customary way of thinking. Because human nature is what it is, there will always be customary ways of human thinking that, although they center on religious themes, do not contain the revelation of God. Thus, for centuries, religious men thought that the Book of Jona was strictly historical. This is why the Church through her scholars must constantly sift our customary ways of religious thinking to determine whether they contain God's revealed word or are merely human ideas about a supposed word of God that is nonexistent.

I say it is unfortunate that this lack of discernment is often present in those who should know better. For, as a result, obligations of faith are often imposed where no obligation of faith exists. People who use the word "tradition" lightly and who are ever ready to invoke the authority of "faith" are the very ones who create crises in faith where such crises should never exist.

INTERVIEWER: Are you saying, then, that the consensus of the faithful for centuries is not enough to substantiate the historicity of the Ascension?

FATHER AHERN: That men have long looked upon Luke's description of the "ascension" as the record of an historical fact is not in itself a reason for subscribing to this view. (The same men were just as insistent that the narratives in the Books of Job and Jona were based on historical events!) The witness of Scripture itself, as well as the liturgies of the early Church, provide many arguments against the historicity of the Lukan "ascension." I would say, therefore, that the matter of Christ's Ascension should be seen in the perspective in which God's word places it—as part of the Resurrection. This alone is a certain object of faith. As far as the reality of a phenomenological event occurring forty days after the Resurrection, this is now a matter for scholarly research. The all-important concern is that, in celebrating the feast of the Ascension, the minds of our faithful should be centered on the essential theological reality of the mystery as part of the Resurrection. Luke's description of the supposed event, whether based on actual occurrence or presented in a purely literary form, has as its only purpose to emphasize the truth revealed by God, that is, that Jesus in His risen life shares the power of His Father.

INTERVIEWER: Does anyone use similar arguments and conclude that the event of Pentecost was not an actual historical occurrence?

FATHER AHERN: Speaking for Catholic exegetes, I am quite sure that no one would question the historical reality of a remarkable divine intervention at Pentecost. The prominence of this event in the life of the early Church places it in an entirely different category from the Ascension as an event occurring forty days after the Resurrection. The history recorded in the Acts of the Apostles is impossible to understand if the events of Pentecost were not an historical reality. Moreover, the reality of the Pentecostal experience is guaranteed by St. Peter's allusion to it in the house of Cornelius (cf. *Acts* 10:46–47).

INTERVIEWER: What was the gift of tongues at Pentecost?

FATHER AHERN: The gift of tongues at Pentecost is more than likely the same gift of tongues referred to elsewhere in the New

Testament writings and treated at length by St. Paul in *1 Cor.* 14:6ff. A person is so overwhelmed by a divinely given conviction that he seems to lose control of himself and to utter incoherent cries. Therefore, St. Paul writes, "If all speak in tongues, and outsiders or unbelievers enter, will they not say that you are mad?" (*1 Cor.* 14:23). So, too, at Pentecost people cried out on hearing the Apostles, "They are filled with new wine" (*Acts* 2:13). Hence, many authors today explain the gift of tongues that came to the Apostles at Pentecost as the overflow of the brilliant illumination that they received from the Holy Spirit on the true character of Jesus as the messianic Son of God. The conviction was so overwhelming that the Apostles cried out with words that others could not understand. The fact that Luke represents them as speaking in languages intelligible to all who were present is seen as a literary device that Luke utilizes to emphasize the universality of the message given to the Apostles in their new knowledge of Jesus. This device had already been utilized in rabbinical literature. In order to stress the universality of the law given to Moses at Sinai, the Jewish rabbis had invented the midrashic story of how the law was heard in seventy different languages throughout the world. Just as this device had been utilized to stress the universality of the mission given to Israel, so it was employed again by Luke to emphasize the universality of the mission given to the Christian Church. This style of writing was very popular among the Jews of the first century; and so the significance of the Lukan literary development would have been readily understood by his readers.

INTERVIEWER: Do you think that there is danger that theologians may become too involved in the biblical approach?

FATHER AHERN: Yes, there is as much danger of this as of the problem we have just discussed. Indeed, it would be a great loss if theologians were to become so interested in the scriptural presentation of revealed truth that they would neglect the responsibilities of their own task. As we have said, every age must make its own response to the voice of God that is always speaking in the Church. The response of the first century, as recorded in the New Testament, was cast in the language and thought-patterns of the contemporary historical situation. That age is long past, and now the Church of today must respond to God as faithfully as the Church of the first century, yet in an altogether different way. Our life situation has changed; we think and speak in our own special way; we have our own set of problems to grapple with. It is the function of the theologian to show us how we of the twentieth century are to respond to the voice of God. The expression of revealed truth in Scripture must now have its counterpart in a corresponding expression adapted to the conceptual forms of the present. This is the function of the theologian. He must be not only a faithful witness to God's word, but also its live and present exponent.

INTERVIEWER: In some seminaries, the dogmatic theologian and the Scripture professor work together very closely in team-teaching. What do you think of this?

FATHER AHERN: I heartily approve of this method. It is a wonderful way to correlate God's voice in the past and men's response to it (Scripture) with God's voice in the present and our present response (theology). However, in actual practice, team-teaching carries with it no assurance of automatic success. If the professors who engage in it are to secure sound results, they must have a very clear understanding of their separate functions, they must actually prepare their work together, and in their conduct of the class they must render obvious to the student the correlation of their two separate treatments. If team-teaching becomes a matter of professors joined only by physical contiguity, it would be far better to discontinue the system and to have only one professor present both the scriptural and theological aspects of the theme discussed. At least he would not work at odds with himself!

INTERVIEWER: Do you have any advice you would like to give to students of theology?

FATHER AHERN: I have only one suggestion to make to students of theology. Confident that their professors will acquaint them with the contents of Sacred Scripture and will bring them to love the inspired word, and confident, too, that their professors will be utilizing what is best in the modern theologians, I put forth as my only suggestion that during the course of theology, they should read from cover to cover the *Summa Theologica* of St. Thomas. There are deficiencies in this work that St. Thomas today would be the first to change. The style of the *Summa* does not make for easy reading. St. Thomas today would be the first to abandon a method of presentation that, in this present time, has lost all vitality and appeal. But his work is still a treasure house where one frequently finds unsurpassed expressions of Catholic doctrine. A student who has read St. Thomas with attention and interest will emerge from college or seminary with a rich store of wisdom and with a confident grasp of the unchanging structures of Faith.

I often smile when I hear men who have never read St. Thomas dismiss him as one who has outlived his day. Little do they realize that many of the developments in modern theology are all to be found fully set forth in the writings of the Angelic Doctor. It is significant that Father Schillebeeckx in explaining the "new" approach to the Eucharist has constantly pointed out his dependence on the insights of St. Thomas. In many instances, the author of the *Summa* is far more modern than the moderns.

❖❖❖

BARNABAS AHERN was born in Chicago, Illionis, on February 18th, 1915. He entered the Passionists in 1932 and was ordained in 1941. He did graduate studies in theology and Scripture at The Catholic University of America, L'Ecole Biblique in Jerusalem, and at the Pontifical Biblical Institute in Rome, where he received his doctorate in 1958. He has taught Scripture at Passionist seminaries in Chicago and Louisville, and at present he is the Professor of New Testament Studies at St. Meinrad's Seminary. He was a *peritus* at the Second Vatican Council and is a permanent consultor to the Pontifical Biblical Commission.

His writings include: *New Horizons: Studies in Biblical Theology; Commentary on Galatians and Romans; Life in Christ;* and numerous articles. He is co-editor of *The Bible Today,* and from 1960 to 1962 he was Scripture editor of *Worship.*

John C. Bennett

*D*r. *Bennett is waiting for me in his faculty apartment at the Union Theological Seminary on Morningside Heights, New York City. From there, we walk over to his office and pass no one on the way. His office is spacious, but the dark paneling gives it warmth. The interview is held in an adjoining room that has a large, highly polished oak table. Sitting there I can see, through the many-paned windows, the quadrangle and English Gothic buildings of the seminary. It is evening in late spring, and the soft shadows of the setting sun on the dark green grass and gray stone of the buildings are reminiscent of Cambridge—with one exception: no dons are in sight. Dr. Bennett is a quiet man, but with a decided air of assurance and control. He speaks softly, but with feeling, and he smiles easily. For a few moments, we discuss his recent article in* Look *on the "death of God" theologians, and then we begin our interview.*

INTERVIEWER: You once wrote that in the United States the "revival of theology has to be distinguished from the so-called religious revival." Do you think that this is still true?

DR. BENNETT: Yes I do. My main point in that article was that the religious renewal and the theological renewal have not moved in the same directions. Clearly, there has been considerable interest in religion in this country; churches have become as important as social centers and statistically more people are going to church. Yet, at the same time it was tending to be a culture-affirming religion without much criticism of the culture in which it was growing. Whereas the theological revival that had preceded it, had its

195

roots in people like Barth and Niebuhr and was based upon a very strong sense of the transcendence of God, the divine judgment on society, sin, and the like. The religious renewal has been rather bland and has lacked the vigor of the theological revival that preceded it. However, I think that both the religious and theological revival have tapered off. The revival of theology is losing its character. The great men like Barth, Brunner, Niebuhr, and Tillich are either retired or dead, and there are no theologians of equal stature who have taken their place. It is true you have a great deal of theological ferment, but there is not much structure to it. One doesn't know what will happen. You have many fine young Protestant theologians who are able and doing first-class work, but no one stands out.

INTERVIEWER: Do you detect any signs that the religious renewal is becoming less vigorous?

DR. BENNETT: There is a feeling, and I think it is quite widespread, that the substance of the Christian faith has never really been grasped properly during the so-called renewal. The "death of God" discussions are a rather extreme symptom of this. The very fact that they have gained so much attention indicates that their slogan at least expresses a certain sense of emptiness or vacuum. This is part of the honest searching that is going on in the church today.

INTERVIEWER: Does the Protestant minister find the "death of God" controversy a difficult pastoral problem?

DR. BENNETT: Yes, I think he does. At least that is the impression that we get here at Union. I am speaking more of the minister who has come up through the critical type of theology and belongs to one of the main denominations. Of course, we have a conservative, very orthodox group in Protestantism, but they are not dominant in the major denominations. I should say that for those denominations who have an ecumenical orientation, the "death of God" theology creates some difficulties. I doubt if there are many people who would be, in any sense, adherents to this movement. After all, there are only three theologians involved, and not one of them, as a person, has a very wide influence. None of them speak for any denomination. They have more publicity than influence. I don't say that I think what they are doing is a good thing, but I personally believe in freedom and getting your problems out into the open. I don't worry about it quite so much as you might expect me to do. In fact, one of the theologians involved is a former student of mine whom I have greatly appreciated.

INTERVIEWER: Is there any reason why the "death of God" issue appeared in Protestantism at this particular time?

DR. BENNETT: These men represent a very extreme Christocentrism that came out, at least in the case of two of them, of the earlier Barthian movement. Karl Barth's theology was wholly Christocentric; he allowed for no approach to faith other than confronting the center that is Christ. There was nothing that supported this—no philosophical preparation that was its foundation. In this respect, it differs greatly from Roman Catholicism. Now the moment this particular emphasis on a purely revelational approach to faith begins to grow weak, then something else will take its place. It's not strange that there is a kind of collapse in some circles of which the idea of the "death of God" is symptomatic. However, they represent the last stages of a Barthian, neoorthodox movement that in the past gave great strength to theology. I wouldn't say that the Barthian approach has to end this way, but I think the result is something that you might expect to have at times. The Barthian background of these men makes them quite different from the ordinary atheist.

INTERVIEWER: Since we are on the subject of Christology, do you think that the rank and file Protestant believes that Christ is truly God in the sense of being of the same substance?

DR. BENNETT: I hesitate to speak for Protestants in general or even for Protestant theologians. However, I would say that any doctrine of the divinity of Christ that tends to make unreal the humanity of Christ, as a person, limited in knowledge, capable of real suffering—any diminution of the real humanity would be resisted. It is through Christ as a truly human figure that God acts in the world and reveals Himself to the world. The doctrine of the two natures has always been historically a difficult one, because the tendency has been for the divine nature to overwhelm the human nature. It is a little like noise overwhelming silence. It has been frequently said by Protestant theologians that the actual, operative Christology of the great tradition has been decidedly Apollinarian.

However, I think that the Protestant Christocentric theologians of an older generation looked upon Christ as divine, although they explained it in their own particular way dogmatically. It was strong in Barth and Brunner. Reinhold Niebuhr was always more liberal in his Christology, although he was very much influenced by certain classical Christian reformation doctrines, especially in his doctrine of man. Niebuhr was never one to emphasize the Christological doctrines. Tillich, of course, was very sophisticated, or at least symbolic, in his approach, and it is difficult to classify him.

INTERVIEWER: Can we say that for Tillich the question of Jesus Christ's divinity is irrelevant because he does not use the traditional categories?

DR. BENNETT: I think that in the second volume of his *Systematic Theology* Tillich attempts to provide the equivalent of that. In his earlier works you had more emphasis on Jesus as the Christ who was the center of history. Yet Tillich later worked with the Chalcedonian formula and tried, admittedly using symbolic rather than substantial terms, to answer the question of Christ's nature. Most Protestant theologians who were brought up in an atmosphere of liberal, critical theology, do have a Christology. It is not so much a matter of a metaphysical sense of the deity of Christ, rather an affirmation of the genuine revelation of God in Christ and the Christ-event as being a redeeming event. From that point, they go off into all sorts of different interpretations. It is more of a dynamic Christology in terms of history than a metaphysical Christology.

INTERVIEWER: Do you consider the problem of Christ a fundamental ecumenical problem?

DR. BENNETT: It certainly is an ecumenical problem that must be honestly discussed by all Christians. I don't know just how far Roman Catholics tend, in their own ways, to demythologize, that is, to develop symbolic interpretations of dogmas. I don't know how far they would be willing to go. I have some Roman Catholic friends who seem to be very strongly influenced by Bultmann, and while they don't necessarily limit their thought to Bultmann, they do absorb a good deal of his criticism.

INTERVIEWER: Is Karl Barth still a major influence in Protestant theology?

DR. BENNETT: There are probably very few "died in the wool" Barthians any more. I know of none in this country, and I know that there are fewer in Europe than there used to be. It is hard to measure these things statistically, but one hears that Bultmann is much stronger than Barth on the continent—at least in Germany. Barth, however, is still read a great deal, and his contribution is immense. I use him in my course on ethics. Part four of his third volume is a very great treatise on Christian ethics.

Most theologians do not accept the exclusivism of Barth's methodology. They don't accept the approach of Barth that sees nothing of significance for faith apart from revelation. He has no place at all for certain preparations in our common experience—not to mention any kind of rational preparation. For some time, there has been considerable objection to a natural theology that is made up of proofs. Proofs never seem to prove that God really exists. They never seem to convince anyone who does not already believe in God. Most Protestant theologians, other than Barth, recognize certain pointers to God in experience—certain questions posed by experience is Tillich's way of putting it. Questions are given us sometimes in philosophy and sometimes in our common human experience to which revelation provides an answer. Barth wouldn't admit such a thing.

INTERVIEWER: Isn't the later Barth with his emphasis on the "humanity of God" more acceptable to contemporary Protestant theology?

DR. BENNETT: I doubt, unless I am mistaken, that Barth has changed his methodology in any significant way. He has, however, changed some of his conclusions. The God of Barth now is not "the wholly other" or "wholly transcendent." This is brought out in his book, *The Humanity of God*. This tendency in his thought goes back to the early forties. At that time, you can find a kind of Christian humanism in some of his writings.

INTERVIEWER: Let us talk about American theologians for a

moment. How would you assess the impact that Reinhold Niebuhr has made on American Protestant theology?

DR. BENNETT: Reinhold Niebuhr has influenced the whole climate of thinking about man, ethics, and especially political ethics. People are influenced by Niebuhr who don't even realize it. I think that it is in this respect that there is a difference between Niebuhr and Tillich. Tillich is a person whose system is admired. People see it, admire it, and learn from it. Theologians often make great use of some of his concepts. But in the case of Niebuhr, I think what you have is a change of climate. People borrow from him without realizing it. This is true at least in the circles in which I live. His Christian realism is a good example of this. Niebuhr is not a systematic thinker; in fact, he is almost self-consciously unsystematic. He is fearful of ontology and fearful of any kind of rationalistic structure. He believes in the use of reason, but he uses reason to interpret the realities he finds, rather than to develop a structure of reason. Fifteen years ago, Niebuhr was certainly as influential as any thinker in this country.

INTERVIEWER: Dean Brauer, dean of the University of Chicago Divinity School, has written that "Tillich will probably have a deeper and more lasting impact on American theology than any other theologian now at work." Do you agree?

DR. BENNETT: I am not at all sure. One of the troubles is that Tillich gives us a whole system that one is inclined to take or leave. Unless one is willing to accept the system as a whole, I am not sure how much basic theology one learns from him. This may, to some extent, limit his influence. Apart from the system, Tillich did have an extraordinary appreciation of so many human interests—philosophy, politics, art, and psychiatry. He illumined everything that he touched. This is true of a book that is appealed to by psychiatrists, *The Courage to Be*, as well as a book like *Love, Power, and Justice,* which has a good deal of social philosophy in it. In many areas, Tillich will have a great influence. How far his central system will be strongly influential in the future, I just don't know. After all, Tillich was very much of a classical philosopher, even though he had a strong existentialist element in his diagnosis of the human situation. Personally, I have not been influenced to a great extent by his system. But Tillich did influence me and many others very much by his methodology. It involves the question and answer process by which you use every conceivable tool of thought to penetrate the human situation and then, the Gospel comes as an answer. He calls it the method of correlation.

INTERVIEWER: As the president of a large and influential seminary, do you detect any cleavage between academic theology and the pastoral needs of the Church?

DR. BENNETT: I think that this tension is found more in Europe than in this country. Our theologians, for the most part, are very much involved in the Church, and their work is oriented toward the Church. It is possible that we will develop more and more institutions where advanced graduate work in theology may be done by scholarly theologians. Yet we must fight against separating scholarly work from the needs of the Church. Here, at Union, we have always had interaction between the training of the ministry and the training of scholars.

INTERVIEWER: What are the practical aspects of the program at Union?

DR. BENNETT: Our student body has two major groups that live together. We have about two hundred and fifty Bachelor of Divinity Students who are being trained primarily for the ministry and another hundred or more students who are doctoral candidates. We have always stressed what we call field education. As a matter of educational policy, not merely from financial necessity, we believe in having our students work in churches or perhaps even take secular jobs. In doing this, they are exposed to the life that they should know more about. We have a program that has been developed gradually over the years. This coming year we will have nearly all our first-year students—about a hundred—working in some thirty churches in the area. There are three students assigned to each church. They are assigned to a minister who receives a small stipend from the seminary and is regarded as a teaching associate in practical theology. The minister is responsible for the guidance of these students and uses them in his church in many different ways. The minister also comes back to the seminary every other week for a seminar to keep in touch with the academic side. Students in the other years also do some field work, but it is more varied. We don't want our students to have the full responsibility for a church before they finish their studies.

INTERVIEWER: The Lutherans have an internship during which theological students leave the seminary after their third year and spend one year working in a parish as a vicar. Is there anything comparable to that at Union?

DR. BENNETT: We haven't worked out the program fully yet, but we have experimented with it. About a quarter of our students choose an internship year, and the numbers are increasing. We are not inclined to require it, rather to encourage it.

We have begun experimenting with still another kind of program and this is under the leadership of Dr. Webber. We allow seven or eight of our students to work with Dr. Webber in some secular field work. These students often undertake this before they have done any academic work in our seminary. They have been admitted to the seminary, but they take no classes. Unlike Roman Catholic seminaries, we get young men who are not sure what they want to do. They come here to find out whether the ministry is their vocation. They are able and promising students, but somewhat unsure of their vocation. This year of field work gives them a chance to find themselves.

INTERVIEWER: Has there been a decline in vocations to the Protestant ministry in the last few years?

DR. BENNETT: That is true on a national level, but here at Union, we seem to be getting more applications than ever. However, the situation here is not as critical as in Scotland and Britain. They are in serious trouble. Here, some denominations suffer more than others. One of the points that needs to be looked at more closely is whether or not we should try to train people for local churches that shouldn't exist. There has not been a sufficient reorganization of the life of the various churches; more churches have to merge. This is very wasteful. A look at the actual church situation indicates that there are too many churches that cannot support a trained minister.

Also, we have a certain number who leave the ministry. Often they leave the local church and find other kinds of work, but most often in other church organizations. Many do additional graduate work and train to be teachers.

INTERVIEWER: Are most of the Protestant ministers in this country theologically trained?

DR. BENNETT: In the major denominations, this is true. There was a time when some denominations, like the Methodists, trained many of their men on the job. But this is passing. Now, most ministers are college graduates who have gone through divinity school. The Pentecostal churches would be the exception. The Baptists, too, are somewhat different. I know that the Southern Baptists have many large seminaries, but I don't know how many untrained ministers they allow to work in their churches.

INTERVIEWER: In the past, Union Theological Seminary was noted for the wide variety of its theological views. Is that still true today?

DR. BENNETT: Yes, it is. Fortunately, we have always emphasized diversity here. On one end of our theological spectrum, you have Daniel Day Williams who represents American empirical theology, influenced by Whitehead, but who is evangelical and Church centered. At the other end of the spectrum, there is Paul Louis Lehmann, who is very much of a reformation theologian and strongly influenced by Barth. He teaches the one required course in theology, and believe it or not, his textbook is Calvin's *Institutes*. He has a great respect for Calvin, and he doesn't try to make his students into little Calvins. But he does believe in the classical structure of theology that is present in Calvin's great system. His idea is to have his students become familiar with Calvin and to interpret him quite freely. We also have a variety of other approaches. For example, there is John Macquarrie, who has been thoroughly exposed to the German existentialism of Heidegger and Bultmann.

INTERVIEWER: Does this wide variety of approaches lend itself to theological eclecticism?

DR. BENNETT: I don't think so. The students do find that they are influenced by one professor more than another and some of the professors have their disciples. Rather, it is extremely useful that there can be a dialogue between them. All of these thinkers are *critical* theologians. Not one of them is authoritarian, and not one of them has an exclusive system. You generally find that when you talk to them, they are not as far apart as their slogans sometimes suggest. The student builds his own structure of thought and develops his own synthesis. The ideal thing would be to have the student have his own center and learn from everybody he can. I don't know whether this means he is eclectic or not. After all, there has always been a great deal of eclecticism in theology. Anyone who has studied the history of doctrine knows that.

INTERVIEWER: Do you think that intercommunion would be useful in establishing a closer ecumenical rapport between Christians?

DR. BENNETT: Perhaps I should first give you my personal background, since I belong to a somewhat left-wing type of church— the United Church of Christ. Actually, the United Church is a merger of two churches: the Congregationalist, which represents the New England tradition, and the Evangelical and Reformed Church, which represents German and Swiss reform groups that came to this country at different times. One of the things we recognize in Protestantism is that the differences in theology do not correspond too much to the differences between denominations. In fact, the doctrinal differences within a denomination will often be greater than the differences between denominations. In the Episcopal Church, for example, you will find a certain, distinctive ethos, but you will also find that the theological thought within that church varies tremendously.

Now about intercommunion. As a person who belongs to the kind of ecclesiastical family that I do, intercommunion is never a problem. I have no doctrines about communion that make it difficult for me to take part in the communion service of another church or to have other Christians take part in my service. We have open communion, and we always have had it—at least in this modern period. With most Protestant denominations, it is no problem. However, the Lutherans (at least the Missouri Synod), Anglicans, and Episcopalians find it a problem. Then, too, the Southern Baptists are often very exclusive. I once heard about a Southern Baptist who went to the Oxford Conference in 1937 and wouldn't take communion from the Archbishop of Canterbury because he hadn't been immersed. I think that intercommunion among all Christians would foster the ecumenical movement. We have only begun to think about this problem in the context of Catholic-Protestant relations. I have a suspicion that Roman Catholics may outflank other groups who reject intercommunion.

INTERVIEWER: Your name has been associated with Christian realism since the days of World War II. How would you explain this ethical approach?

DR. BENNETT: By way of preface, I would like to refer to an article that appeared in *America*, April 30th, 1966, with the somewhat unfortunate title: "Christian Realism in Vietnam." I was originally asked to write that article by the Methodist journal, *The Advocate*. I had been a member of a group influenced by Reinhold Niebuhr who supported the Second World War. I was also a member of the editorial board of *Christianity and Crisis*. *The Advocate* wondered why a Christian realist who opposed pacifism in the Second World War would now make common cause with pacifists regarding the Vietnam war. That is the background of the article and why I mentioned in a parenthesis that I apologize for perpetuating the label. It was simply to indicate the problem of consistency. If a pacifist writes an article condemning war, everyone knows that he is against war. But when someone like myself writes such an article, immediately a question arises.

INTERVIEWER: How would you describe Christian realism?

DR. BENNETT: Yes, to get to your original question. Christian realism is not an epistemological realism, although it might turn out to be that in the end. Primarily, it's a realism about human nature and human history, freedom from utopianism, from a belief in panaceas, as well as from cynicism. History is very tragic in places, and evil generally is very stubborn. One of Dr. Niebuhr's frequent assertions is that problems are not solved, but you can learn to live with them. You get proximate solutions and you learn to adjust to your problems. That's what Christian realism is as I understand it.

INTERVIEWER: Paul Ramsey, in the same issue of *America*, questions the "realism" behind the sweeping moral judgments made by the Christian realists of today. He argues that one should not define an action as "intolerably evil in itself" and then say that it can be performed in some circumstances.

DR. BENNETT: I would say that there are certain things that are intrinsically evil, but they may be by-products of a policy that may not be the worst policy considering the circumstances. In other words, I might have to say of them in some circumstances that, as by-products of an action to overcome a still greater evil, they would not be sufficient to cause me to reject the action. Yet they should put an overwhelming burden of proof on the acceptance of such action. You have to see things in their context. I would agree with Ramsey when he seems to say that the *direct* destruction of noncombatants is intrinsically evil. On the other hand, he can allow for the destruction of a tremendous number of noncombatants *indirectly*, as a by-product of other actions. I say that there is something unrealistic about this. Take, for example, nuclear war. The by-products of nuclear weapons in terms of fallout, fire, and pestilence are so enormous that if you allow this thing to happen at all, regardless of your intentions, you immediately become involved in something that is so inherently evil that it cannot be tolerated. Yet, Ramsey is willing to leave that question open. He thinks that limited nuclear war should be allowed. I question that seriously. I doubt that you can have tactical nuclear weapons in isolated situations without grave danger. With the increased tendency toward escalation, I don't see how it can be given moral sanction.

INTERVIEWER: Would you say that all war is intrinsically evil?

DR. BENNETT: There are many things that are intrinsically evil.

Whether they represent the worst evil is another thing. I would say that all killing in war is evil. But this doesn't make it necessarily in all circumstances the worst evil if it is the only way of preventing some greater catastrophe. The reason I supported the war against Hitler was because it would end Hitler's extension of tyranny by agression. When you see an evil like that, you have to take steps to prevent it. The war against Hitler and the war against the Communists in Vietnam are not parallel. Hitlerism was primarily a military threat. Communism of all sorts is only secondarily a military threat. What is at stake in the resistance to Communism is not the same as what was at stake in our resistance to the National Socialism of Hitler. Communism has shown that it is capable of change. It is not monolithic. We ought to stop exaggerating the evil of Communism; it is not the worst fate that can come to any country. I do not think that the United States has the responsibility for a military counterrevolution on all continents against all wars of liberation.

INTERVIEWER: Is it fair to describe your ethical approach as situationalism?

DR. BENNETT: No, but I believe in taking the situation very seriously. I don't believe in applying abstract law without recognizing the way it must be applied. In most instances, what you have is a tension between opposite goals or moral criteria and their adjustment—for example, a conflict between freedom and order. The Catholic emphasis on prudence in moral action is not far removed from what is often meant by situation ethics. The extreme situationalists, however, don't have enough structure. They go on intuition too frequently. When a situationalist decides that he must do something in a particular situation and waives one of the obvious laws or moral criteria, he is not always sufficiently aware of the value of the laws that he has waived. He is in danger of becoming a law unto himself.

❖❖❖

JOHN COLEMAN BENNETT was born in Kingston, Ontario, Canada, on July 22nd, 1902. After his preparatory education at Phillips

Exeter Academy, he went to Williams College where he received his B.A. in 1924. He took his graduate work in theology at Union Theological Seminary and at Mansfield College at Oxford. In 1930, he began his professional teaching career at Auburn Theological Seminary in Auburn, New York. In 1930, he was named Professor in Christian Theology at Pacific School of Religion in Berkeley, California. He was ordained to the ministry of the Congregational Church in 1939. He returned to Union in 1943 to teach social ethics. In 1960, he became the Reinhold Niebuhr Professor of Social Ethics and in 1963 was named President of Union. He is editor of *Christianity and Crisis*. He is married and has three children.

Dr. Bennett is a frequent contributor to religious periodicals. His books include: *Social Salvation; Christian Ethics and Social Policy; Christianity and Communism; The Christian as a Citizen;* and *Christians and the State.*

Christopher Butler

His closely cropped hair, round face, and horn-rimmed glasses give Bishop Butler a decidedly monastic look. In his Oxonian accent, pitched somewhat high, but confidently emphatic, he speaks articulately, spicing his conversation with witty understatements and colorful turns of phrase. A graciously urbane person, he is a relaxed conversationalist.

The evening of the interview, Bishop Butler looks well-rested despite a day in meetings at a theological conference at the University of Notre Dame. I meet him after dinner, and we go directly to his room. A few copies of the London Tablet *lie open on his desk, along with his breviary and a draft of a speech with corrections neatly written in a miniscule script. After filling his pipe painstakingly, he lights it and settles down in a comfortable chair. Puffing contentedly, with a small, flat can of tobacco and a box of matches at his side, he awaits my opening question.*

INTERVIEWER: In Rome, at the end of the Council, you said in a public address that the *Decree on the Appropriate Renewal of the Religious Life* was a summons to revolution. What did you mean by that?

BISHOP BUTLER: The Decree, of course, considers the religious life in the light of the *aggiornamento* in general. It spells out the meaning of the word *aggiornamento* by talking about adapted renovation of religious life. It takes the criteria for adaptation, I think, from the notion of renovation. When it gets back to what it means by renovation, it appears that this means recovering the *spirit* in which the founder of your religious institute created the body to which you belong. There is stated, or could very easily be evoked from the document, the distinction between the spirit and purposes of the founder's creation and the actual contingent form into which he put it. As I see the meaning of the document, religious are entitled to regard as contingent and expendable not only all the accretions that have been added to the founder's original institution, but even the contingent forms in which he expressed his spirit. Religious are to try to re-express that spirit in forms that are relevant and contemporary.

INTERVIEWER: Is that revolution?

BISHOP BUTLER: *Technically,* it's not revolution, because it's a question of going back to primal sources. But the practical consequences will look very much like revolution if we take this seriously and accept with both hands the invitation that has been offered us by the Church.

INTERVIEWER: Perhaps a more fundamental question deals with the desirability of religious life. Do you think that there is any place for religious life in the changing Church?

BISHOP BUTLER: It is a little difficult for me to give a revolutionary answer to that question since I was one, in a general way at least as a Council Father, who passed the *Constitution on the Church*. As you know *De Ecclesia* has consecrated a chapter to the religious life and seemed to give a kind of rationale of it. I feel that that limits one a little here. However, I can say that since religious life has been such a feature of the life of the Church virtually speaking throughout the ages—certainly you get that idea from St. Cyprian in the third century writing his treatise on virgins, and the virgins of that time were the forerunners of religious life as we know it—that I think it would be very difficult to say that the religious life has no more than a merely transitory and passing value in the Church for a particular age. What I think is much more difficult, even after having decided that one has to find room for the religious life in the Church, even in the *aggiornamento* Church, is to find a rationale for it. In recent discussions, these difficulties have been accentuated. I had always thought that

I knew more or less what the religious life was, although I was rather doubtful how I would give a definition of monasticism as a species of religious life. However, after these discussions, I came away feeling completely agnostic about the definition of religious life altogether.

INTERVIEWER: What of the suggestion of situating religious life between the lay state and the clerical state?

BISHOP BUTLER: You cannot locate it in this way. You are applying the wrong criteria if you try to find a place for it between Sacred Orders and the lay state. Obviously, the vocation to religious life appears to come to men whether they are lay or sacerdotal. Or supposing that they are laymen at the time, it may come *along with* a vocation to the sacerdotal state. It seems to me that it has to be seen more in the charismatic order than in the sacramental order. There is a sacramental distinction between the clergy and the laity. But the religious life, although it sounds rather paradoxical to put it like this, is a kind of institutionalized charism.

INTERVIEWER: Who, then, is a religious?

BISHOP BUTLER: A religious is a person who has become aware of and has responded to a more special invitation from God to take Christianity at its *maximal significance,* instead of trying to get past with the minimal interpretation. Then, having seen and responded to it, he has wished to safeguard himself against future temptations to relapse on the minimizing basis of things by committing himself for the future, as well as for the moment, by vows.

INTERVIEWER: It seems that you are implying that the lay person is not committed to the maximal exercise of Christianity.

BISHOP BUTLER: I think all Christians are called to it, but what makes a bit of difference with religious is that he has become in some special way *conscious* of that vocation. He has apprehended it as something that appertains to him personally. He has wished to make a response to it, and he has desired to commit himself to it by an *engagement,* which helps keep him from any failure.

INTERVIEWER: How is the religious any different from the dedicated Christian who, conscious of his baptismal character, makes every effort to grow in the love of God?

BISHOP BUTLER: Leaving aside the question of the *public* nature of the religious vocations in the Church, I agree that both have become conscious of the call to holiness and both of them have willed to make apposite responses. But the religious has added the feature of dedication, by which he commits himself for the future. Now if anybody does that, whether or not he plays a role in the public life of the Church as a religious, he is dedicated basically in the same way as a religious, provided he has committed himself to the future.

INTERVIEWER: What do you think about the traditional way of speaking of the religious life as a state of perfection?

BISHOP BUTLER: The term comes out of a world of discourse that is so alien to us these days that it is more misleading than helpful.

INTERVIEWER: Do you think it is theologically inaccurate?

BISHOP BUTLER: I suspect that if you take it in its full theological depth, it meant for the medieval people who invented this way of talking much the same sort of thing that I mean by the engagement of oneself for the future in a maximal practice of Christianity. This is what the *status perfectionis* means.

INTERVIEWER: How do you relate this to the monastic state?

BISHOP BUTLER: It is difficult enough to settle on what one means by a religious, but it's more difficult to decide what one means by a monk. If you look the world over you find an extraordinary variety of interpretations of what monasticism means. This is not merely a modern phenomenon; other ages had a similar problem. This is partly due to the fact that monasticism grew up almost spontaneously in an age that had not developed a conceptualized theology. It is rather like—if I may use an analogy—comparing the British Constitution with the American Constitution. The British Constitution is, practically speaking, undefinable because it is the result of gradual growth. It goes back to periods long before men reflected scientifically on their experiences and their intentions. Whereas the American Constitution came from a highly sophisticated age and was a written constitution from the first. Therefore, you might compare the Society of Jesus with the American Constitution, since both came from a sophisticated time and were able to define themselves at the moment they came into origin. But monasticism just grew in the Church. It is extremely difficult to look back and to decide what was the basic and not merely the accidental structure.

I was talking about this problem very recently with Canon Charles Moeller. He said that one of his theology professors, who had spent a lifetime studying the Fathers of the Desert and early monasticism, told him that nothing is more difficult than to elucidate the historical origins and theological basis of monasticism.

INTERVIEWER: What are your own observations on the nature of monasticism?

BISHOP BUTLER: Yes, to return to your question. In Rome, I think it was at the end of the second session, a group of us got together to discuss this question. Some were already a bit frightened about certain proposed changes in Canon Law that applied to monks. Someone suggested that the formal object of the monastic vocation was simply *vacare Deo*—to have time for God, to be open to God. Other Orders and Congregations in the Church have specific work, particular ways in which they serve God. But the whole point about monasticism is that there is no special way. It is just *vacare Deo*— dedication to God in and for Himself.

INTERVIEWER: Do you agree with that explanation?

BISHOP BUTLER: Well, I thought it was rather good until the Abbot President of a missionary monastic group said: "Well, if that is monasticism, then we are not monks." Another view was given by the Abbot of Montserrat who said that the thing that really makes a monk is the special place he gives to *lectio divina*— prayer in the wide sense. He explained that while the monk does work like anybody else, what makes him a monk is the "Work of God," the *Opus Dei,* the official public recitation of the Divine Office. The Rule of St. Benedict supports this and gives great emphasis to *lectio divina*. It is this dedication to a kind of meditative absorption of the whole Christian spiritual tradition in *lectio divina* that constitutes the specificity of the monk. Whether that's the case or not, I don't know, but it's the latest suggestion that I've heard of a positive kind.

INTERVIEWER: One frequently hears the criticism that the monastic state is a great waste of talent, time, and effort, a kind of religious escapism from the needs and responsibilities of the world.

BISHOP BUTLER: Yes, this is often heard. One answer can be found in the *Constitution on the Church,* which says that the religious life is a witness to the transcendental claims of Christianity. It says that the religious life "not only witnesses to the fact of a new and eternal life acquired by the redemption of Christ," but it "foretells the resurrected state and the glory of the heavenly kingdom." The same document insists that the religious life can be of great advantage to the salvific mission of the Church.

INTERVIEWER: Hasn't the time come for immediate renewal of the religious life?

BISHOP BUTLER: I think it is a time for drastic measures. I think that *most* certainly. One of the things that really rather upset me at the Council was that whenever the question of religious came up, there was an extreme supersensitiveness on the part of some religious superiors. They seemed to have an *esprit de corps* that was almost neurotic. I felt that they were consistently refusing even to make the effort to get down to the theological depths of the problem. They were continually taking refuge behind Canon Law. One of the first things we have to do is to delegalize the whole thing. We have to get down to the theological view and leave aside the legalistic view.

INTERVIEWER: How do you explain this sheltering behind Canon Law?

BISHOP BUTLER: I am not sure how to explain it. I suspect that it indicates a fear of the action of the local hierarchy or the local bishop. For the older Orders, of course, the obvious defense against the bishop is exemption. But exemption is a pure invention of Canon Law. The bias that some religious show to Canon Law distorts the true picture of things.

We also have to get behind some of the second-rate theologizing of what we used to call the Scholastic Tradition. I am becoming extremely skeptical about the old divisions that we've been used to, the distinctions between the active and contemplative life and the mixed life. I don't believe that that has any deep roots in tradition. If you study the Fathers, you will discover that they meant something different by the active and contemplative life than the scholastic theologians.

INTERVIEWER: Do you have any practical suggestions on how monastic life might be renewed?

BISHOP BUTLER: There is a tremendous amount of "clearing of the decks" to be done. To get down to particulars, we should begin with the Divine Office, which plays such a prominent part in our lives. For nearly all monks today, the articulation of the daily office into eight separate hours is no longer authentic. It no longer corresponds to a vital need. It was done in St. Benedict's time when they followed the seasons of the year and the hours of the sun and lived in a rural community. A much more meaningful way of dividing up the office for us would be to take a leaf out of the *Constitution on the Liturgy* and to see Lauds and Vespers as the two hinges on which the whole office revolves. That way you have a morning and an evening office, and you can add something in the way of a "little hour" at mid-day. Besides that I think that we need a solid block of prayer with the psalms and *lectio divina* that could be put at any convenient hour. This type of articulation rings much truer.

INTERVIEWER: The younger generation would agree with that.

BISHOP BUTLER: I am very interested in the younger generation, although I don't pretend to understand it. It would be absurd for anybody of my age to pretend to. I do seem to glimpse certain things about them and I think that they have a horror, which I can respect as I understand it, for anything that is phony—anything that is hypocritical, unauthentic. They feel that we are preserving the present structure of the monastic office just for the sake of preserving. For them, the present articulation of the office doesn't make sense. They almost shriek with repulsion when, for instance, we say Sext and None in one fell swoop and start off twice in the course of ten minutes with *Deus in adiutorium meum intende,* which is obviously the beginning of a new time of prayer. It's like bad music to them. Something should be done about this.

INTERVIEWER: Do you think that the psalms are still authentic vehicles of prayer?

BISHOP BUTLER: The psalms, I feel (and perhaps I'm a bit old-fashioned about it) are the inspired prayerbook of the Church and they have a permanent value. They are so remote that they are easier to universalize and to apply to new situations than some modern prayers would prove to be.

INTERVIEWER: What of the readings from the Fathers?

BISHOP BUTLER: This is something else. I agree that the Fathers for the most part are not helpful. Perhaps better selections could be found. Let us take, for example, the homilies in our office that are supposed to be the exegesis for the Scripture of the day. Now if there is one thing that is quite clear about the Fathers, it is that their exegesis was nearly always wrong! It's one of the most remarkable things about the Fathers. I don't know why the strict conservative who thinks that tradition is an independent channel of preserving revelation hasn't insisted more on this point. The early Fathers always get the right results by the wrong exegetical method.

INTERVIEWER: The vow of stability, that unique Benedictine vow whereby one promises to live in a particular monastery, is being re-examined by the monks themselves. I recently met a monk who justified his nearly two hundred days of absence from the monastery in one year by the argument that the essential part of the vow of stability is the stability of the heart or loyalty and not merely the geographic stability of place. What are your thoughts on stability?

BISHOP BUTLER: Lord Walsingham, foreign diplomat in the reign of Elizabeth I, used to describe his job as being to lie abroad in the service of her majesty. I think that the formal element in stability is the *stabilitas cordis*—stability of the heart. Now we are getting down very near the basic roots of the monastic problem. Monasticism had its genesis in a cultural background entirely different from what we are growing into at the present day. Stability meant a great deal more and had a great deal more positive value in those days than it has today. It meant that you grew into a total local environment that was only doing rather better and more deliberately what everybody tended to do in those days. There wasn't much instability in the life of the ordinary person. Today, we live in a world where the horizons are so widened and the socialization has become such, that the old idea of local stability does not have the same role to play in monasticism as it used to. I say this with great hesitation, because I am convinced that *local* stability has an obvious value. It makes the *stabilitas cordis* not merely a kind of pious velleity, but a positive incarnational thing. As men, we do form a concrete, human family in our local monastery, and we interact with one another directly in a very obvious way. It could be that because the world is going so socialized and so universalized that it needs a counterpoise that monasticism offers.

INTERVIEWER: You don't feel that the uniqueness of Benedictine monasticism is in jeopardy if a liberal view of stability is adopted?

BISHOP BUTLER: What is most specific in monasticism, compared with other forms of religious life in the Church, is allegiance to the local abbot. In Orders like the Dominicans or Franciscans your allegiance would be to a superior who rules thousands of people all over the world. He is a remote figure, and few of his subjects have any contact with him. Even if a Benedictine spends half a year outside the monastery, he does know his abbot personally and has a personal link with the other brethren in the monastery. This *does* make a great difference.

INTERVIEWER: On the other hand, the Dominicans, Franciscans, or Jesuits also have their local superior, and they live in a community structure. While it's true that monasticism insists *more* on the communitarian aspect of life, can it still do so if it accepts a very wide view of stability that does not stress the *local* aspect— the permanence in a *particular* place?

BISHOP BUTLER: It is very difficult to conceptualize such things. But in my own abbey, for instance, we have a certain number of parishes where the monks are in charge, and they spend years outside the monastery. I feel that the relationship between the monk in the distant parish and his abbot is of a human quality different from the relation between a friar and his local superior. Apart from the pope, there is no higher superior for a monk than his abbot.

INTERVIEWER: Declericalization is a primary goal in the present religious renewal. How does this apply practically to monasticism?

BISHOP BUTLER: The separation in monastic life between the

clerical family and the lay brotherhood is in itself an absolutely outrageous thing! Here we must get back to the spirit of the founder. If there is one thing about which I am absolutely certain it is that St. Benedict conceived of monastic life as a way of being a *Christian, not* a way of being a priest. You might be a priest as well, but it is accidental to your monastic vocation. The present state of things in monasticism in the West is a bit of a scandal. It almost amounts to a dictation to the Holy Ghost. You tell the Holy Ghost that He may not give a full monastic vocation to anybody unless he couples it with a quite different thing, which is a sacerdotal vocation.

INTERVIEWER: Historically, the tendency to clericalize goes back to the eighth or ninth century.

BISHOP BUTLER: It did begin as early as that, but I think that the monstrosity of the lay brother probably came in about the end of the eleventh century or the beginning of the twelfth. In a legalized form it was a Cistercian invention. It is helpful to remember that we do belong to the *Catholic* Church and that Eastern monasticism has never fallen into this awful abyss.

INTERVIEWER: Let us for a moment discuss the subject of theology. As an Englishman and a theologian, do you think that modern theology has successfully answered the challenge put forth by linguistic analysis?

BISHOP BUTLER: No.

INTERVIEWER: Do you think theology has a duty to answer?

BISHOP BUTLER: Yes, there is a duty. I would like to preface my remarks by saying that I am not a professional philosopher. I am inclined to think that linguistic analysis is a rather provincial phenomenon and a rather transitory stage in the total history of philosophy. It will probably have done some good in much the same way as the Greek Sophists in forcing men to be careful in their use of language and to reflect upon their use of language. *In toto,* linguistic analysis is not too important, but in the actual situation, it happens to be important because it controls a great deal of the higher culture of the West in its more sophisticated side. I don't think that we have faced up to it yet.

INTERVIEWER: Perhaps Bernard Lonergan's contributions in theological epistemology may be useful here.

BISHOP BUTLER: I personally think that Lonergan's contribution in his book, *Insight,* and his previous articles on the *Verbum,* constitute something of an absolutely epoch-making scale in the life of the Church. One of his most important contributions has been to force us back, through an examination of the problems of hermeneutics, to a realization that a *critical* metaphysics is something that is indispensable for man, for baptized man, and for Christianity.

In his discussion of Plato, Lonergan remarks that in interpreting Plato, you can reach a position in which the only possible interpretation of Plato is the reproduction of an exact, critical text of the Greek of Plato. After indicating that this is not really a sane solution to the problem of exegesis and hermeneutics, he then goes on to show that unless you have a reflexive, critical metaphysical position of which you can be absolutely certain, you can have no criterion by which to test your interpretation. This is a vitally important issue for Christianity, which is continually engaged in a task of reinterpreting the foundation of its doctrine.

INTERVIEWER: Some theologians fear that the theology that seems to be emerging from the Council is nonprofessional, shallow, jargon theology that does not seriously meet the issues.

BISHOP BUTLER: There is a danger that this might take place. The Church, of course, is always in a state of unstable equilibrium. A reaction against the manualistic scholasticism was overdue, and it came with a great flourish. It came with such a rush that now there's been a swing of the pendulum to another extreme. In one of the speeches that I made at the Council for which I am not sorry, as I am for some of the others, I tried to suggest that the Council was witnessing a confrontation of two theological approaches: the old deductive, scholastic approach and the newer approach that is based on an historical method. However, it is not a question of a genuine "either-or." We don't have to reject the deductive approach in order to adopt the historical method. But what we are feeling about for, or at least *should* be feeling about for, is a higher synthesis. In the end, we shall need a new scholasticism that won't necessarily be a new Thomism.

INTERVIEWER: You mean that we will need a new metaphysics?

BISHOP BUTLER: I mean that we will need a new systematic conceptualization in theology. Strictly speaking, we don't need a new metaphysics, because I happen to believe that there is truth in the phrase, *"philosophia perennis."* Here is where Lonergan has shown us the way. What Thomas is to Aristotle, Lonergan is to Thomas. There is a real continuity there, a real identity of the sort that Newman refers to when he says that here below for things to make progress is to change and to be perfect is to have changed often; and in changing often, you succeed in maintaining your own identity. There is a real metaphysical continuity from Aristotle to the present, but now we need a fresh conceptual systematization. Ultimately, the human spirit can't get along without that, although I doubt whether the moment has come for it yet. We are in such a state of dynamic change that it is not wise to fetter things too soon.

INTERVIEWER: Will we arrive at it in this century?

BISHOP BUTLER: No. I should think that perhaps in about 250 years.

INTERVIEWER: In the meantime, what will be the task of theology?

BISHOP BUTLER: To begin with, there is a fresh task, or at least the permanent task has increased its scope enormously of collecting, sifting, and classifying data. You remember how Lonergan divides up the intellectual process. First of all, there is the perception; then you arrive at the stage of organization and understanding of the data, which eventually leads to a judgment. What we want theologically is the judgment. But many of our theological judgments were inherited from the Middle Ages and are based not only on a far too narrow range of data, but also on a range of data that mixes, in a grand sort of confusion, things that are of the essence of sacred tradition with purely contingent medieval factors. All this has got to be broken down and looked at afresh. The Church today faces not only Europe and the Graeco-Roman culture, but the whole world, which must include the various Eastern traditions. There is also much work to be done in the real understanding of the Bible itself and primitive tradition. This is going to take a long time. You can't hurry this very much because it's a question of maturation and of an attitude of the mind.

INTERVIEWER: Do you foresee any dangers inherent in the challenge facing future theologians?

BISHOP BUTLER: The principal danger of the period is going to be that we may have almost lost contact with our metaphysical substratum in the process. This brings us back to a subject that we discussed earlier—the function of monks and other religious in the Church. It is a curious thing, not really curious, but rather remarkable, but I think that in so far as people are really trying to pray at a deep level, they become sensitively aware of the metaphysical dimensions of our natural existence. This is something that religious can contribute. One of the things that I am frightened about in the Church at the present moment is the superactivism that is developing and that could go into an unholy alliance with kerygmatic theology. This would leave us with a terribly superficialized Christian consciousness. We are living in a decadent period as regards reflective, philosophical thought. I don't see any easy way of dealing with that particular problem, and perhaps the right thing to do is to pursue the avenues that seem to offer some promise for the moment.

INTERVIEWER: Can polemical theology be justified any more?

BISHOP BUTLER: I find it difficult to answer that one, since I have spent so much of my life in controversy. However, I should say that polemical theology should play a subordinate role, even though it does help to clarify one's own mind. Yet it is very easy to exceed the bonds of charity when one gets too polemical.

INTERVIEWER: Today's theologian will certainly have to face the problem of authority in the Church. Some feel that the Council has precipitated this crisis.

BISHOP BUTLER: Broadly speaking, the Council has precipitated such a crisis. The crisis was in the womb, so to speak, before the Council opened, but the Council brought it well and truly to birth. By the end of the first session, people realized that the image of theology as a monolithic structure was now irretrievably over-thrown, destroyed, and disintegrated. From that moment onward, the crisis of authority and obedience was inevitable—partly because we had been putting across a claim for authority that was completely untenable, as the Council has shown. It was one of the most dramatic and exciting things throughout the Council to find that you only had to force the issue onto a fully theological level to discover that very often the conservatives hadn't a foot to stand on. This is very worrying, because then you have to face the question: "Well look, where do you find *terra firma* in the whole problem of authority?"

INTERVIEWER: And the answer to that question?

BISHOP BUTLER: Well, that's another story. I believe that the *terra firma* is the dogmatic definitions of the Church that claim infalli-bility. But one might say: "Why should we stop there? Why not relativize the infallible definitions, too? Is the notion of infallibility still viable in the modern world?" Now I hold that emphatically it is, and that unless you are prepared to accept the definitions of the Church from the Council of Nicea to the Assumption of Our Lady as infallible, then there is no stopping ground short of com-plete and utter liberalism. I agree (in part!) with the celebrated Canadian Presbyterian, Doctor Machen, who said that whereas, of course, Roman Catholicism is an extremely corrupt form of Chris-tianity, it *is* a form of Christianity; Liberalism is a different re-ligion altogether.

INTERVIEWER: A critical area in the problem of authority is the question of religious assent—that assent given to an authoritative but noninfallible statement of the Church.

BISHOP BUTLER: First of all, let's clear away a possible miscon-ception. We must distinguish between the practical disciplinary aspect and the claim on the speculative intellect. Having made that distinction, I think that there is probably some real value concealed behind the idea of religious assent. But it is extremely difficult to state it in a way that is itself satisfying to the speculative intellect, because a thing is either certainly true or not certainly true. If it is not certainly true, then it is questionable. The furthest you can go there is to say: "I am myself not infallible; this comes from the highest authority and with all the apparatus of authority backing it up I should be prepared to give an assent to the notion that probably the Church is stating a truth here."

INTERVIEWER: The presumption, then, is in favor of the Church?

BISHOP BUTLER: Yes, but it is only a presumption, and all presumptions fail against a contrary certainty. We are speaking all along only of noninfallible teaching and only of the speculative intellect.

INTERVIEWER: What action could a person take who, as a qualified expert, has a legitimate doubt about the objective truth of an authoritative statement of the Church?

BISHOP BUTLER: You have to be very careful in your public, external behavior, because there is a duty of not "rocking the boat." There is a genuine and valuable *esprit de corps* that we have to consider. Also there is the question of possible scandal to the faithful. If you have objective reasons for your doubt, then you have a perfect right to make these reasons discreetly known in the right quarters.

INTERVIEWER: How does one carry this out in practice?

BISHOP BUTLER: I agree that it is much more difficult these days. In *principle,* I feel that my answer is correct. Thirty years ago, I remember coming across a young Catholic who said about a particular Church teaching: "I just can't take this." He had given up frequenting the sacraments. After considerable discussion, I finally told him, and I don't think I was being disloyal to the Church in any way, that if he was sure that his position contradicts the official position, then he should fall back on my distinction between infallible dogma and any other kind of teaching.

INTERVIEWER: Wouldn't this lead to a gradual disregard for any Church teaching that is not infallible? It seems to minimize the role of the Church as teacher, guide, and protector.

BISHOP BUTLER: I know exactly what you mean, but I don't think that such a conclusion necessarily follows. We have to review what we mean by the infallibility of the ordinary *Magisterium.* I am sure that when they talk about it they are talking about something that is real, but I think they apply to the ordinary *Magisterium* categories and concepts that only apply properly to the extraordinary *Magisterium*. The latter started its eventful history in 325 A.D. with the *homoousion* of Nicea. Already, by the end of the second century, you have Irenaeus saying that the Church is always safe in following the universal episcopate. Now if you take Irenaeus' remarks and interpret them in the light of the attitude that we have learned to adopt regarding infallible definitions, then you make Irenaeus mean that every specific thing that happens to be said unanimously by the whole hierarchy is infallibly true. But I doubt very much whether he meant that or that he thought in those terms. What he meant was that you are safe when you *sentire cum ecclesia*. That is, you believe that God overrules things in such a way that the *Magisterium* doesn't take the Church irreparably or even gravely away from the path of truth.

INTERVIEWER: As a concluding question, Father Abbot, would you describe the path that led you to the Church.

BISHOP BUTLER: The one thinker who, humanly speaking, saved my Christianity was Frederic von Hugel. I read him before I was a Catholic. At that time, I was tempted to think that Oxford Hegelianism, which is now very much despised, might be the real answer to the problem of existence. Von Hugel restored my faith in the possibility that Christianity might, after all, have the answer. That was one of the turning points in my life.

INTERVIEWER: Did Newman influence you in any way?

BISHOP BUTLER: Once I was able to see the meaning of Christianity, I found in Newman the reason to become a Catholic. He made it possible and necessary for me to become a Catholic. I had hardly taken the step when, I recall, I had a conversation with the clergy in a presbytery in England. I discovered with a shock that Newman was regarded as being completely out as regards philosophy and theology—a good man, no doubt, but not at all Catholic.

✤✤

CHRISTOPHER BUTLER was born on May 7th, 1902 in Reading, England. He attended Reading School and St. John's College, Oxford

University. He received the Gaisford Greek Prose prize and the Craven scholarship award at Oxford. He was a tutor at Keble College, Oxford, from 1925 to 1927 and the following year the Classics Master at Brighton College. In 1926, he became a deacon in the Church of England. Two years later, he entered the Catholic Church, and, in 1929, joined the Benedictine community at Downside. He was ordained in 1933. From 1940 to 1946, he was Head Master of Downside School. He was elected Abbot of Downside Abbey in 1946, and president of the English Benedictine Congregation in 1961. He was a member of the Doctrinal Commission at the Second Vatican Council. In November 1966, he was named auxiliary bishop of Westminster.

Bishop Butler's writings have appeared in many journals. He has written the following books: *The Originality of Matthew; Why Christ?; The Church and Infallibility; The Church and the Bible; Prayer, an Adventure in Living;* and *The Idea of the Church.*

Markus Barth

A quiet parlor facing the glass enclosed cloister garth of St. Anselm's Benedictine Abbey in Washington, D.C., is the scene of this interview. Markus Barth looks weary this evening as he enters the room, takes of his beret and rain coat, and stretches out in an overstuffed chair. He has good reason to be tired. This afternoon, he delivered a two-hour lecture on justification in St. Paul at the Catholic University, and he answered students' questions for another hour.

A tall, lean man, Dr. Barth has graying and thinning hair. His thick glasses give him a sad expression. But this look quickly changes when he begins to talk in a friendly and engaging manner. His face lights up as he speaks excitedly in short, sudden bursts. One is taken by surprise to hear him use American colloquialisms and slang in his pronounced Swiss-German accent. We talk for several hours, and then at about nine, I drive him to the National Airport for a flight to New York where the next morning he has a committee meeting of the World Council of Churches.

INTERVIEWER: The first question is an obvious one, and perhaps you have been asked it before. Are you a Barthian?

DR. BARTH: My father once said "Barthians are the bane of my life." The term was first used in the mid-Twenties. There were Barthians in Denmark, and my father was invited there to give a series of lectures. While there, he got into many arguments with the Barthians. Karl Barth is no more a Barthian than St. Paul was a Paulinist or Luther a Lutheran. If I am a Barthian, then I am certainly one according to the flesh. But I should like to be the son of my father also according to the spirit.

INTERVIEWER: How would you define a Barthian?

DR. BARTH: A Barthian is a reader and admirer of Karl Barth who somewhere in the course of the many volumes of his writings got stuck and stopped thinking. He takes one phase in my father's development or a phrase from his works and absolutizes it. There are many varieties of Barthians depending on what parts of my father's writings they like. Some concentrate on the early period, when the *Commentary on Romans* was written; others on the first volumes of his *Dogmatics;* others on his political writings; still others on his booklet on Mozart. At any rate, I believe that they most often misinterpret my father. For they frequently fail to follow the way he points out; rather, they enjoy having found a resting place at the wayside in the shade.

INTERVIEWER: Were you influenced greatly by your father?

DR. BARTH: Yes, indeed. I owe him almost all that I know about theology. It would be hard to measure the extent of his inspiration and guidance. He corrected me often and never ceased to stimulate me with new ideas. He once told me that his *Dogmatics* was not an answer to certain questions, but an attempt to discover a method to ask questions. I learned from him that he is a good theologian who is a good listener. A theologian will always be ready to hear what the Bible says. The Bible is relevant and does not have to be made so.

INTERVIEWER: Critics say that the earlier Barth emphasized the "otherness" of God, while the later Barth is more Christological. Do you agree?

DR. BARTH: There are several critical periods in my father's career in which he stressed certain things more than others. It is true that when he was younger he emphasized the abyss between God and man in an effort to protect the unique character of God's nature. His *Commentary on Romans* contained a strong and a strange message. But since 1932, in his *Church Dogmatics,* he gave much greater emphasis to Jesus Christ Incarnate. In fact, I think he was always Christological in his thinking. But as he got older, he became more joyful in his study of the Incarnation. In his early years, he might have said that men saw Christ's glory *in spite of* the Incarnation, but in his later years, he became aware that we saw Christ's glory *because of* the Incarnation.

INTERVIEWER: How does your theological approach differ from your father's?

DR. BARTH: I will explain by first giving a little background information. Unlike my grandfather, Fritz Barth, my father was not a New Testament specialist in the technical sense of a historical-critical exegete. New Testament studies have become my field of interest, while my brother Christoph chose for himself the study of the Old Testament. My father was and is a preacher; because of the immense task of preaching, he worked in the dogmatic field. He never earned a Ph.D., but he has received eleven honorary degrees. I have made some infantile attempts here and there to correct my father. For example, in 1943, he wrote a book: *The Church Doctrine on Baptism*. A little later, Cullmann replied with another doctrine of baptism. His was a kind of Lutheran counter-attack to what he thought was the extreme Calvinism of Karl Barth's teaching. This debate fascinated me, and so I set to work to find out just what the New Testament writers individually or as a group were saying to the modern propositions on baptism and older beliefs. After studying the issue, I concluded that some of the questions that my father and Cullmann were asking were not the decisive issues treated in the New Testament. For example, the distinction between the ontic and the noetic did not fit into the witness of the Bible that is primarily concerned with the covenant relationship between the free God and redeemed man. Thus, I wrote the book, *Die Taufe—ein Sakrament?*, which placed much stress on the definition of baptism found in *1 Peter* 3:21 and resulted in a more radical exposition of the nature of baptism than my father's. Baptism became now a cornerstone in the realm of ethics. For a little while, I disagreed quite seriously with my father. I was brash enough to tell him that not one stone of his doctrine on baptism would remain unturned.

INTERVIEWER: How did he react?

DR. BARTH: First he laughed at my boldness and pointed out my exaggerations. But in the last lectures he gave at Basel, shortly before his retirement and his trip to the United States in 1962, he reconsidered the doctrine on baptism. He presented the place and meaning of baptism in a way that was very different from, though not wholly inconsistent with his earlier treatment. His results were even more radical than those of my book. But these lectures have never been published; the manuscript of some two hundred pages is in one of his desk drawers. He does not want to have them published before his death. Though he would like to work on the manuscript and to edit it, his reduced health and energy do not permit him the labor. While he still is carefully following the political trends—with special interest and joy those inaugurated by *Vatican II*—he is at present not doing any theological writing.

INTERVIEWER: Bishop Pike, in reviewing your book, *Acquittal by Resurrection,* said that it was an important book "which helps us to bridge this enormous gap that appears to exist between theology and humanity." Do you think that there is such a gap?

DR. BARTH: I think that a theology that is not human and humane is not theology at all. Theology has to deal with God Incarnate. God has already bridged the gap when He became man. The God we deal with in theology is the God that loved man and became one of us. In the whole of the Old Testament no less than in the New Testament, God tells the people that He is their God and they are His people. Theology that is true to its task does not have to reach out to humanity. By its very nature, theology deals with God who contacts humanity.

INTERVIEWER: Since God is man's Covenant Partner, theology must be incarnational.

DR. BARTH: Very much so. The God of whom we speak in theology was not ashamed to be called the God of Abraham. Then His name grew and He became the God of Abraham and Isaac. It grew even more and He was the God of Abraham, Isaac, and Jacob. In the continuing revelation, God draws closer and closer to men. He is not ashamed to be called their God. Finally, God is in Jesus Christ, in the cradle, among the sick, the criminals, the dead— even on the cross. If He is not ashamed to place Himself so low, then theology should not be ashamed to be human.

INTERVIEWER: To phrase it another way, can we say that there is no theology without anthropology?

DR. BARTH: In one of his latest writings my father suggested that true theology is theanthropology. In my book, *Conversation with the Bible,* I tried to show that God not only reveals Himself but He also reveals who man is. In the Gospel of St. John, we have the statement of Pontius Pilate: "Behold the man." Note that this pagan calls Jesus Christ *the* man, not just *a* man. The intention of St. John in reporting the *"Ecce homo"* was to show that Christ is the true man. He is *the man* who acknowledges that God is right in His judgment and who receives the crown of thorns. If we want to know what it is to be human, we had better look at Christ. Though we may perceive various aspects of humanity when we study psychology, physiology, and sociology, we arrive at what is essentially human only when we study Jesus Christ.

INTERVIEWER: In many of your writings, you have been critical of Bultmann's interpretations. Do you disagree with his view of the Resurrection?

DR. BARTH: I consider it the primary task of a biblical scholar to look for the intention of the sacred authors in order to try and understand why they said certain things and to ward off impositions caused by later traditions and by supposed requirements of modern man. If we use the same Old Testament texts as a key to the event and meaning of the Resurrection that the New Testament writers allude to when they wrote about the Resurrection, then we must not only wonder at Bultmann's efforts to connect the Resurrection with mystery cults and Gnostic notions, but seriously question his religio-historical and existentialist interpretation of this event. Bultmann believes that our knowledge of Gnosticism and the mystery cults on one hand, and of modern man's psyche and predicament on the other, help us to see that Paul and John, when they spoke of the Resurrection, used strange and time-bound forms of teaching and imagery to convey the Gospel to the Gentile world. Bultmann thinks that the Christological pattern of humiliation and exaltation, of dying and rising, is bound up with the Gnostic redeemer myth and has had its day as much as that myth.

INTERVIEWER: What approach do you take to the Resurrection?

DR. BARTH: I think that we have to understand it in terms of the Old Testament. God's revelation through His faithful servants to a sinful people follows a special pattern. Joseph went down into the well and came up again; he went into prison and came out again; Israel went into Egypt and out again, and then it was redeemed. All the servants of God follow this route, as scholars like Ed. Schweizer have pointed out by reference to *Wisdom of Solomon* 2-5. So Christ, as exemplary man, the Messiah, died the death of a criminal and then rose again from the dead. In view of the number of Old Testament witnesses, I see no reason to take refuge in the testimony of Gnostic myths to explain Pauline and Johannine theology. Bultmann heartily cares for modern man and his acceptance of the *kerygma*. But I doubt whether the contents of the *kerygma* need be evaporized, and whether the resulting vapors alone will be powerful enough to heal mankind or even help certain individuals. Actually, Bultmann allegorizes the Resurrection when he demythologizes it. Demythologizing is the modern form of allegorization—done for the same reasons with the same tricks as were formerly employed by the Hellenistic interpreters of Homer and by the Alexandrian interpreters of the Bible. While there are indeed texts in the Bible that were written down for allegorical interpretation—as, for example, the dreams of Pharaoh and some parables— Paul preached Christ crucified and risen for one reason and purpose only: The two events of Calvary and of Easter were for him as for all Jews and Gentiles the sum, the means, the full revelation of God's work on behalf of man. They were not just a mythical garb into which he wrapped his witness to Christ in order to sell it the better on the contemporary religious market places. The Resurrection for Paul was certainly connected with the cross. He was convinced that Jesus Christ was raised as really as He had been crucified and that by His Resurrection He was justified by God (*1 Tim.* 3:16).

INTERVIEWER: Have Bultmann's views seriously affected American Protestantism?

DR. BARTH: He appears to be especially popular with some American Methodists. A possible reason for his growing influence upon theologians in this country is this: He allows them to do certain things with a good conscience that up till now they had held and done with a bad one. There has always been a strong tendency in American preaching to demythologize, that is, to moralize, to rationalize, to repeat platitudes. American Protestants in great numbers have tacitly done away with the Resurrection and the second coming of Jesus Christ. Before Bultmann came, they had many practical, but hardly any scholarly arguments to embellish their eclecticism and skepticism. But Bultmann came and appealed to their yearning for philosophical and academic respectability. I doubt whether this purification of conscience agrees with what the Epistle to the Hebrews calls purification of conscience!

INTERVIEWER: Some would say that Bultmann's startling claims had a good effect in that they made people realize that biblical theology is extremely important.

DR. BARTH: I agree. For this reason our generation owes a great debt to Bultmann. He was and is courageous and consistent enough to acknowledge that exegesis, dogmatics, and philosophical thought mutually influence and condition one another. But my father's *Commentary on Romans* had already performed a similar service. Harnack was genuinely shocked at some of the things my father said. He thought this was the end of historical, critical science, and he predicted my father would be a new Marcion. Many Christians have been shaken from their complacency by Bultmann, many by Karl Barth, many by Bonhoeffer—others were apparently waiting for Bishop J. A. T. Robinson. Upon hearing that nobody should accept the meaning of the virgin birth and the Ascension of Jesus Christ as children accept for true the absurdities of fairy tales, many people were forced to reconsider their good or blind faith, to examine themselves, and to find out whether they had relied upon something more solid than simple credulity.

INTERVIEWER: Does Bultmann's demythologizing lead him to a denial of the supernatural?

DR. BARTH: Bultmann in his theology of the New Testament speaks of the act of God that happens on the cross and in the *kerygma*. This act is something that happens beyond the realm of what man might manage; it is beyond the world of reason or *physis*. Bultmann does not call it supernatural—such a word is not in his vocabulary, and he is wise in avoiding it—but he says that God acts. Shubert Ogden and F. Buri have criticized Bultmann for retaining mythological elements in his teaching, even the "action of God" on Calvary and in the preaching of the Word. They say that he is inconsistent. But I would say that it is precisely this seeming contradiction that makes him a Christian. He seeks to attest to the living God, not to a God-idea which, of course, cannot act. Also he cannot say, as some fools do, that God is dead. I have a theory that the identity of man is constituted by the inconsistencies and contradictions that he combines and with which he tries to live. No man is *just* a rationalist, or an idealist, or a Marxist, or an existentialist. There are many elements that make up a man. Bultmann is a good illustration of the fact that the acknowledgment of the living God makes man human.

INTERVIEWER: Is Bultmann's concept of faith traditional?

DR. BARTH: The gift of faith is according to Bultmann an act of God that implies obedience, fear, love, and freedom. Faith is always related to the historical event of the cross. God meets us there, and we encounter God in Jesus of Nazareth; faith is the acknowledgment that in this man who looks like a rabbi and speaks with prophesy, we find God. Thus, faith is the opening of man's mind, heart, and will toward God and toward all that God will bring about. It is at the same time the miracle of finding authentic selfhood, true existence, and a loving relationship to our fellowman. By freeing man from his servitude of this world, from pride and from death, faith makes him responsive to the Creator and his creatures. Untraditional in this concept of faith is the separation of faith from the sacraments and other so-called "objective" events, and the existentialist nomenclature and the dependence upon slogans like encounter, opening to the future, authentic being. Traditional is—on the positive side—the orientation toward God and Jesus Christ, also eventually toward the neighbor, and—on the negative side—an individualist and abstract inclination that is present already, not in *Heb.* 3–4 and 11, not in *Rom.* 3–5 or in Galatians, and certainly not in the theology of St. James, but in the time-honored distinction, combination, and discussion of *notitia, assensus, fiducia* and the like. Personally, I feel indebted to Bultmann for opening the issue of faith anew. While his treatment of the Resurrection and his rugged individualism should be a warning to us all, he strives honestly to show that the totality of man's life is determined by God's act. God wills that man enjoys freedom and lives from love courageously.

INTERVIEWER: Did Catholic authors like Durrwell and Lyonnet influence you in your study of the Resurrection?

DR. BARTH: Very much so, for I discovered that they asked the same questions that I did. The central question was: What does St. Paul mean when he says that Christ *was raised for our justification?* There are some Protestant authors who say that this statement was but a traditional formula that has its roots in an early liturgy; however, they argued that we shouldn't take this expression too seriously, because Paul might as well have written that Christ *was delivered* for our justification. Indeed, Paul may well have taken over this formula from tradition. But even if he did, it must have made sense to him. Durrwell and others wondered what was the precise meaning of it. I felt the same way, but I couldn't find in Protestant commentaries a serious treatment of the problem. The Catholic exegetes you mentioned are among those who are about to do more than just catch up with Protestant exegesis. However, there is at least one point on which I cannot agree with Father Lyonnet. In an essay on justification, he says that the judgment vocabulary employed by Paul for describing the justification of the sinner does not fully serve the apostle's purpose. Lyonnet believes that when Paul says righteousness he doesn't mean judgment, but only a father's mercy. Though Calvin on one occasion takes the same stand ("In heaven we don't have a judge but a merciful father"), I do not think that the Pauline texts support this assumption. Rather, Paul follows those prophets and psalms that praise the triumph of God's faithfulness even *in* His judgments.

INTERVIEWER: You once wrote that "through the Resurrection man is vindicated against all powers hostile to humanity." Isn't the overwhelming presence of evil in the world an apparent contradiction to this statement?

DR. BARTH: The question you asked is a Jewish argument against the faith of Christians. It is argued that if Jesus were the Messiah and if His Resurrection were the beginning of a new age, then the world would have changed. But look around and you see that it hasn't! Therefore, some say, Jesus is just another one of the Messianic pretenders. To answer this objection, which is as old as Christianity itself, we must go back to the Old Testament. In Daniel we have the vision of the four beasts: the lion, the bear, the leopard, and a dreadful-looking animal with iron teeth and horns. These animals represent the powers of this world (be they political, economic, psychic or of any other sort) in their demonic dimension. These animals were slain and divested of their power when God's kingship was established in heaven and upon earth. The Son of Man appears on a cloud and to Him is given dominion, glory, and kingly power. He establishes a reign of peace among the nations. In *Psalm* 22, we find a desperate cry to the Lord to save His servant who is surrounded by lion-like bulls and dogs. Like Daniel, the psalmist knows of deliverance. He praises God and asks everyone to praise the Lord who rules over all the nations and who protects His followers. This same notion is found in the first chapters of Hebrews where the author insists that the Lord will give rest to those faithful to Him. He quotes from *Psalm* 110, which says that the Lord's enemies will become a stool for His feet. Still the author proves to be a realist and faces (in *Heb.* 2:8b) the objection that "we still do not see that everything is subjected to Him." This is his reply: though we don't *see* the submission of all power, it is still true. For "we see Jesus, who for a little while was made lower than the angels, crowned with glory and honor because of the suffering of death, so that by the grace of God He might taste death for everyone." We are told that by His death and Resurrection Jesus has conquered the powers that are hostile to humanity—even though this might not be evident to historians, sociologists, or readers of newspapers. With Cullmann we might put it this way: The devil is already chained, but he is still on a long chain. He seeks to behave and roar as if he were free, but he is still on the chain.

INTERVIEWER: Can we conclude from the above statements that

the Resurrection acts as a norm of morality for the Christian?

DR. BARTH: Yes, the mysterious event of the Resurrection is an answer to all questions concerning right and wrong. For the Stoic and for some philosophers of law today natural law or the conscience of man is ultimately determinative of right and wrong. The natural law is something to fall back on when the positive law goes bankrupt. For the New Testament writers, the *judgment of God,* which was passed in the death and the Resurrection of Christ, is the legal constant. This righteous judgment ending with acquittal is the moral and historical ground on which the writers of the New Testament think about marriage, obedience to the state, fellowship, and such things. The history made by God, that is, the knowledge of God's judgment, gives them an advantage over the Stoics. While the natural law of the Stoics is an elusive thing that cannot be defined, the New Testament writers acknowledge and proclaim that historical events change all things drastically. The death and Resurrection of Christ is "the greatest drama ever staged," to borrow a phrase from Dorothy Sayers.

INTERVIEWER: You once said that "we are all Augustinians." In what sense did you mean that?

DR. BARTH: The Augustinian influence is so omnipresent that I don't know where to begin. One aspect of Augustine is that in the quest for authentic being we must begin by looking into our souls—the soul is made the criterion of what happens to me and how I react to it. Another aspect of Augustine is his emphasis on the social Gospel—to be a Christian is to get involved. The Christian should not despair of the evil he sees in the world, but he must get involved so that he can do something that can change the evil to good. This is the idea of the *City of God* where he speaks of the glorious calling of the Church as opposed to the decay found in the crumbling Roman empire here below. Then there is a strong Neoplatonic strand in Augustine—in his *Confessions* he speaks of his indebtedness to Plato—where he takes up the dualistic Manichean pattern. The distinction of the spiritual from the the earthly world, of the visible from the invisible, provides him with a metaphysical problem that was far from the issues faced by the patriarchs, the prophets, and the psalmists. Augustine super-imposed an ontological and metaphysical scheme upon his under-standing of Word and Sign, Grace and Church, Soul and Freedom that made the teaching of the Western Churches indigestible to Jews and that eventually led to the split between Orthodox, Roman, and Protestant Christianity and that equated faith in Jesus Christ with the acceptance of a time-bound world-view or philosophy that was to be overthrown by discoveries and theories of later times. The various Augustinian themes are still being discussed and are still proving divisive in Christian theology. Many Catholics and Protestants still believe that the penetrating and helpful in-sights of Augustine might be applied to contemporary problems and can help solve them. I doubt the wisdom and success of this procedure.

INTERVIEWER: Why don't you think that Augustine is a natural, common ground for ecumenical understanding?

DR. BARTH: There is some danger in basing the ecumenical movement on an Augustinian foundation. It's true that Protestants and Catholics might feel at home with Augustine, but what about the Orthodox Christians and the Jews? If the ecumenical move-ment seeks the unity of God's people in God's service and in the witness to God before the world, we cannot make it exclusively ecclesiastical and exclude the Jews. The ecumenical movement started by Pope John and encouraged by Pope Paul now is some-times viewed with suspicion by Jews. They feel that if Christians unite, there will be in the long run a terrible persecution of the Jews. I don't think that Augustine can solve the common prob-lems that Western Christians, Eastern Christians, and Jews face today. More than him, we need the witness of the Old Testament to the Messiah and to the ways and victory of God's righteousness upon earth, and more than him, we also require and request the aid of the Jews to make us free from the all too many pagan shackles that mar the Church, its theology, its conduct.

INTERVIEWER: Origen has been suggested as a possible rallying point.

DR. BARTH: Yes, I know that some feel that Origen would have equal appeal to the East and West. Origen is too ambiguous. He is a docetist and an adoptionist; a sacramentarian and a biblicist; a milleniarist and a spiritualist. He has something for everybody, and everybody must have something against him. In no way could he be a genuine unifying force. This does not mean that his, or Augustine's, or Anselm's, or Thomas', or Luther's, or Calvin's, voice need not be heard anew in our search for unity. But it does mean that—on the ground of *Eph.* 4:13—our unity is to be found in a better obedience and faith to God and service to the world, rather than in any reliance upon a person or system of the past.

INTERVIEWER: Do Protestants feel comfortable with St. Paul?

DR. BARTH: Not in America, so it seems to me. Americans don't like to think systematically, abstractly, or philosophically. Paul appears to look to many like a producer of dogmatic propositions. Most Americans are pragmatists, and their theology can't help but be pragmatic. European theology, on the other hand, is more idealistic, didactic, and deductive. How many Europeans avoid asking the question: "What good will it do to others or to the world, if I believe this or that?" St. Paul is still the patron saint of many Europeans, especially German Protestant theologians, though his teaching is very different from the theories on faith and justification that have been produced in those quarters. I believe that Americans might find a genuinely biblical footing if they would really study and follow St. James. His is a type of wisdom theology that has most ancient roots in Israel's history and theology and that may have great appeal to Americans though it will also sharply criticize them.

INTERVIEWER: You have done special study in the critical problem of justification by faith in St. Paul. What conclusions have you reached?

DR. BARTH: Faith can have three basic meanings in St. Paul. It can mean faith on God's part—His faithfulness in upholding the covenant even when Israel breaks it; it also means the faith or perhaps better, the fidelity or faithfulness of Christ; and finally it means man's faith—the response given by the Spirit of God so that man may praise the gift and revelation of God.

INTERVIEWER: Which of these would Luther accept?

DR. BARTH: Luther puts most emphasis on the third—man's acceptance and complete, blind trust in God. It is man's openness, rather his passivity to let God do what He must do. Luther rightly felt that a troubled conscience could be consoled by letting God have His way. In this area, Luther was a mystic. But a danger lurks in the one-sided emphasis: Faith may easily become an end in itself, even faith in faith, a sort of fideism or an attitude that is independent of history, of the community, and of ethical responsibility and action. Calvin, however, added something different. He agreed with Thomas' commentary on Titus and Luther in saying that justification is "by faith alone," but he emphasized that there is also the gift of sanctification. The same God who justifies also sends the Spirit to give new life to the redeemed. This new life involves new obedience. Lutherans argued that Calvin introduced the law through the back door in the name of sanctification and that he ended up being a legalist.

It is interesting to note that in Bible translations and commentaries, with one recent exception, the term *pistis Christou Iesou* is always interpreted as faith *in* Christ, rather than faith *of* the Messiah, Jesus. Only R. N. Longenecker (in *Paul, Apostle of Liberty*) quotes a series of authors who (on the basis of *Heb.* 2-3 and many Pauline passages) speak of Jesus Christ's faith. There is a faith that at the same time is fully human and fully divine, which is not only passive but equally active. It is the faith of the God-man. By His faith we are justified. It is His faith that is spread abroad by the Spirit that He gives from on high. This faith is not private or quietistic, but social and active. The question immediately to be asked is this: How could so patent a fact be overlooked for so long? If anybody, then the professional exegetes may have been guilty of gross neglect.

INTERVIEWER: What are the exegete's responsibilities?

DR. BARTH: The exegete has only one responsibility: to seek the truth by listening to biblical texts. As long as he seeks truth at this place, his work will be ecumenically oriented. For the Bible itself is a collection of ecumenically oriented literature. God's revealed truth creates diversity within the unity of service and witness. An exegete should look at his texts without holy or unholy prejudices and use all the knowledge at his disposal to arrive at the precise meaning of the divine message. This is an over-whelmingly hard task; sweat, tears, and blood are found on the path to its fulfillment. No exegete should be hampered either by petty, insignificant restrictions imposed upon him by church officials or by the ambition to please his own or other people's latest philosophy. Nor should he strive to make newspaper head-lines. Like Jerome, he will do his best work in the seclusion of his study, but like a lion he may at times have to roar publicly. In this age of biblical renewal, the exegete has a special role to play. He must play it in all honesty and humility.

INTERVIEWER: You mentioned that your father was criticized for his views on justification.

DR. BARTH: Yes, members of the Dutch Gereformeerde church severely criticized him for the supposed universalism of his presenta-tion of St. Paul's message of justification. American "Fundamen-talists" joined them in the assumption that Karl Barth preaches unconditional salvation that eliminates faith. They misread St. Paul, my father, and other authors. Berkouwer's book *The Triumph of Grace* is a noteworthy exception.

INTERVIEWER: Can we say that in St. Paul there is an appreciation of the social, communitarian aspect of justification as well as the individual aspect?

DR. BARTH: St. Paul's doctrine of justification is neither individual-istic nor quietistic. St. Paul speaks always of a social event, that is, of the Jews and Gentiles that are made *one* in Christ. We cannot say that there is the mystical Paul who talks about oneness in Christ and a legal Paul who speaks about justification. The unifica-tion of Jews and Gentiles in Christ through His death and Resur-rection and justification by faith is all one action. In *Eph.* 2:11-22; *Gal.* 2:11-21; *Rom.* 3-4; 9-11 Paul speaks of justification in such terms that its social, ethical character shines equally bright as its gracious and spiritual essence. The Church consists of Jews and Gentiles, free men and slaves, laborers and managers who sit at the one table together. The Church is a representative union of all men. Individual men are justified by sharing in the justification of the community. It is impossible to distinguish between, or separate, the righteousness of the individual members of the whole body of Christ and of the totality of mankind that is represented by the Church. The Church is a society. It is not a static, closed community, but a growing body. In St. Paul, the Church grows quantitatively in numbers and qualitatively in faith and good works.

INTERVIEWER: Do you have any suggestions to make concerning the importance of ecumenism in seminary education?

DR. BARTH: I would say that ecumenics is not one, separate field of study in the seminary curriculum. We must teach all theological subjects in an ecumenical orientation. Still we shall be realistic and humble only when we realize that the theological material that we try to communicate to the students is too bulky. We cover so many things so superficially that the students end up with having almost nothing. We need more courses that go into depth in selected, important areas of theology and fewer shallow survey courses. We should have training courses for men who are already out in the ministry. A postgraduate program that does not lead to an additional degree, but fills existing or emerging gaps, is essential if we are to keep our men aware of the progress in theology. After a man is ordained and has some experience in the ministry, he may be eager to come back and take a few good courses. I am also very much in favor of voluntary class attendance in the seminary. If a student can read the necessary books and is able to pass the examination, why should he come to a dull class, the highlights of which are quotations from textbooks? The lectures and seminars conducted by professors should introduce the student to doing careful, necessary, daring research; in these meetings, he himself should dare to stick his neck out—as is expected of every Christian in today's world.

INTERVIEWER: Do you think that the theological language used today is an obstacle or a help to communication?

DR. BARTH: The problem of communication is of critical importance. But the subject matter of communication is still more decisive than the method or methods chosen for its presentation.

If I used all the methodological tricks, but did not know *what* I really had to and wanted to say, all my striving and success would be in vain. I recognize that among the words we use to communicate biblical concepts, many are no longer adequate. It is difficult to make the man on the street understand what we mean by "realized eschatology," "total depravity," or "anthropology." The Bible uses simple words, but we theologians have preferred complicated ones. It is a pity that we have transformed theology into a kind of *kabbala*. We throw about Greek and Latin words as if everyone knows what they mean. We take words from Aristotle, Plato, or the Roman legal system and fail in the meantime to explain what a biblical statement actually may mean, or where its as yet unsolved mysteries might be located. The narrative style of the Bible is still a better form of communicating ultimate things than our well-meant definitions, deductions, and systematizations.

❧❧

MARKUS BARTH, the son of Karl Barth, was born on October 6th, 1915, in Safenwil, Switzerland. He received his university training in Berne, Basel, Berlin, and Edinburgh and was granted his doctorate in New Testament from the University of Göttingen in 1947. From 1940 to 1953, he was parish minister of the Evangelical Reformed Church in Bubendorff, Basselland, Switzerland. He came to this country in 1953 and has taught at the Presbyterian Theological Seminary, Dubuque, Iowa, and the University of Chicago. At present, he is Professor of New Testament at the Pittsburgh Theological Seminary. He is married and has five children.

Among Dr. Barth's writings are: *Das Abendmahl, Passamahl, Bundesmahl, und Messiasmahl; Die Taufe—ein Sakrament?; The Broken Wall; Was Christ's Death a Sacrifice?; Acquittal by Resurrection;* and *Conversation with the Bible.* He is also the author of many articles in various theological journals.

Yves Congar

Ah, Mon Père, we meet at last. What kind of questions are you going to ask me? Come now to my room and we will have a little talk, but, please, without your tape recorder." With these words, Father Congar greets me one morning after breakfast at the Morris Inn on the campus of the University of Notre Dame where we are both attending a theological conference. He is wearing a light-gray, double-breasted suit with a clerical collar that makes him look more like an Anglican vicar than a Catholic priest. Walking slowly with a cane, he brings me to his room on the second floor. A small altar is in one corner. His desk is covered with papers, books, and several small bottles of medicine. "Some days I cannot walk at all," he remarks as he painfully eases himself into a chair. Sitting there, he looks frail and tired, but as we discuss some of the subjects to be covered in our interview, he becomes excited and interested. His English, while decidedly Gallic, is adequate. In making an important point, his "passion française" becomes more evident as he occasionally raps on the desk for emphasis.

Later on in the day, I return for our interview (this time with the tape recorder). I begin by asking him about his student days before he entered the Dominicans.

INTERVIEWER: You might begin by telling us something of your intellectual formation.

FATHER CONGAR: I attended the seminary at the Institut Catholique for three years from 1921-24. I was only seventeen—quite a young boy. At that time, I came under the influence of some very strict Thomists. Abbé Lallement, for example, who was and still is teaching at the Institut, is a very saintly priest, but a narrow Thomist.

INTERVIEWER: Wasn't Jacques Maritain at the Institut at that time?

FATHER CONGAR: You are correct. I have a great admiration for Maritain and the role that he has played in the spiritual movement of the last fifty years. At times, I have wondered if one ought not to distinguish in him two men. There is the Maritain who is the man of broad vision and who wrote about art, politics, the Jewish problem, etc. Then there is, I should say was, the Maritain who wrote *Antimoderne* and that rather bad book, *The Three Reformers*.

INTERVIEWER: Why bad?

FATHER CONGAR: As you know, the book is about Luther, Descartes, and Rousseau. Unfortunately, the book is a good example of an *a priori* method. I doubt that Maritain has read more than thirty pages of Luther. He has not really tried to understand the *positive religious meaning* of his desire for reform. Now, in my opinion, nothing serious will be done on the ecumenical level as long as, while still denying the errors that I am the first to criticize, we do not recognize the profound religious intention of Luther and the Reform.

INTERVIEWER: Do you think that Maritain's wife, Raïssa, influenced him at all?

FATHER CONGAR: They lived *together* an intense intellectual and spiritual life. I knew Raïssa, and I have a glowing memory of her—first at Versailles in 1921-22, then at Meudon. Although I was a young seminarian at that time, I was admitted to the monthly Sunday afternoon meetings. On these visits, Maritain would explain a text, not from St. Thomas, but from John of St. Thomas. It was all very orthodox, and men like Kant, Leibnitz, or Hegel were always considered in a bad light because they failed to recognize a minute distinction that was made by St. Thomas in the *ad tertium* or *ad quartum* of some article.

INTERVIEWER: Your philosophical formation, then, gave no importance to the moderns.

FATHER CONGAR: I was brought up with a kind of contempt for all moderns. Everyone who had written after St. Thomas was rejected. Men like Blondel, Laberthonnière, and Maréchal were considered as contributing nothing to philosophy. I have read nothing of Maréchal. Blondel and Laberthonnière have always interested me because of the contribution they have made to theology. I am convinced that in time the importance of Blondel will grow even greater. When I realized that these men had great minds and had much to say, I began reading them earnestly. However, by that time it was too late. I can say that I had no real philosophical formation.

INTERVIEWER: Did you know Garrigou-Lagrange very well?

FATHER CONGAR: Oh yes. I belonged to a kind of intellectual fraternity before I became a Dominican. It was a spiritual fraternity, a Thomist fraternity. In September every year, we had a retreat that was preached by Garrigou-Lagrange. He impressed me very much with his profound grasp of the spiritual life, but most of all by his strong sense of affirmation. As a young man, I admired his positive spirit.

INTERVIEWER: Didn't you also study philosophy after you became a Dominican?

FATHER CONGAR: Since I had already studied philosophy for three years, I had only to take one year more after I entered the Order. The one man who could have perhaps opened my mind to modern philosophy, Father Roland Gosselin, was my teacher for only five or six months. That was not enough. And so I never entered into the philosophical mind and the philosophical attitude of the moderns.

INTERVIEWER: However, you did receive an excellent theological education.

FATHER CONGAR: Yes, I did. I must insist that *I believe* in theology very, very, very strongly. I am convinced that theology is necessary in the present condition of the Church. At Le Saulchoir, where I studied theology from 1926-31, the true notion of theology was that which Père Ambroise Gardeil explained in his book of 1909: *Le donné révélé et la théologie.* This book should be translated into English. The very title of this book is extremely important, for theology depends on *le donné*—the data of revelation. This includes the Scriptures, the Fathers, the liturgy. In a word, the whole tradition of the Church. Theology must always be related to *le donné,* for this is where it receives its life and criterion.

INTERVIEWER: Do you feel that you and Father Karl Rahner have a different theological method?

FATHER CONGAR: I have read your interview with Father Rahner, and it is clear that his theology is different from mine. Father Karl Rahner has a philosophical basis that I do not possess. His approach to theological and pastoral problems shows this quite clearly. He generally proceeds from concepts that he examines thoroughly and then specifies. Or he might examine the conditions that, *a priori,* render a problem accessible and soluble. Thus, he is able to take a new look at a problem and to hit upon an essential aspect of it in a new way. But he is also able, for example, to write an article on Catholic Action without citing one papal text. Nevertheless, he does know history well, the witness of tradition, and even his Denzinger. I have a great admiration for him, and even, I may say, affection. I also admire his intellectual courage and his extraordinary human feeling that, in the course of an extended discussion, shines through in a kindly but mischievous smile. He played an important role on the Theological Commission of the Council from the second session on, and everyone paid attention to what he said.

INTERVIEWER: Father Chénu's approach is closer to your own.

FATHER CONGAR: Yes, it is. Father Chénu, who is ten years older than I am, and my colleagues at Le Saulchoir feel that theology is *intellectus fidei.* Theology is the unfolding of faith in human reason, and it embraces the resources and methods proper to reason. It depends on the data of revelation, *le donné,* but it is not solely concerned with the past. Theology must answer the questions that men have. At times, it is in the most classic theological questions, the Trinity for example, that the questions of modern man afford new developments. I agree with Rahner that theology cannot be merely deductive; I am also critical of this form.

INTERVIEWER: You are considered to be a progressive or liberal theologian. Personally, do you feel that you are quite avant-garde?

FATHER CONGAR. Absolutely not. I hope that I am open-minded and that I recognize the problems of our time. But I am a man of tradition. This does not mean that I am a conservative. Tradition, as I understand it, is like the Church herself. It comes from the past, but looks forward to the future and sets the stage for a new eschatology. It is in this sense that the *Constitution on Divine Revelation* (cf. no. 8) speaks of it. Tradition is not constant and static; it grows and builds. I remember that Paul Claudel compared tradition to a man walking. In order to walk, you must have one foot on the ground and one in the air. If you have both on the ground, you don't move; if you have both in the air, you fall. Tradition always tries to answer current problems; it grows and renews itself. Nothing is more silly than to think that all has been said in the past.

INTERVIEWER: Would you still insist that you are a Thomist?

FATHER CONGAR: It is true that I am a follower of St. Thomas. I owe St. Thomas the best of all my work. Yet, for me St. Thomas does not have to be slavishly followed. For instance, on specific points concerning the Sacrament of Orders or the nature of the episcopate, I disagree with St. Thomas. But that is insignificant. If St. Thomas lived today, he would know facts that he did not know before. For me, St. Thomas is a master of thought, and he can form the mind and the judgment. In all his writings, he showed that he had a great respect for the truth. He was a model of loyalty and intellectual honesty and looked for the truth wherever he could find it. He was not one merely to repeat conclusions that he formed once and for all. All his life, he searched for new texts and for new translations from the Greek or the Arabic. As a man of dialogue, St. Thomas frequently entered into discussion with the "heretics" of his day. St. Thomas is the symbol of open-mindedness, the genius of reality. We should remain faithful to his spirit.

INTERVIEWER: Do you think that St. Thomas should still be studied in seminaries?

FATHER CONGAR: Of course. St. Thomas is mentioned explicitly in the decrees on the training of priests and on Christian education. In the case of the profane disciplines, autonomy of research is insisted upon and St. Thomas is presented as one authority, although not the only one. In the case of the sacred sciences, St. Thomas is proposed as a master. This does not mean simply repetition and the exclusion of other theologians. Rather, it means that we study under his guidance; we follow his spirit. I doubt that a better intellectual guide can be found.

I am distressed when I see young clerics, sometimes even seminary professors, trying to invent a new synthesis from scratch, to meet the needs of modern man, as they say. However, history has shown us that the first serious study of a subject consists in finding out what has been thought and created before us. If you are a musician, your first step is to study Bach and Mozart. So in theology we must begin by studying St. Augustine and St. Thomas. These are the classics. They are not the terminal point, but the point of departure and the foundation for future work.

INTERVIEWER: Speaking of classics, your aricle on *"Théologie"* in the *Dictionnaire de Théologie Catholique* is a classic source for the nature of theology. That appeared almost thirty years ago. If you had to rewrite it today, would you make any major changes?

FATHER CONGAR: I prepared this article in 1938 when Pius XII was pope. As for the historical part, some changes would have to be made because there has been progress in several areas. For example, scholars have shown the relationship between the monastic tradition and the scholastic tradition of the medieval universities. Already, in 1938, I did not believe very much in the so-called "theological conclusion." I had drawn away from the system of Father Marin-Sola. Today, with the exception perhaps of the Spanish and the Roman theological schools, creative theology does not follow the traditional schema. Have I ever followed it myself? To be sure in an article for the *Dictionnaire* it was necessary to classify established positions. However, if the classical system of theological reasoning is more abandoned today than followed, I personally have remained faithful to my major insights of 1938. It is for this reason that I have agreed to re-edit the article with some changes for

Doubleday and Company. One of the main ideas in that article was to distinguish between the two acts of theologizing. The first is the *auditus fidei* of which the scientific form is positive theology. This would include the knowledge of tradition, Scripture, the Fathers and the *Magisterium*. Secondly, there is the *intellectus fidei* that corresponds to speculative theology. This is the work of reflection and construction that helps us see how the truths are linked together. You must search for an organic structure.

INTERVIEWER: This is what St. Thomas means by *sacra doctrina*, does he not?

FATHER CONGAR: For St. Thomas, *sacra doctrina* means the whole complexus of divine, saving truth. It means Scripture and tradition, preaching, and catechizing. Theology as a science is only a function of *sacra doctrina* and preaching is higher than the science of theology. The end of theology for St. Thomas is eschatological. Faith itself, he insists, is a participation in the knowledge that God has of Himself. By faith we can have in our minds what the *beati* or *comprehensores* see in heaven—the *visio Dei*. But we only participate in it obscurely. St. Thomas defined dogma as *"perceptio veritatis tendens in ipsam."* Theology is born from the "already" and the "not yet." It is *already* a certain imitation of the knowledge of God possessed by the blessed, but it is trying its utmost to approach more effectively what it does *not yet* possess.

INTERVIEWER: What do you see as the greatest challenge facing modern theology?

FATHER CONGAR: The most important work today is to show the unity between theology and anthropology. They are always related. My friend, Rabbi Abraham Heschel, sums it up nicely when he says that "The Bible is not a theology for man, it is an anthropology for God." I believe that in fact it is both. I have quoted that sentence many times. It means that you cannot separate God and man. In the Bible, the affirmations about God are linked to the affirmations about man. And why should this be so? Because the content of revelation is not God as He is Himself exactly. God revealed Himself in the temporal revelation of the Incarnation and established a unique relation between Himself and man. Theologians like Rahner and Schillebeeckx might seem to be studying man more than God. But this is a false impression. They study God in light of modern anthropology, and I agree completely with this approach.

INTERVIEWER: Isn't this approach especially valuable for the problem of atheism?

FATHER CONGAR: Yes, it is a response to atheism. For many people today, atheism is not the negation of God, it is the affirmation of man. But they wrongly reason that one cannot affirm man and his great role in the world without saying that God is dead. This is false, and we must show them why it is false.

INTERVIEWER: As a working theologian you have published very much. How many articles have you written?

FATHER CONGAR: Oh, I don't know exactly.

INTERVIEWER: A hundred?

FATHER CONGAR: Several hundred at least, maybe more.

INTERVIEWER: How many books have you written?

FATHER CONGAR: Fifteen large or medium books, a dozen smaller ones. Theologians today do not have the time to write great tomes. We are constantly being asked to write articles, to attend congresses and academic conventions, and to give lectures. It is possible to collect the various talks and put them into a book. Nowadays, theologians are publishing *kleine Schriften*. Rahner has collected several of his articles and published them in his five volumes of *Schriften zur Theologie;* Schillebeeckx has four volumes; and I have four.

INTERVIEWER: Have you developed over the years any special method in your writing?

FATHER CONGAR: When I taught at Le Saulchoir every year, I would give a few lectures on my method of working. Briefly it is this: First of all, you must have questions. What a seed is to nature, questions are to the mind. You can either ask yourself these questions (like the *Utrum sit?* of St. Thomas) or you can get the questions from men around you. Since I am a Dominican and Dominicans are apostolic men, preachers, then the questions of my contemporaries are the main source for me. Secondly, you must learn to profit from every circumstance. You have to mull over the questions. Whether you are in bed, or walking, or in the refectory, you should think about the questions. What happens is that gradually, step by step, the answer is forming itself within your mind so that finally your ideas come to maturity and you are able to write them down accurately.

INTERVIEWER: Are you able to set aside part of the day for writing?

FATHER CONGAR: If I have the time. I never lose a second. But I do not always have the time to work in that way. Every day I receive about fifteen letters. Some ask for advice; others request me to read a manuscript or approve a particular article. I also give many lectures and preach frequently.

INTERVIEWER: Do you keep a journal?

FATHER CONGAR: Not regularly. I keep a journal only on special occasions. For example, when I am involved in some special historical event. Thus, at the Council I kept a journal.

INTERVIEWER: Were you able to do any writing during the war?

FATHET CONGAR: None at all. I was drafted into the army in 1939, and in November of 1940 I was taken prisoner by the Germans. I was a prisoner for five years. I tried to escape several times, but I was always recaptured. I was very opposed to the Nazis, and five times in the camp I gave a series of lectures against them. They knew it, but they never said anything to me. For a year and a half, I was in a special fortress in Saxony and for two years in a special camp with Communists, Jews, and political prisoners.

INTERVIEWER: Could you tell us how you came to start the *Unam Sanctam* collection?

FATHER CONGAR: At the beginning of 1935, I was aked to work on the results of a major investigation that the review, *La vie intellectuelle,* had pursued for three years on the present causes of unbelief. This led me to the conclusion that as far as this unbelief depended on *us,* it was caused by a poor presentation of the Church. At that time, the Church was presented in a completely juridical way and sometimes even somewhat political. I wanted to remedy this state of affairs. I decided to start a series of theological works that would examine a number of ecclesiological themes that were profoundly traditional, but had become more or less overlooked as the formal *De Ecclesia* tract developed. I sought to restore the genuine value of ecclesiology by viewing, as far as possible, the totality of Catholic doctrine and by using the rich resources of tradition and applying it to the current problems in the Church. The series *Unam Sanctam* was announced in the periodical, *La vie intellectuelle,* November 25, 1935. The first volume appeared in 1937 and was published by Editions du Cerf. I felt that such a series would fill a genuine need and would give a solid and serious theological foundation to a movement that had begun under the inspiration of the Holy Spirit. *Unam Sanctam* looks at the *mysterium Ecclesiae* from many different aspects, but always keeping in mind its organic unity.

INTERVIEWER: Do you think that the *Unam Sanctam* series has come up to your expectations?

FATHER CONGAR: Yes, I would say so. The first volume was written by me, and it was my first book, *Chrétiens désunis. Principes d'un oecuménisme catholique.* It was translated in 1938 under the title: *Divided Christendom.* So far sixty volumes have appeared, and among the authors you will find de Lubac, Batiffol, Bardy, Vonier, Bouyer, H. Rahner, Dumont, Leclercq, and Le Guillou. Pope Paul VI alluded to the work done by myself and others in his first encyclical, *Ecclesiam Suam.* There he pays tribute to "those scholars, who especially during the last years, with perfect docility to the teaching authority of the Church. . . . have with great dedication undertaken many difficult and fruitful studies on the Church."

INTERVIEWER: Looking over your life and your numerous writings, what do you consider your greatest contribution to theology?

FATHER CONGAR: [Here he paused for a long time and became very pensive. Finally, he went on in a very slow and deliberate way.] I have but one desire in my life: to fulfill God's plan for me. I wish to take my place in the plan of God. My whole life has consisted in offering myself totally, bodily, mentally, and spiritually to the Will of God. I have no plan for myself; I have only tried to do what God wanted of me. [Then, he continued in a lighter vein.] However, I have not done too badly. Without any merit on my part, I have been fortunate to have written accurately on several theological points that have proved to be decisive in the Church today. There is ecumenism, the laity, tradition, and Church reform. However, it was often difficult for me to advocate these views. Especially in the fifties. . . .

INTERVIEWER: You suffered much for your opinions?

FATHER CONGAR: Suffering is not easy for me; I would prefer not to discuss it. But I will say that I always did what I considered my duty and nothing else. When I am convinced that something is true, then no one, not even a pope can make me deny it. To be sure, if the pope or my superiors were to tell me that I was mistaken, I would think seriously about it and consider their remarks in an attentive and docile way. For me, truth is absolute. This is the main reason why I would not be a Communist. During the war, I had frequent conversations with Communists, and in Paris I have talked to some Marxists. I discovered that for them the truth is always changing. For them the truth is relative because it is only historical. This is the essence of dialectical materialism. But I believe what is true is *always* true.

INTERVIEWER: In your conversations with Marxists did you ever feel that their theories could contribute something to the Church?

FATHER CONGAR: There is no doubt that they have influenced the Church. One of the French Marxists once said that Communism has produced that unknown thing—Christians. They forced us to be Christian. Not to be simply Catholic, in the sociological meaning of the word, but to be truly Christian. This means to believe in the Gospel and to live according to the Gospel.

INTERVIEWER: Can any comparison be made between the Communist's notion of community and the Church's understanding of this term?

FATHER CONGAR: The two realities are situated on different levels. Nevertheless, there exists, in my opinion, a certain material correspondence between the end of history as the Communists see it and the end of history that we affirm will be realized in the Kingdom of God. History seeks two things. First of all, it seeks the overcoming of all opposition between men, between classes, between nations, between man and the state, and between spirit and nature. This is precisely what the Kingdom of God does. Secondly, history looks for integrity: the victory of life over illness and death; the victory of truth over ignorance; and the victory of justice over injustice. Does not the prophet Isaias tell us this? Human history and the Kingdom of God have the same goals, but we know that human history cannot achieve these ends by itself. We know that the grace of God and the help of the Holy Spirit are needed. The Communists believe that these goals are in the power of humanity, and this is where they differ from us. There exist, of course, many other very serious points of divergence.

INTERVIEWER: Have you ever talked with Jean-Paul Sartre?

FATHER CONGAR: No, I don't know him personally. Of course, I have read some of his works as well as Simone de Beauvoir, but what they say is so opposed to what I believe and know to be true that it is very painful for me to read them.

INTERVIEWER: Yet Sartre has had a great influence on the French intellectual world.

FATHER CONGAR: Yes, perhaps so. But it is difficult to say whether certain movements owe their life to Sartre or whether Sartre is only the spokesman of a movement already widespread. Camus also has had a great influence. I have more sympathy for Camus; his humanity is more genuine.

INTERVIEWER: Your ecclesiology has always exhibited an ecumenical dimension. Your doctoral dissertation, for example, was on the unity of the Church. Could you tell us something about the "ecumenical vocation" that you received as a young man.

FATHER CONGAR: There were many circumstances that prepared me for ecumenical work. As a boy in Sedan, a small village in the Ardennes, I had many Jewish and Protestant friends whose parents were friends of my parents. In 1914, our church in Sedan was intentionally burned by the Germans. The Protestant pastor, M. Cosson, let the Catholics use a Protestant chapel in the suburbs of the city. For almost six years that became our church, and in that chapel, I received or at least recognized my priestly vocation. I am also grateful to our Curé, Canon R. Tonnel who preached so well, and to Canon D. Lallement who taught me the beauty of the religious life. I also occasionally visited the Abbey of Saint-Wandrille, which was then in exile on the banks of the Semoye. My dear mother's wonderful example cannot be overemphasized. She had a very broad vision of the Church and a deep sense of what the Church is.

In preparing for my priestly ordination, which took place on July 25th, 1930, I became very interested in the theology of the Eucharistic Sacrifice. I read frequently Chapter 17 of St. John. While meditating on this chapter, I recognized definitely a call to work so that all who believe in Christ may be one.

I am grateful that God has called me to do His will. My special inspiration to work for Church unity cannot be understood apart from my interest in ecclesiology or for that matter apart from my religious vocation. I must say that from the beginning I have had really only one vocation that was at the same time priestly and religious, Dominican and Thomist, and ecumenical and ecclesiological.

INTERVIEWER: Catholicity has been a favorite theme in your writings over the years. Do you see any development in this notion today?

FATHER CONGAR: Dogmatically speaking, the Church is catholic. But the *structure* of the Church needs to become more catholic. I recall an incident that took place at the end of the pontificate of Pius XII that brings this out. The Holy Office had permitted a few Catholic observers to attend an ecumenical meeting with a group from the World Council of Churches. Rome suggested that the meeting be held in Assisi. We notified our Protestant friends in Geneva, and they answered that it was too far to go. Now these people are used to having their meetings everywhere. If we had said that the meeting would be in London, Evanston, or Ceylon, they would have asked when the next plane left. But for them, Assisi was too close to Rome. They were fearful. The Vatican Council itself was held in Rome and the conciliar commissions scarcely worked outside of Rome. Practically, the Catholic Church has an imperial structure, not a world-wide structure. For me this is one of the practical interests in the principle of collegiality. The Protestants at the Vatican Council often told us that it is useful that the pope is the supreme power and that Rome is Rome. But they felt that the Church must have a structure that is more in accord with the structure of the world. We must rid ourselves of thinking of the Church in terms of the Roman Empire—a capital city with provinces. The Church must become more catholic and recognize the differences in nations, cultures, and mentalities. Collegiality, I am confident, will do just that.

INTERVIEWER: The question of integrating the college of bishops with the supreme power of the pope is widely discussed today by theologians. How do you approach this problem?

FATHER CONGAR: It is a question of integration, and it is also a question of determining exactly what is the subject of supreme power in the Church. This cannot be adequately solved on the judicial level alone. As you know there are several positions. I eliminate at the start what amounts to a pure pontifical monarchy. It does not have consistent support either in the New Testament or in Christian antiquity. In recent years, some (K. Rahner and O. Semmelroth) have formulated the idea of a single power that is always collegial. Father W. Bertrams criticizes them by saying that *if* the supreme power is always that *of the college, then* how could the pope be dependent on the college of bishops and yet still possess *personally* the "fulness of power"? Vatican I affirms papal supremacy, and the New Testament (*Matt.* 16; *John* 21) shows that Peter personally and independently of the other apostles received full pastoral power. Bertrams then discusses the rather common explanation of two inadequately distinct subjects of supreme power. I have noticed that those who hold this view also say that there cannot exist a college without a head and that there can be no ecumenical council without the pope. But they never make the complementary application, namely that the pope is inconceivable without the college, that is without the rest of the bishops and the Church. The pope is always the head of the college and he always acts as such. Jimenez Urresti holds the thesis, which he supports with strong argumentation, that the pope is head of the Church *because* he is head of the college.

INTERVIEWER: What do you think of Rahner's position?

FATHER CONGAR: I wonder if the Rahner-Semmelroth thesis makes ample provision for the teaching of Vatican I? How can we say that every act of the pope's must be considered as an act of the college, since he is the head of the college? It seems to me that one must say that the pope receives the supreme power from a source other than that of head of the college, although he always exercises this power as head of the college. For that reason, I hold the theory of the two subjects inadequately distinct. The supreme power exists in both the pope and the college of bishops, but in different ways. The pope possesses real episcopal power over the whole Church (this is clear from Vatican I), not to administer the ordinary affairs of the dioceses, but to intervene only that the unity of the Church may be preserved.

Interviewer: Does not Father Bertrams present the arguments for the two subject theory in too juridical a framework?

Father Congar: Father Bertrams is a canonist, and he has not sufficiently considered the ontological aspects of the problem. The whole problem cannot be solved or even properly asked if we stay on the juridical level. In that category, we can only make affirmations of identity or subordination: relations "according to under and over." We must go on to ontology. The pope and his power are inseparable from the Church, from the apostolic succession of the college of bishops or college of apostles. As far as *power,* the pope has no superior; he is the head of the body of bishops. But we must not forget that he is bound to the Church, to its faith, outside of which there would be no pope or power. In this sense, on the radical level of ontology, the pope *depends* on the Church and has no power *over* her. Surely, one cannot eliminate from ecclesiology the unanimously recognized theme of the possibility of a heretical or schismatic pope. It might appear to be an unreal hypothesis, but it is a theme that is *necessary* to work out properly the position of the pope in the overall view of ecclesiology.

Interviewer: What of the hypothesis of a complete disagreement between the pope and an ecumenical council?

Father Congar: The hypothesis of an ecumenical conciliar assembly voting for a doctrine in a morally unanimous way and of the pope alone holding the contrary in such a way as to stop the assembly of the bishops seems to me impossible to maintain. In any event, that is not the way Paul VI understood his interventions in the Council according to a letter published in *La civiltà cattolica*, No. 2775 (1966, I). There is a limit to the personal power possessed by the pope that puts him over the assembly of the bishops and renders him independent of the college from a *juridical* point of view. This limit is communion in the faith. From an *ontological* point of view, the pope is not *over* the Church nor the college, but he is *within*. The *"supra"* has the limit of the *"cum."* No analogy taken from the constitutions of human societies and no purely juridical formulation is adequate for the *sui generis* supernatural reality that is the Church. Rather, we must look for its model in the mystery of the Trinity where we have perfect communion and circumcincession of the Divine Persons.

In summary, I would say that on the juridical level the *title* by which the pope possesses supreme power is proper and personal to him. It is something different from the title of member (head) of the college of bishops. It is independent of the college. But the *reality* that is thus given is nothing other than that of head *of the college* and head *of the Church*. The pope is inseparable from the college and the Church. He can no more be conceived of being independent of them than they can exist independently of him. Thus, the exercise of the power of the pope (received and possessed personally) is linked with the Church, although it is the power of the head of the Church *and* of the college.

INTERVIEWER: Some have said that you invented the term collegiality.

FATHER CONGAR: I know that Msgr. Lattanzi and others have said that I started the discussion on collegiality. This is entirely false. I did, it is true, put the word *collegiality* into the theological vocabulary. But the context was quite different from that of bishops.

INTERVIEWER: What were you writing about?

FATHER CONGAR: When I was writing my book on the laity, which appeared in 1953, I found that in the tradition of the Church, a communitarian structure always accompanied the hierarchic structure. I discovered that in the practical life of the Church decisions were always made in community. I found numerous texts in St. Cyprian and St. Leo, for instance, that insisted that *"nulli populo invito detur episcopus."* A bishop is not given to a community against their will. It was in studying texts like this that I formulated the communitarian or collegial idea. I even proposed to translate the orthodox term *sobornost,* to the degree that it is valid, as collegiality.

INTERVIEWER: The idea of the local community, the particular local Church, is emphasized in the *Constitution on the Liturgy.*

FATHER CONGAR: That is true, but I find that Constitution a little lacking in the theology of cult. What precisely is Christian cult? Generally, we think of cult in terms of the Old Testament and just add: "Through our Lord Jesus Christ, etc." But our Christian cult is quite different from the ritual cult of the Old Testament. It is a cult of faith by which we receive the gift of God. We return God's gift to Him as a thanksgiving and to men as a fraternal service, *diakonia.* For me, that is Christian cult. The *Constitution on the Liturgy* gives us a good picture of the Christian community, but it does not insist enough on the point that the true subject of liturgical action is the community as such, the *ecclesia,* the Church. The Council of Trent says of the Eucharist: *"Offert ecclesia per manus sacerdotis."* The Church, then, is a community and offers the Eucharist through the hands of the priest. When we say that the Church is a community, we mean that every living member is taking part and determining the whole life of the Church, not in an individualistic way, but in solidarity with others and in relation to the hierarchic structure of the Church.

INTERVIEWER: In your book on the laity you wrote that "theology properly so called is pre-eminently a clerical, priestly, learning." In the light of Vatican II would you modify that statement at all?

FATHER CONGAR: My idea behind that statement is quite simple. I believe that a layman could be as good a theologian as a priest. The example of men like Gilson or Maritain is quite eloquent, although they want to be known as philosophers and deny being theologians. I think that laymen should be able to teach theology even in universities. In the United States, you have women religious who are theologians. I do not mean that theology should be monopolized by the clergy. But I do think that the priesthood gives a *special* grace in regard to theology for two reasons. First of all, the priest can enter into the mysteries of Christianity in a unique way since he celebrates them. Secondly, a priest, by his calling, must be *more* a man for others. We read in this morning's Mass about forgiving our enemies. A priest cannot have enemies. I have always had as a practical rule of life never to treat anyone in such a way that he would not be able to ask me to hear his confession. Of course, laymen should not have enemies either. A layman can defend his view more rigidly and forcefully than a priest. I think that priests, all things being equal, have a more balanced view. However, I do not want to insist on this. It is not an important point, but rather a side remark. Since you have asked the same question to Father Rahner, it is good that I say something about it.

INTERVIEWER: The celibacy of the clergy is the subject of much discussion these days. What are your feelings on this problem?

FATHER CONGAR: The question is very difficult. Very difficult indeed. There are two questions that should not be confused. One is the problem of ordaining married men and the other is permitting priests to marry. In twenty years, I think we will have a married clergy in the sense that the Church will ordain married men.

INTERVIEWER: Do you think the married diaconate is a step in that direction?

FATHER CONGAR: Two years ago the Council approved a married diaconate, but since that time nothing has happened. It shows that it is a difficult problem. But I am confident that soon some practical implementations of the Council's approval of married deacons will take place. Last October in Rome, I was invited to attend a small congress that dealt with the diaconate, in which I gave a talk on the various ministries in the Church. There is more than the priestly ministry. In fact, most of the true ministries in the Church are performed by laymen. Would it not be possible to consecrate laymen to read the lessons at Mass, to teach religion in our schools, and to take care of the sick?

INTERVIEWER: You are not in favor of priests marrying after ordination?

FATHER CONGAR: No. I am quite opposed to it. There is no foundation for it in the tradition of the Church, not even the Eastern Church. It has always been forbidden.

INTERVIEWER: Would you allow for any exceptions to this?

FATHER CONGAR: I see no reason why exceptions cannot be made. But they would be the extraordinary thing. We must not forget that priestly celibacy is a Church law and not a divine law. There is no theological difference between a married priest, as in the East, and an unmarried priest. Both are priests in the full sense. It was interesting at the Council to read some of the *modi* of the bishops. I was one of the redactors of the decree on the priesthood, and many of the *modi* presented seemed to say that an unmarried priest was more a priest than a married priest. This is theologically not true, and the Commission refused to go along with it.

I would say that permission may be occasionally given for priests to marry. Some men discover the question of sexuality after their ordination, when they are in their late thirties. At this time, there is no honest exit from the priesthood. I think there should be some honest exit, either by reducing one to the lay state and allowing him to marry, or very rarely, to allow him to remain as a priest and function as a priest, at least in those places where Catholics would accept it. In nations like France, I think the latter would be difficult, although working people might accept it. But I don't think that the people in the small country villages would like it very much. In any hypothesis, that should only be an exceptional thing. There are other ways of answering the difficult problems that celibacy at times brings us. We should look for more developed human maturity before ordination, more intense forms of common life, and other things like this. I beseech God to preserve in His Church, in the midst of the aphrodisiac and hypersensualized world in which we live, the gift of religious and priestly chastity!

❖❖❖

YVES MARIE-JOSEPH CONGAR was born in Sedan (Ardennes), France, on April 13th, 1904. He attended schools in Sedan and Rheims, and for three years (1921-1924), he studied philosophy at the Institut Catholique. In 1925, he entered the Dominican Order and studied philosophy and theology at Le Saulchoir, which at that time was located in Belgium. On July 25, 1930, he was ordained. From 1931 to the outbreak of the Second World War, he taught fundamental theology and ecclesiology at Le Saulchoir. In July, 1939, he was drafted into the French army and on Armistice Day, a year later, was captured by the Germans. He spent the next five years in various prison camps. From 1945 to 1954, Father Congar returned to his teaching at Le Saulchoir, which was located near Paris. During the next two years, he spent time in Jerusalem, Rome, and Cambridge. In 1956, he joined the Dominican monastery in Strasbourg where he now resides.

Father Congar published *Chrétiens désunis* in 1937, which became a classic in Catholic ecumenism. He has written extensively in theological journals and among his books in English are: *Divided Christendom; Lay People in the Church; The Mystery of the Church; Our Lady and the Church; Laity, Church, and World;* and *The Mystery of the Temple.* He is editor of the *Unam Sanctam* series and from 1935 to 1951 was editor of *Revue des sciences philosophiques et théologiques.*

At the Second Vatican Council, Father Congar was a *peritus* and a member of the Theological Commission. He is a consultor of the Missions' Post-Conciliar Commission and of the Secretariat for Non-Christians. He is a member of the Executive Editorial Committee of *Concilium* and a member of the academic committee of the ecumenical institute founded by Pope Paul VI in Jerusalem.